BOOK 1

AQA GCSE ENGLISH LANGUAGE

DEVELOPING THE SKILLS FOR LEARNING AND ASSESSMENT

Helen Backhouse
Beverley Emm

CONSULTANT: DAVID STONE

OXFORD
UNIVERSITY PRESS

CONTENTS

CONTENTS

CONTENTS

The Assessment Objectives

Assessment Objective (AO)		Exam Paper and Question assessment coverage
AO1	• Identify and interpret explicit and implicit information and ideas.	Paper 1 Question 1 and Paper 2 Question 1
	• Select and synthesize evidence from different texts.	Paper 2 Question 2
AO2	Explain, comment on and analyse how writers use language and structure to achieve effects and influence readers, using relevant subject terminology to support their views.	Paper 1 Question 2 and Paper 1 Question 3 and Paper 2 Question 3
AO3	Compare writers' ideas and perspectives, as well as how these are conveyed, across two or more texts.	Paper 2 Question 4
AO4	Evaluate texts critically and support this with appropriate textual references.	Paper 1 Question 4
AO5	Communicate clearly, effectively and imaginatively, selecting and adapting tone, style and register for different forms, purposes and audiences. Organize information and ideas, using structural and grammatical features to support coherence and cohesion of texts.	Paper 1 Question 5 and Paper 2 Question 5
AO6	Use a range of vocabulary and sentence structures for clarity, purpose and effect, with accurate spelling and punctuation.	Paper 1 Question 5 and Paper 2 Question 5
AO7	Demonstrate presentation skills in a formal setting.	n/a
AO8	Listen and respond appropriately to spoken language, including to questions and feedback on presentations.	n/a
AO9	Use spoken Standard English effectively in speeches and presentations.	n/a

AQA GCSE English Language specification overview

The exam papers

The grade you receive at the end of your AQA GCSE English Language course is entirely based on your performance in two exam papers. The following provides a summary of these two exam papers:

Exam paper	Reading and Writing questions and marks	Assessment Objectives	Timing	Marks (and % of GCSE)
Paper 1: Explorations in Creative Reading and Writing	**Section A: Reading** Exam text: • One unseen literature fiction text Exam questions and marks: • One short form question (1 x 4 marks) • Two longer form questions (2 x 8 marks) • One extended question (1 x 20 marks)	Reading: • AO1 • AO2 • AO4	1 hour 45 minutes	Reading: 40 marks (25% of GCSE) Writing: 40 marks (25% of GCSE) Paper 1 total: 80 marks (50% of GCSE)
	Section B: Writing Descriptive or narrative writing Exam question and marks: • One extended writing question (24 marks for content, 16 marks for technical accuracy)	Writing: • AO5 • AO6		
Paper 2: Writers' Viewpoints and Perspectives	**Section A: Reading** Exam text: • One unseen non-fiction text and one unseen literary non-fiction text Exam questions and marks: • One short form question (1 x 4 marks) • Two longer form questions (1 x 8 marks and 1 x 12 marks) • One extended question (1 x 16 marks)	Reading: • AO1 • AO2 • AO3	1 hour 45 minutes	Reading: 40 marks (25% of GCSE) Writing: 40 marks (25% of GCSE) Paper 2 total: 80 marks (50% of GCSE)
	Section B: Writing Writing to present a viewpoint Exam question and marks: • One extended writing question (24 marks for content, 16 marks for technical accuracy)	Writing: • AO5 • AO6		

What sorts of texts and stimulus tasks will the exam papers include?

Paper 1

Section A: Reading will include the following types of text:

- A prose literature text from either the 20th or 21st century
- It will be an extract from a novel or short story.
- It will focus on openings, endings, narrative perspectives and points of view, narrative or descriptive passages, character, atmospheric descriptions and other appropriate narrative and descriptive approaches.

Section B: Writing will include the following stimulus:

- There will be a choice of scenario, either a written prompt or a visual image related to the topic of the reading text in Section A. The scenario sets out a context for writing with a designated audience, purpose and form that will differ to those specified on Paper 2.
- You will produce your own writing, inspired by the topic that you responded to in Section A.

Paper 2

Section A: Reading will include the following types of text:

- Two linked sources (one non-fiction and one literary non-fiction) from different time periods (one 19th century and one from either the 20th or 21st century, depending on the time period of the text in Paper 1) and different genres in order to consider how each presents a perspective or viewpoint to influence the reader.

Section B: Writing will include the following stimulus:

- You will produce a written text to a specified audience, purpose and form in which you give your own perspective on the theme that has been introduced in Section A.

Spoken Language

As well as preparing for the two GCSE English Language exams, your course also includes Spoken Language assessment. This is **not** an exam. Instead your teacher sets and marks the assessments.

There are three separate Assessment Objectives covering Spoken Language – AO7, AO8 and AO9. At the end of your course you will receive a separate endorsement for Spoken Language, which means it will not count as part of your GCSE English Language qualification.

Introduction to this book

How this book will help you

Develop your reading and writing skills

The primary aim of this book is to develop and improve your reading and writing skills. You will be doing this in the context of the Assessment Objectives which underpin the requirements of the exam papers that you will be taking at the end of your course.

Explore the types of texts that you will face in the exams

In your English Language exams you will have to respond to a number of unseen texts. In order to prepare you for the range and types of texts that you might face in the exam, this book is structured thematically so you can explore the connections between texts. The unseen texts in your exam papers will be of different types (fiction and non-fiction), from different historical periods (from the 19th, 20th and 21st centuries) and will, in some instances, be connected.

Become familiar with the Assessment Objectives and exam paper requirements

Assessment Objectives are the skills that underpin all qualifications. Your GCSE English Language exam papers are testing six Assessment Objectives (see pages 5 and 6). Chapters 1 to 5 of this book take the same approach – each chapter develops your reading and writing skills addressing the same Assessment Objectives. This revisiting of Assessment Objectives and supported practising of tasks, in different thematic contexts and with different texts, will ensure that your skills improve and that you're ready to start your exam preparation. Chapter 6 pulls all the skills together that you have been practising in order to help prepare you for the sample papers at the end of the book.

Monitor progress through assessments

Chapters 1 to 5 in this book include end-of-chapter assessments that enable you to demonstrate what you have learned and help your teacher assess your progress. The sample papers at the end of the book give you the opportunity to bring together all that you have been learning and practising in a 'mock' exam situation.

> **A note on spelling**
> Certain words, for example 'synthesize' and 'organize', have been spelt with 'ize' throughout this book. It is equally acceptable to spell these words and others with 'ise'.

How is the book structured?

Chapters 1 to 5

Chapters 1 to 5 develop your reading and writing skills within different themes. Each chapter opens with an introduction to the theme which explains the skills you will be developing and includes an introductory activity.

Each chapter then includes a range of fiction, non-fiction and literary non-fiction texts, from different historical periods, to help you develop your reading skills. Each chapter covers all the same reading Assessment Objectives and across the chapters you will encounter a range of text types from all of the historical periods that your exam paper texts will be taken from at the end of your course.

Your writing skills are also developed throughout every chapter, including a focus on improving your technical accuracy (also known as SPAG – Spelling, Punctuation and Grammar). This is done in the context of the chapter to help embed these vital skills into your writing.

Chapter 6

Chapter 6 pulls all of the skills together that you have learned throughout the course, revisiting key points and providing you with revision practice. The chapter and book concludes with full sample papers, which are for practice only and do not constitute the final AQA examination papers, to enable you and your teacher to see how much progress you have made.

What are the main features within this book?

Activities, Stretch and Support

To develop your reading responses to the wide range of texts included in this book, as well as developing your writing skills, you will find many varied activities. The 'Support' feature provides additional help with some activities, while the 'Stretch' feature introduces further challenge to help develop a more advanced response.

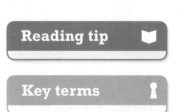

Tips, Key terms and glossed words

These features help support your understanding of key terms, concepts and more difficult words within a source text. These therefore enable you to concentrate fully on developing your reading and writing skills.

Progress check

In addition to the summative end-of-chapter assessments, you will also find regular formative assessments in the form of 'Progress checks'. Through peer and self-assessment, these enable you to assess your learning and establish next steps and targets.

Further GCSE English Language and GCSE English Literature resources

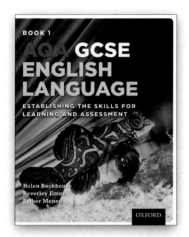

AQA GCSE English Language Student Book 1: Establishing the Skills for Learning and Assessment

This Student Book focuses on establishing students' reading and writing skills. Structured around engaging themes in the context of the Assessment Objectives, with regular formative and summative assessments, and an embedded focus on SPAG, this book also includes:

- the same core structure as Student Book 1: Developing the Skills for Learning and Assessment
- clear and accessible teaching explanations
- additional support and steps in the activities
- models of writing with a further focus on technical accuracy.

AQA GCSE English Language Student Book 2: Assessment Preparation for Paper 1 and Paper 2

Student Book 2 provides you with exam preparation and practice. The book is divided into Reading and Writing sections (like in the exams) and further divided into chapters which guide you through a range of questions. The book features:

- a range of texts and tasks similar to those you will encounter in the exams
- marked sample student responses at different levels
- opportunities for self-assessment and peer-assessment
- sample exam papers.

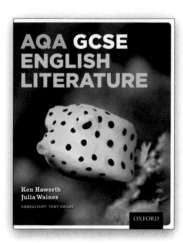

AQA GCSE English Literature Student Book

This Student Book provides in-depth skills development for the English Literature specification, including:

- coverage and practice of the poetry anthology and unseen poetry requirements
- advice and activities to support Shakespeare, the 19th-century novel and modern prose and drama
- sample student responses at different levels and practice tasks
- Stretch and Support features to ensure all students make progress
- clear, student-friendly explanations of the Assessment Objectives and the skills required to meet them.

AQA GCSE English Language and English Literature Teacher Companion

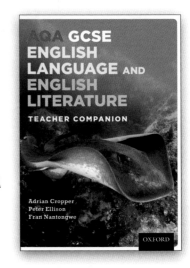

The Teacher Companion provides support for teachers to help them plan and deliver their GCSE programme, including:

- specification insight and planning guidance to aid planning and delivery of the specifications
- teaching tips and guidance for effective lesson delivery to all students of the material in Student Book 1, with additional support for differentiation and personalization
- exam preparation guidance and planning, with links to English Language Student Book 2 and English Literature Student Book
- links to, and guidance on, the additional resources on Kerboodle.

AQA GCSE English Language and English Literature Kerboodle: Resources and Assessment

What is Kerboodle?

Kerboodle is a brand new online subscription-based platform provided by Oxford University Press.

Kerboodle: Resources and Assessment

This AQA GCSE English Language and English Literature Kerboodle: Resources and Assessment provides support and resources to enable English departments and individual teachers to plan their GCSE courses and deliver effective, personalized lessons. Resources include:

- Teaching and learning materials, linked to the corresponding Student Books and Teacher Companion, including:
  - Differentiation, personalization and peer/self-assessment worksheets and teaching resources
  - A bank of assignable spelling, punctuation and grammar interactive activities to improve technical accuracy
- Assessment resources, including:
  - Marked sample answers and mark schemes
  - Editable versions of the end-of-chapter Student Book assessments and sample exam papers

- Professional development materials, including:
  - Seven specially-commissioned film-based CPD units devised by Geoff Barton, with classroom lesson footage, additional interviews and supporting written resources
  - A SPAG guide for GCSE teaching
- Planning resources, including:
  - Editable sample schemes of work and medium-term plans, with guidance on what to consider when planning your GCSE course
  - CPD units supporting discussion around departmental GCSE planning
- Digital books, including:
  - Student Books 1 (*Developing*) and 2, and the English Literature Student Book in digital format
  - A bank of tools enabling personalization

1 Bugs

Bugs.
Cockroaches...
spiders...
grasshoppers...
snails.
You either love
them or you hate
them.

Perhaps you're turning your nose up already at the thought of these creepy crawlies. Maybe you're the sort of person whose skin crawls at the sight of a centipede with all those wriggling legs. Bugs are evil, slimy things that make you squirm, you might think.

Or maybe you love the little critters? Some people are fascinated by bugs. They study them, keep them as pets and even eat them as a delicacy. Did you know Mexico has over 500 species of edible insects, and in Columbia, roasted *hormigas culonas* (large-bottomed ants) are a speciality?

In this chapter, you will encounter many different attitudes to the insect world by reading a range of writing from different genres and across different centuries.

The chapter is divided into three units:

- Fascination
- The land of make believe?
- Assessment.

Fascination focuses on people who devote their lives to bugs, sometimes to the point of obsession, and *The land of make believe?* deals with the fine line between what is real and what strays into the world of imagination.

In these first two units you will learn a number of reading and writing skills, and in the final unit, *Assessment*, you will be able to put these skills into practice to make sure you have understood them.

By the end of the chapter you may have fallen in love with cockroaches, spiders, grasshoppers or snails – or you may hate every single one of them with a passion!

Skills, Assessment Objectives and examination coverage

All the skills covered in this chapter focus on the Assessment Objectives and are directly relevant to the requirements of English Language.

Reading skills include how to:

- identify and interpret information and ideas
- select and summarize evidence from the text(s) to support your views
- analyse how the writer uses language for emotive effect, rhetorical questions and imagery
- examine how the writer uses whole text structure and sentence forms to achieve effects
- compare writers' ideas and perspectives
- evaluate what the writer does to make their writing successful, in particular the creation of character and atmosphere and the use of humour.

Writing skills include how to:

- communicate imaginatively, in particular through narrative and descriptive writing
- organize your ideas so that your writing is shaped and accurate.

Activity

a. We all have very different reactions to bugs. With a partner, discuss your experience of bugs and how you feel about them.

You might like to consider:

- bugs in movies and on TV
- apps and computer games involving bugs
- bugs encountered on holiday
- childhood experiences of bugs.

b. Join with another pair to share your experiences. Are your feelings towards bugs mostly positive or negative? Why?

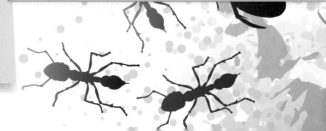

Fascination

This unit focuses on people who are fascinated with bugs: they study them, protect them, even become obsessed with them. Sometimes the result is amusing – but sometimes it is deadly!

1 All creatures great and small

If you asked someone to recall the last time they saw a bug of any kind, it's likely they would reply: 'On TV. I watched *I'm A Celebrity… Get Me Out Of Here!* and they ate those witchety grubs in the bush tucker trial. It was disgusting!'

We watch this programme and pity the poor celebrities who have to endure such misery, but do we think of the living creatures they are so disgustingly devouring? Probably not. In the following newspaper article, Chris Packham, a TV wildlife expert, is interviewed about this subject.

Autumnwatch presenter Chris Packham slams *I'm A Celebrity…* for 'killing animals and cruelty to bugs and insects'

TV wildlife expert Chris Packham has blasted *I'm A Celebrity… Get Me Out of Here!* for being cruel to bugs and insects. The host of BBC2's *Autumnwatch*, who controversially called for giant pandas to be allowed to die out, says he is appalled by how the show's bosses and celebrities abuse animals in the Aussie outback. The 48-year-old, who shot to fame on the BAFTA-winning BBC1 children's programme *The Really Wild Show*, says it is wrong that creatures are killed for entertainment purposes.

Chris told *Yours* magazine: 'The people working on *I'm A Celebrity… Get Me Out of Here!* have no regard for creatures' lives. If a celebrity trod on a cat it would be on the front page of every newspaper but they jump up and down on as many cockroaches, spiders and bugs as they like. From the first series I've been nothing short of appalled by the way they abuse animals. What sickens me more than anything is when people say "But they're only insects." I happen to really like insects and more than anything I like life. There's not a single living organism on this planet that wants to die. […]

'Other aspects of the programme like the physical trials can be entertaining but I don't find the treatment of creatures excusable at all. The insects are wriggling as they shove them into their mouths. Surely they have feelings? They do have nervous systems – for example witchety grubs and mealworms shy away from heat.

'There is a lunatic divide whereby it's okay to slaughter as many bugs as we like but if it is anything cute and furry it immediately makes front page news. […] If a celebrity were genuinely starving I'd have no problems with it. But when they are doing it for entertainment it's no more than exploitation. I'd like to see the animal aspects of the programme taken out. I'm sure there are enough brains in the programming department to come up with different challenges that are equally exciting but don't involve killing creatures.'

The information and ideas contained in this article are both explicit and implicit. If something is explicit it is clearly stated, and all you have to do is retrieve it, but when something is implicit it is just suggested and you have to **interpret** the text to work it out for yourself.

Activity 1

a. Look at the first paragraph of the article. One explicit piece of information about Chris Packham is that he is a TV wildlife expert. Find four other explicit pieces of information about him in this paragraph.

b. Now look at the second paragraph. This contains both explicit and implicit ideas to convey Chris Packham's views about the treatment of insects. What do you understand about his views from this paragraph?

c. What further points does Chris Packham make in the rest of the article to develop his views about the way creatures are treated?

d. Chris Packham acknowledges: 'Other aspects of the programme like the physical trials can be entertaining...' How does this attempt to present a more balanced argument affect our views of him? Where else in the text does he do this?

e. Chris Packham concludes the article by saying: 'I'm sure there are enough brains in the programming department to come up with different challenges that are equally exciting but don't involve killing creatures.' What can you interpret from this comment about his **opinion** of the people who make *I'm A Celebrity... Get Me Out Of Here!*?

Stretch

Chris Packham says: '...when they are doing it for entertainment it's no more than exploitation.' How does the fact that this is happening to these creatures in the name of entertainment make it worse?

Reading tip

To show you understand a text, you are expected to interpret as well as identify the ideas and information.

Activity 2

Using all the work you have done so far, write your response to the following question:

What do you understand about Chris Packham's views from the article? Use your own words but also quote from the text to support what you say.

Language is deliberately chosen by the writer to add to your understanding of a text and make you feel a certain way. Chris Packham feels very strongly about how creatures are treated in *I'm A Celebrity… Get Me Out Of Here!* and this is conveyed in this article through his use of **language for emotive effect**. He chooses specific words to make us respond at an emotional level in the hope that this will persuade us to agree with his views.

Activity 3

a. Look at the headline and the first two paragraphs. Select some examples of language used for emotive effect that show how strongly Chris Packham feels. Record your examples in a grid like the one started below, and explain the effect on the reader.

Language for emotive effect	Effect
The host of BBC2's *Autumnwatch* says he is 'appalled…'	The word 'appalled' tells us that Chris Packham is horrified by the way animals are treated in this TV programme and he finds it disgusting.

b. Chris Packam says: 'There is a lunatic divide whereby it's okay to slaughter as many bugs as we like.' What effect do the words 'lunatic divide' and 'slaughter' have on the reader? Add these examples to the grid and include your ideas about effect.

Support Think of the **connotations** of the word 'lunatic'. Then look back at the original article to see how Chris Packham uses the word and what he is talking about at the time.

c. Look at any language used for emotive effect in the rest of the article. Select some further examples and explain the effect on the reader. Add your ideas to the grid.

d. Compare your grid with a partner's. Discuss how the examples you have selected demonstrate the strength of Chris Packham's feelings. Consider alternative effects and add them to your grid.

Reading tip

When discussing the effect of language, it is important to consider the context in which the words and phrases are used.

Another way that Chris Packham conveys how strongly he feels about the way creatures are treated in *I'm A Celebrity... Get Me Out Of Here!* is by using a **rhetorical question**. This engages the reader at a personal level and again persuades us to agree with his views.

Activity 4

a. Identify the rhetorical question in the third paragraph.

b. What is the context in which this rhetorical question is used? How does it help to persuade us to agree with his views?

Activity 5

Using all the work you have done so far on language for emotive effect and rhetorical questions, write your response to the following question:

How does the use of language show how strongly Chris Packham feels about the treatment of insects in *I'm A Celebrity... Get Me Out Of Here!*?

Stretch Chris Packham is known for his controversial views regarding wildlife. For example, he believes we should allow giant pandas to become extinct. Conduct some research to find any other controversial views he holds and decide whether or not you agree with them.

2 Obsession

Key term 🔒

Mood: the feeling or atmosphere conveyed by a piece of writing

The opening of a novel is important – a strong beginning will grab the reader and, with any luck, carry them all the way to the final page. The opening of a short story is even more critical. The first paragraph has to set the scene, launch the plot, and establish the **mood** and the characters. It has to transport the reader into a different world, and fast!

The following extract is the opening of a short story called 'The Snail Watcher' by Patricia Highsmith. It gives the reader a number of clues about the character of Mr Knoppert.

Extract from 'The Snail Watcher' by Patricia Highsmith

When Mr Peter Knoppert began to make a hobby of snail-watching, he had no idea that his handful of specimens would become hundreds in no time. Only two months after the original snails were carried up to the Knoppert study, some thirty glass tanks and bowls, all teeming with snails, lined the walls, rested on the desk and windowsills, and were beginning even to cover the floor. Mrs Knoppert disapproved strongly, and would no longer enter the room. It smelled, she said, and besides she had once stepped on a snail by accident, a horrible sensation she would never forget. But the more his wife and friends deplored his unusual and vaguely repellent pastime, the more pleasure Mr Knoppert seemed to find in it.

'I never cared for nature before in my life,' Mr Knoppert often remarked – he was a partner in a brokerage firm*, a man who had devoted all his life to the science of finance – 'but snails have opened my eyes to the beauty of the animal world.'

If his friends commented that snails were not really animals, and their slimy habitats hardly the best example of the beauty of nature, Mr Knoppert would tell them with a superior smile that they simply didn't know all that he knew about snails.

*brokerage firm – a business that buys and sells stocks and shares

Activity 1

a. Which of the following descriptions apply to Mr Knoppert at the start of the story?

> displays his snails throughout the house

> obsessed with his new hobby

> knows a lot about snails when he starts to collect them

> very odd

> works as an accountant

> smug

> likes to be right all the time

b. Draw a spider diagram with 'Mr Knoppert' in the centre and place your chosen descriptions for him in the surrounding bubbles. Select evidence from the text to support your choices and attach a quotation to each bubble.

c. Compare your spider diagram with a partner's. Discuss your chosen descriptions as well as your supporting quotations to see if you agree.

d. Mr Knoppert's wife and friends are also mentioned at the start of the story. With your partner, discuss how this adds to our understanding of Mr Knoppert.

> Mr Knoppert

The writer includes many details to develop a character so that the reader becomes increasingly engaged and cares what happens to them. As the story of 'The Snail Watcher' progresses, Mr Knoppert's behaviour becomes more and more extreme. He is particularly fascinated by the breeding habits of the snails: he watches their mating rituals and reads encyclopaedias to acquire more knowledge. In the following extract, the females have finally laid their eggs and Mr Knoppert waits with much anticipation for the baby snails to be born.

Extract from 'The Snail Watcher' by Patricia Highsmith

He had to go and look at the eggs every hour that he was at home. He looked at them every morning to see if any change had taken place, and the eggs were his last thought every night before he went to bed. Moreover, another snail was now digging a pit. And another pair of snails was mating! The first batch of eggs turned a greyish colour, and minuscule spirals of shells became discernible on one side of each egg. Mr Knoppert's anticipation rose to a higher pitch. At last a morning arrived – the eighteenth after laying, according to Mr Knoppert's careful count – when he looked down into the egg pit and saw the first tiny moving head, the first stubby little antennae uncertainly exploring the nest. Mr Knoppert was as happy as the father of a new child. Every one of the seventy or more eggs in the pit came miraculously to life. He had seen the entire reproductive cycle evolve to a successful conclusion. And the fact that no one, at least no one that he knew of, was acquainted with a fraction of what he knew, lent his knowledge a thrill of discovery, the piquancy of the esoteric. Mr Knoppert made notes on successive matings and egg hatchings. He narrated snail biology to fascinated, more often shocked, friends and guests, until his wife squirmed with embarrassment.

Activity 2

a. In the extract on page 19, the writer includes many details to show the development of Mr Knoppert's character. List the details that convey how obsessed he has become with the snails by this point in the story.

b. Compare your list with a partner's. Consider any alternative ideas and add them to your list.

Support

Think about how often he watches the snails, his reaction when the babies are born and how he feels about knowing so much about them.

Stretch

Consider the sentence: 'And the fact that no one, at least no one that he knew of, was acquainted with a fraction of what he knew, lent his knowledge a thrill of discovery, the piquancy of the esoteric.' Look up any words that you don't understand and explain how this quotation adds to your understanding of Mr Knoppert's character.

Activity 3

Using all the work you have done so far, write your response to the following question:

How successful is Patricia Highsmith in conveying Mr Knoppert's growing obsession with snails? Give your own opinion and quote from both extracts to support what you say.

The writer also includes details to create a particular atmosphere. In 'The Snail Watcher', the snails continue to breed and eventually take over the study: every inch of the floor, the walls and even the ceiling is covered in snails. In the following conclusion to the story, the writer creates a surreal atmosphere of horror as Mr Knoppert becomes trapped in the room.

Extract from 'The Snail Watcher' by Patricia Highsmith

He crawled to the door, heedless of the sea of snails he crushed under hands and knees. He could not get the door open. There were so many snails on it, crossing and re-crossing the crack of the door on all sides, they actually resisted his strength.

'Edna!' A snail crawled into his mouth. He spat it out in disgust. Mr Knoppert tried to brush the snails off his arms. But for every hundred he dislodged, four hundred seemed to slide upon him and fasten to him again, as if they deliberately sought him out as the only comparatively snail-free surface in the room. There were snails crawling over his eyes. Then just as he staggered to his feet, something else hit him – Mr Knoppert couldn't even see what. He was fainting! At any rate, he was on the floor. His arms felt like leaden weights as he tried to reach his nostrils, his eyes, to free them from the sealing, murderous snail bodies.

'Help!' He swallowed a snail. Choking, he widened his mouth for air and felt a snail crawl over his lips on to his tongue. He was in hell! He could feel them gliding over his legs like a glutinous river, pinning his legs to the floor. 'Ugh!' Mr Knoppert's breath came in feeble gasps. His vision grew black, a horrible, undulating black. He could not breathe at all, because he could not reach his nostrils, could not move his hands. Then through the slit of one eye, he saw directly in front of him, only inches away, what had been, he knew, the rubber plant that stood in its pot near the door. A pair of snails were quietly making love in it. And right beside them, tiny snails as pure as dewdrops were emerging from a pit like an infinite army into their widening world.

Activity 4

a. In a small group, discuss how the writer successfully creates an atmosphere of horror by her use of detail.

In particular, you could think about:

- the situation Mr Knoppert is in and what he says, does, thinks and feels
- the behaviour of the snails
- how the writer uses language.

Some examples have been highlighted for you to begin your discussion.

b. Which details do you find particularly effective and why?

> **Stretch**
>
> Sentence structure can also add to the atmosphere being created. For example, the use of repetition in 'He could not breathe at all, because he could not reach his nostrils, could not move his hands' creates an effect of increasing panic. Find some other examples of effective sentences in the extract that help to create atmosphere.

Activity 5

Write your response to the following question:

To what extent do you think the writer has been successful in creating an atmosphere of horror at the end of the story? Give your own opinion and quote from the text to support what you say.

Skills and objectives

3 Caught in the spider's web

You are going to write an imaginative short story suggested by either the poem or the picture below. You do not need to take the poem or picture literally: 'suggested by' means you can use them as a starting point to stimulate your imagination.

- To communicate imaginatively, focusing in particular on creating character and atmosphere **(AO5)**

- To write clearly and accurately **(AO6)**

> **'The Spider and the Fly' by Mary Howitt (1829)**
>
> 'Will you walk into my parlour?' said the Spider to the Fly,
> 'Tis the prettiest little parlour that ever you did spy;
> The way into my parlour is up a winding stair,
> And I've a many curious things to show when you are there.'
>
> 'Oh no, no,' said the little Fly, 'to ask me is in vain,
> For who goes up your winding stair
> – can ne'er come down again.'

Key term 🔒

Structure: the organization of the text, how it is introduced, presented and concluded; structure also includes how paragraphs and ideas are grouped or linked together

Stage 1: Planning

Before starting to write a narrative, you need to consider:
- plot: what is the sequence of events in your story?
- setting: where and when will your story take place?
- characterization: who is the story about?
- viewpoint: who is narrating the story?
- **structure**: how will your story begin, what conflict will be encountered and how will it be resolved?
- atmosphere: what mood do you want to create?

**Activity ① **

> Make notes in answer to the above questions for a short story of your own suggested by either the poem 'The Spider and the Fly' or the picture of the spider above. Discuss your notes with a partner, adding any ideas for improvement.

Creating character and atmosphere

Remember, when you are creating your characters and atmosphere, you need to decide how you want your reader to respond and the details you need to include to achieve this effect.

Activity 2

a. With a partner, discuss the differences between the two paragraphs below. How does the use of detail included by the writers help to create very different impressions of character and atmosphere?

> It was night. Occasionally, the moon cast shadows across the bedroom floor, but then it disappeared behind a cloud and the room was encased in darkness once more. Hannah heard an owl hoot in the distance and then silence. Death hung in the air like an omen. She pulled up the bed covers and hid beneath them, trembling with fear.

> It was a bright summer's day. Occasionally, a gentle breeze tinkled the wind chimes that glittered in the sunlight. Amy heard her mum laughing loudly in the garden and knew her father was telling awful jokes again. The sun scattered happiness all around. She headed over to the barbecue, smiling, and happily joined in the family fun.

b. Decide how you want the reader to respond to your characters and atmosphere and make a note of some details that will achieve this effect.

 Support — Think about the personality of your characters as well as their physical features.

 Stretch — You may want to vary your atmosphere at different stages in the story – for example, lull your reader into a false sense of security just before a scary climax.

Stage 2: Writing

Activity 3

Using all the work you have done so far, write your response to the following:

Your favourite magazine is running a creative writing competition. Write an imaginative short story suggested by the poem 'The Spider and the Fly' or the picture of a spider opposite.

Stage 3: Proofreading

Activity 4

When you have finished your short story you need to proofread your work. Check that what you have written is clear, accurate and includes a range of vocabulary. Make any changes that would improve your demonstration of AO6 skills. **SPAG**

Writing tip

Remember, **SPAG** effective communication is the most important skill. If you make too many mistakes in spelling, punctuation and grammar, you will not be able to communicate your ideas effectively.

4 The collecting bug

Skills and objectives

- To examine how the writer uses whole text structure and sentence forms to achieve effects **(AO2)**

- To compare writers' ideas and perspectives **(AO3)**

Writers shape and structure their ideas in order to help the reader understand their meaning. They do this by considering two things:

- whole text structure
- sentence forms.

Whole text structure

A successful piece of writing has an overall framework for readers to navigate: a clear beginning that engages the reader, a middle that contains a number of connected ideas and an effective conclusion. Paragraphs are coherent, fluently linked and organized for impact.

In the following newspaper article, the writer's argument follows a logical sequence in order to convince the reader that collecting cockroaches can be fun.

The creepy subject of Darren's collecting bug

The day Darren Mann left primary school his teacher presented him with a parting gift – four hissing cockroaches. It was a wonderful present, he recalls. They make lovely pets.

It's very much a minority view. Few creepy crawlies have a poorer public image than the humble cockroach. Associated with poor hygiene and the spread of disease, it's a target for extermination wherever it raises its ugly head.

But it has a passionate defender in Darren Mann. He keeps about two thousand of the little beasts in a garden shed at the family home, where he spends hours every day feeding them sliced apple and specialist food prepared for pet rats. He likes nothing better than to put his hand into a squirming tankful and let them tickle his fingers.

The very thought makes environmental health officer George Makin cringe. He says that the common cockroach is rapidly moving up the public enemy list. He has recently had to close down several food premises and has no hesitation in describing the cockroach as a health hazard, a carrier of diseases like salmonella that must be rooted out and eradicated wherever it is found.

That's by no means easy. Cockroaches are among the great survivors of the animal kingdom. They'll eat almost anything, including each other and the paste used to stick on wallpaper, and they can live in the tiniest crack in a skirting board.

Darren believes cockroaches are being unfairly maligned. He's not convinced that they are a major cause of the spread of salmonella and he says that it's their lifestyle, scuttling far and wide in search of food under cover of darkness, that makes them unloved. Despite the dirty brown appearance of the British cockroach, all cockroaches actually spend almost half their waking moments cleaning themselves, he reveals.

Darren's parents are quite happy about several thousand cockroaches living at the bottom of the garden. And Darren's girlfriend takes it in her stride too. 'She thinks they're quite cute actually,' he says, 'although she tends to scratch a bit when she comes out of the shed.'

As an insect collector who can't pass a stone without lifting it to see what's underneath, Darren is about to broaden his horizons. Next month he's off to Madagascar with a party of fellow enthusiasts to study some of the more exotic species of cockroach in their natural habitat. He's itching to get there.

Activity 1

a. The writer has used eight paragraphs in the article. Rearrange the following paragraph summaries into the correct sequence.

> Darren's interest started because of a gift of four cockroaches from his teacher.

> An environmental health officer believes cockroaches are a health hazard.

> Darren is about to travel abroad to study other cockroaches.

> Darren's family are happy with his hobby.

> Most people dislike cockroaches because they think they are dirty and spread disease.

> Cockroaches are great survivors and are difficult to exterminate.

> Darren likes cockroaches and looks after 2000 of them.

> Cockroaches are actually clean insects and Darren thinks people dislike them just because of their lifestyle.

b. How does the opening paragraph engage the reader?

c. Where does the writer change focus in the article and why does he do this? What effect does this have on the reader?

d. How is the closing paragraph effective?

Writing can be shaped in many different ways. One possible text structure, used in this article, is to begin with something small and zoom out to something much bigger: it starts 'in a garden shed' and ends with Darren 'off to Madagascar'. It also constantly shifts between a narrow focus on Darren – for example, 'spends hours every day feeding them' – and wider general information, such as 'Cockroaches are among the great survivors of the animal kingdom'.

Activity 2

a. Which of the following text structures also apply to this article?

- Zooming in from something big to something much smaller
- Shifting between different times
- A gradual introduction of new characters at significant points
- Moving from inside to the wider outside world
- Following a cyclical shape, that is, shifting focus through a series of points and ending up back at the beginning
- Combining external actions with internal thoughts
- Shifting between different points of view
- Moving from the wider outside world to inside
- Shifting between different places
- Developing and reiterating: focusing on a dominant point of view by expanding and repeating it

b. With a partner, discuss how the structure of the article adds to its success.

Sentence forms

A successful piece of writing also has a variety of sentence forms. Different types of sentences can be used to create different effects.

There are four main types of sentences.

- A simple sentence is made up of a single clause. It has a subject and one main verb. For example,
'It's very much a minority view.'

> This is short for 'it is'. 'It' is the subject; 'is' is the verb.

- A compound sentence is made up of two or more simple sentences joined together. For example,
'They'll eat almost anything and they can live in the tiniest crack in the skirting board.'

> This could stand alone as a simple sentence.

> This is a conjunction that links the two clauses together.

> This could also stand alone as a simple sentence.

- A complex sentence has a main clause (which could stand alone as a simple sentence) and a dependent clause (which could not stand alone as a sentence on its own). For example,
'The day Darren Mann left primary school his teacher presented him with a parting gift.'

> This clause cannot stand alone. It is dependent on the main clause.

> This is the main clause. It could stand alone as a sentence.

- A minor sentence is a short sentence consisting of very few words used deliberately to create an effect. For example, 'Four hissing cockroaches!'

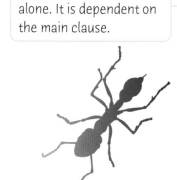

Activity 3

In small groups, look at the sentences above and discuss why they are effective.

Support Look at where each sentence comes in the article. Is it being used to set the scene, or to shift the focus of the argument, or to give lots of information, or to take us by surprise?

Activity 4

Using all the work you have done so far on both whole text structure and sentence forms, write your response to the following question:

How has the writer structured the article to engage the reader?

Darren Mann started his cockroach collection in the 1980s, but collecting insects first became popular back in the 19th century. In the following extract, Charles Darwin, a famous naturalist, recalls how much he enjoyed this hobby while at university.

Extract from *Autobiography of Charles Darwin* by Charles Darwin

No pursuit at Cambridge was followed with nearly so much eagerness or gave me so much pleasure as collecting beetles. It was the mere passion for collecting, for I did not dissect them, and rarely compared their external characters with published descriptions, but got them named anyhow. I will give a proof of my zeal*: one day, on tearing off some old bark, I saw two rare beetles, and seized one in each hand; then I saw a third and new kind, which I could not bear to lose, so that I popped the one which I held in my right hand into my mouth. Alas! it ejected some intensely acrid fluid, which burnt my tongue so that I was forced to spit the beetle out, which was lost, as was the third one.

I was very successful in collecting, and inventing two new methods; I employed a labourer to scrape, during the winter, moss off old trees and place it in a large bag, and likewise to collect the rubbish at the bottom of the barges in which reeds are brought from the fens, and thus I got some very rare species. No poet ever felt more delighted at seeing his first poem published than I did at seeing, in Stephens' 'Illustrations of British Insects', the magic words "captured by C. Darwin, Esq."

*zeal – enthusiasm

Both the newspaper article about Darren and the extract from Charles Darwin's autobiography deal with the subject of collecting bugs, but they are written in different centuries and from different perspectives.

Activity 5

In small groups, discuss the similarities and differences of collecting insects in the two texts.

In particular, you could analyse:

- each collector's attitude to their hobby
- how involved each collector is
- the lengths to which they go for their hobby
- others' involvement in their hobby
- the writers' use of structure and language.

Activity 6

Using both sources, write your response to the following question:

Compare how the writers convey the experience of bug collecting. Use your own words but also quote from both texts to support what you say.

The land of make believe?

Skills and objectives

This unit deals with the fine line between what is real and what is imagined. Some writers present fiction in a factual way whereas others recall facts so vividly that they sound like fiction.

5 Industrious fleas

- To identify and interpret ideas and information **(AO1)**
- To select and synthesize evidence from different texts **(AO1)**

A flea is about 2 mm long – no bigger than the full stop underneath this exclamation mark! So it may come as a surprise to learn that in the Victorian era, a popular pastime was attending something called a flea circus, a sideshow act that amazed and entertained the masses who flocked to watch the fleas performing tricks. The most famous trainer of the time was Signor Bertolotto, who held an exhibition in London to show off exactly what his fleas could do.

This advertisement, persuading people to attend Bertolotto's exhibition, appeared in a newspaper in the 1820s.

It was Signor Bertolotto's intention to close his Exhibition for the season by the 30th August, but the unabated concourse of visitors has determined him to keep it open for a few weeks longer, with the following attractions:

———— • ◆ • ————

A BALL ROOM in which two Fleas dressed as Ladies, and two as Gentlemen Dancing as Waltzers; twelve Fleas in the Orchestra playing on different Instruments of proportionable size, the Music is audible. Four Fleas playing a game of Whist. [...]

———— • ◆ • ————

The Three Heroes of Waterloo! The Duke of Wellington, Napoleon Bonaparte and PRINCE BLUCHER, riding on Fleas, with Gold Saddles, etc. Two Fleas deciding an Affair of Honour, sword in hand; another Flea dressed with a Blue Petticoat, pulling up a Bucket from a Well. [...]

———— • ◆ • ————

Any comment on the merit of this Exhibition would be useless; the unparalleled success it has obtained during the last two years, is sufficient proof that it deserves (as it has obtained) the public patronage.

In this next extract from a short story, Charles Dickens describes a meeting of 'The Mudfog Society for the Advancement of Everything', where a committee member is reporting on a visit to the 'Industrious Fleas' exhibition opposite.

Tip ✓

The skills you are practising with this text can be applied to any fiction or non-fiction text from any century.

Extract from 'The Mudfog Papers' in *Bentley's Miscellany* by Charles Dickens

He had been induced to visit an exhibition in Regent Street, London, commonly known by the designation of 'The Industrious Fleas'. He had there seen many fleas, occupied certainly in various pursuits [...], but occupied, he was bound to add, in a manner which no man of well-regulated mind could fail to regard with sorrow and regret. One flea, reduced to the level of a beast of burden, was drawing about a miniature gig*, containing a particularly small effigy of His Grace the Duke of Wellington; while another was staggering beneath the weight of a golden model of his great adversary Napoleon Bonaparte. Some, brought up as [...] ballet-dancers, were performing a figure dance (he regretted to observe that, of the fleas so employed, several were females); others were in training, in a small cardboard box, for pedestrians – mere sporting characters –and two were actually engaged in the cold-blooded and barbarous occupation of duelling; a pursuit from which humanity recoiled with horror and disgust.

*gig – a carriage normally drawn by horses

Both the advertisement and the extract from the short story deal with the 'Industrious Fleas' exhibition, although the advertisment appeared in a real newspaper in the 1890s and the short story came from the imagination of Charles Dickens and is a work of fiction. Some of the information and ideas are similar in both, although the attitudes towards the exhibition are very different. When **synthesizing**, you need to select evidence from both texts and interpret and make connections between the information and ideas.

Key term 🔑

Synthesize: to combine information and ideas from different texts and produce new material

Activity 1

a. List the performing fleas that appear in both texts. Which flea acts are just in the advertisement and which are just in the short story extract?

b. Look at the opening paragraph of the advertisement. What can the reader interpret about the success of the exhibition from this part of the text? Select another quotation from the final paragraph which supports your interpretation.

c. Now look at the short story extract. What do 'a beast of burden' and 'staggering beneath the weight' tell us about the committee member's reaction to Bertolotto's exhibition? Select another quotation which supports your interpretation.

d. Discuss your interpretations and selected quotations with a partner to see if you agree.

Reading tip

When synthesizing information in two texts, you can highlight the connections between them by using words such as 'both', 'is similar to', 'on the other hand', 'however' and 'whereas'.

Activity ②

Using the work you have done so far, write your response to the following question:

Summarize the different attitudes to the 'Industrious Fleas' exhibition in the two texts. Use your own words but also quote from both texts to support what you say.

Support
Try to go beyond the explicit information and ideas that are clearly stated and look beneath the surface at what is implied. You have to focus on the 'different attitudes' to the 'Industrious Fleas' exhibition in each text, which means you will need to read between the lines and interpret.

Stretch

In order to fully interpret implicit ideas, sometimes it is necessary to recognize that writing is **satirical**, otherwise the reader will miss the whole point of what is being said.

Dickens was a great advocate for social reform and he invents the Mudfog Society in order to satirize the unfair way Victorian society treated the poor and how inadequately committees responded to the problem. He uses fleas as **symbols** of the lower classes and describes how they are being exploited. Although his story is fiction, he writes in a factual style to sound more official and in doing this he is also mocking the behaviour of committees as well as society in general.

In the following extract, the committee member continues his report by offering some solutions to the problem. They are presented as serious suggestions, and the fact the reader recognizes how ridiculous they are contributes to the satire.

Key terms

Summarize: to give the main points of something briefly

Satirical: uses humour, exaggeration or ridicule to criticize human behaviour

Symbol: something that is used to represent something else; often a simpler portrayal of something more complex or abstract

---

Extract from 'The Mudfog Papers' in *Bentley's Miscellany* by Charles Dickens

He suggested that measures should be immediately taken to employ the labour of these fleas as part and parcel of the productive power of the country, which might easily be done by the establishment among them of infant schools and houses of industry[1], in which a system of virtuous education, based upon sound principles, should be observed. [...] He proposed that every flea who presumed to exhibit, for hire, music, or dancing, or any species of theatrical entertainment, without a licence, should be considered a vagabond[2], and treated accordingly. [...] He would further suggest that their labour should be placed under the control and regulation of the state, who should set apart from the profits, a fund for the support of [...] disabled fleas, their widows and orphans.

[1]houses of industry – workhouses
[2]vagabond – tramp

Activity 3

How does Charles Dickens satirize Victorian society in 'The Mudfog Papers'?

Skills and objectives

- To analyse how the writer uses imagery to achieve effects **(AO2)**
- To select evidence from the text to support your views **(AO2)**

Key terms

Fact: something that can be proved to be true

Imagery: the use of figurative or other special language to convey an idea and create a particular effect on the reader

Metaphor: a comparison showing the similarity between two quite different things, stating that one actually *is* the other

Reading tip

Always consider the context when analysing imagery and be precise when commenting on the effect.

6 Invasion!

Writers of literary non-fiction sometimes blur the distinction between **fact** and fiction. What they write is factually accurate, but the style in which they write it often reads like an imaginative story, with **imagery** and inventive language used.

Look at the **metaphor** in the extract below. The extract is taken from a piece of literary non-fiction written by Gordon Grice. He is remembering a time when a cloud of grasshoppers invaded the countryside of Oklahoma, America, where he grew up. As he was driven along the highway, the grasshoppers became trapped in the car's windscreen wipers.

> **Extract from *Deadly Animals: Savage Encounters Between Man and Beast* by Gordon Grice**
>
> Their wings, coffee-coloured fans striped with yellow at the outer edges, lodged in our wipers and fluttered in the onrushing air.

When analysing the effect of a metaphor, you first need to consider which two things are being compared and why. In the example above, the comparison is between grasshopper wings and fans, and although these two things are very different, there has to be a point of similarity for the metaphor to work.

Activity 1

a. With a partner, discuss possible points of similarity between grasshopper wings and 'coffee-coloured fans striped with yellow at the outer edges'. What effect is the writer trying to achieve by using this metaphor?

b. Now read the comments on the effect of this metaphor made by four students. They are ranked in order, with Student A's comment being the weakest and Student D's the best. Note how each student's comment is better than the previous one.

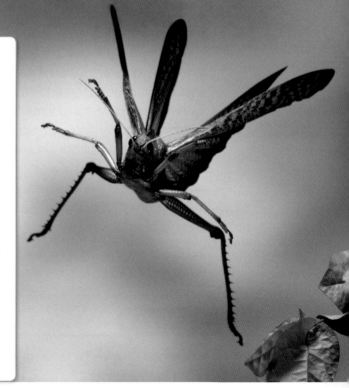

Student A

The writer uses this metaphor to create a picture in our minds.

This is true but the comment is too generalized. It could apply to any metaphor in any piece of writing.

Student B

The writer uses this metaphor to tell us that the grasshopper wings are beautiful.

This explanation is more precise but not yet clearly linked to what is happening in the text. The beauty of the grasshopper wings and the beauty of fans is not the point of similarity that makes this metaphor effective.

Student C

The writer uses this metaphor to suggest that the grasshopper wings are beautiful but fragile and that the insects are easily destroyed by the car's wipers.

This explanation develops the comment made by Student B and is clearly linked to what is happening in the text. The fact that both grasshopper wings and fans are made from delicate materials and therefore can be easily destroyed is a clever point of similarity given the context of the metaphor.

Reading tip

The use of the word 'suggest' shows that Student C is beginning to interpret the effect of the image. Other useful phrases include: 'This means…', 'This lets us know…', 'This indicates…', 'This implies…' and 'This makes me think…'.

Student D

The writer uses this metaphor to suggest that the grasshopper wings are beautiful but fragile and that the insects are easily destroyed by the car's wipers. 'Onrushing air' implies the car is travelling at speed, meaning the grasshoppers are trapped on impact and stand no chance. They are 'lodged' in the wipers and, like fans, their wings can do nothing except flutter. The word 'fluttered' makes it sound positive, like the delicate, graceful movements of ladies' fans, not the frantic struggle to escape of dying insects.

This is the best response of all four students. It takes Student C's comments and develops them further into a detailed and perceptive answer.

Look at how Gordon Grice uses a **simile** in the following extract, when remembering how the cloud of grasshoppers covered the wooden fence posts in great numbers.

Key term

Simile: a comparison showing the similarity between two quite different things, stating that one is *like* the other

---

Extract from *Deadly Animals: Savage Encounters Between Man and Beast* by Gordon Grice

When a stationary grasshopper got bumped, it would draw its legs in tight and shift its footing, like a rider crowded on a bus.

Activity 2

a. Re-read the four student comments on Grice's use of metaphor. Now write a similar comment that each of the students might make about Grice's use of simile. Rank your comments in the same way, with Student A's comment being the weakest and Student D's the best.

Support

Consider which two things are being compared and why. What effect is the writer trying to convey by comparing a grasshopper on the fence with a passenger who is 'crowded on a bus'?

b. Discuss your comments with a partner. Do you both agree that your four student comments are in the correct rank order?

Stretch

Read the full account of *Deadly Animals: Savage Encounters Between Man and Beast* by Gordon Grice. It deals with animal attacks on humans in a witty and extremely engaging way, although be warned – the details are graphic!

Now read Grice's original paragraphs, which contain both the metaphor and the simile.

Extract from *Deadly Animals: Savage Encounters Between Man and Beast* by Gordon Grice

One summer when I was a teenager the grasshoppers were everywhere. Every patch of weeds along the alley would erupt like a pan of popping corn if I set foot in it. When we drove the highway, we inadvertently slaughtered dozens. The collisions speckled our windshield with the clear hemolymph that served them as blood. Their wings, coffee-coloured fans striped with yellow at the outer edges, lodged in our wipers and fluttered in the onrushing air. Sometimes an entire grasshopper, or most of one, would lodge there as well, struggling to get free as the wind tore it to tatters.

They could be found in unaccustomed places that summer. I saw two or three swimming in the dog's water dish. The rosebushes took on the riddled look of lace, as though the grasshoppers had tasted the leaves and found them unappealing but serviceable. In the country, the cedar posts of barbed wire fences seemed to shimmer with heat, but a second glance showed the effect was no mirage. The posts were simply crawling with grasshoppers moving up or down for no obvious reason. They moved with great caution, edging past each other. When a stationary grasshopper got bumped, it would draw its legs in tight and shift its footing, like a rider crowded on a bus.

Activity 3

Using all the work you have done so far and any other examples of language in the text that you find effective, write your response to the following question:

Analyse Gordon Grice's use of imagery in his recollection of the grasshopper invasion.

7 Fireflies at dusk

You are going to write a description suggested by the picture below. You do not need to take the picture literally: 'suggested by' means you can use it as a starting point to stimulate your imagination.

A description is a picture made of words. It needs to contain vivid details so that the reader can experience every aspect of the person, place, thing or event being described.

The writer achieves this through the use of:

- sensory details that appeal to the reader's senses – what they can see, hear, touch, smell or taste
- effective vocabulary choices – specific adjectives and adverbs and powerful verbs that bring the description to life
- imagery, such as similes and metaphors
- organization of ideas.

Stage 1: Planning

Skills and objectives

- To communicate imaginatively, focusing in particular on description **(AO5)**
- To write clearly and accurately **(AO6)**

Activity 1

a. Look at the picture of the girl and the fireflies and make a note of anything that captures your interest. Use your imagination to consider when and where the scene is set, who the girl is and what she might be doing.

b. Think about the mood evoked by the picture. Make a list of words that capture this mood or atmosphere.

Sensory details

One way to make a description come to life is to include sensory details. What initially captured your interest about the picture was probably what you could see, but using the other senses helps to create a more complete picture for your reader.

Activity 2

a. Look at the following two sentences. With a partner, discuss which is more effective and why.

> There were some noises coming from the trees.

> Everything was silent, except for the sound of a night owl hooting, and she could hear her footsteps padding on the grass.

b. Look again at your notes on what initially captured your interest about the picture of the girl with the fireflies. Add any specific sound details, and then do the same for touch, smell and taste if they are appropriate.

Effective vocabulary choices

Another way to make a description come to life is to include effective vocabulary. Adjectives and adverbs are particularly useful as they provide interesting details to engage the reader.

Activity 3

a. Look at the highlighted words in the following sentence. With a partner, discuss what they add to the mood.

> Everything was eerily silent, except for the distant sound of a night owl hooting, and she could hear her footsteps padding softly on the grass.

b. Look again at your notes and add any adjectives and adverbs that will help you to create a more effective description of the picture.

You also need to be precise in your choice of vocabulary; selecting one word rather than another can completely alter the effect on the reader.

Writing tip

Remember to start your description in a way that captures your reader's interest immediately.

Activity 4

a. Look at the following two sentences. With a partner, discuss how the highlighted words affect the meaning.

> Fireflies radiated in the air as the girl wandered through the misty woods.
>
> Fireflies disturbed the air as the girl crept through the haunted woods.

b. Look again at your list of words that capture the mood of the picture. See if there are more sophisticated words that you could include instead, and add any other words you now think are appropriate.

Imagery

Another way to make a description come to life is to include imagery. Look back at your work on similes and metaphors in *Invasion!* (pages 32–35). Remember, you need to compare two things that are very different but have a point of similarity in order for the simile or metaphor to work. For example, 'Their wings, coffee-coloured fans striped with yellow at the outer edges, lodged in our wipers and fluttered in the onrushing air.'

Activity 5

Think of one or two similes or metaphors you could include in your description of the girl with the fireflies picture and add them to your notes.

Support Your point of similarity may be based on appearance, sound, behaviour or anything else of interest that your two things have in common.

Organization

Finally, you need to make sure that your writing is structured. There are a number of ways you can organize a description, including:

- Order of importance, where the most important details are included at the beginning or at the end. This is best used when describing a person or thing.
- Chronological order, where details are included in the order in which they happen. This is best used when describing an event.
- Spatial order, where details are included according to location, such as from left to right or from front to back. This is best used when describing a place.

Activity 6

Think about how best to organize your description. Look at all your notes and make a plan of where your ideas will best fit.

Stage 2: Writing

Activity 7

Using all the work you have done so far, write your response to the following:

Your school or college is inviting entries for a creative writing competition. Write a description suggested by the picture on page 36.

Stage 3: Proofreading

Activity 8

a. When you have finished writing your description, you need to proofread your work. Check that what you have written is clear and accurate.

b. Share your description with a partner. See if there are any further changes that could be made to improve your demonstration of AO6 skills.

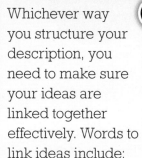

Writing tip

Whichever way you structure your description, you need to make sure your ideas are linked together effectively. Words to link ideas include:

- adverbials showing order of importance: 'initially', 'more impressively', 'best of all'
- adverbs of time showing chronological order: 'meanwhile', 'finally', 'afterwards'
- prepositions showing spatial order: 'beside', 'nearby', 'beyond'.

8 A place in the slime-light

It's a competitive world. From the international glory of the Olympic Games to the humble primary school sports day, we humans battle one another to be first past the post. We want to be the best. But bugs are different: they don't have the same need to prove themselves – their 'winners' tend to be the strongest, fittest specimens of their species. That is, until humans become involved, and suddenly bugs have to win as well – or at least their owners do!

The following is the opening paragraph from a newspaper article that takes a light-hearted look at the competitive world of snail racing.

- To evaluate how effectively the writer uses humour (**AO4**)
- To compare writers' ideas and perspectives (**AO3**)

As the world follows the Ashes, one village is all set for the snail-racing championships... ready, steady, slow!

by David Leafe

Flash and I have only just met, but I know we are going to make a great team. Yes, his personal hygiene could do with some improvement and he's not very talkative – in fact, he really needs to come out of his shell. But he does have one irresistible feature: his membership of the species Helix Aspersa. In other words, he is a common or garden snail. And in the small village of Congham in Norfolk, on this warm July afternoon, that makes him very sought-after indeed.

Key terms

Irony: the use of words that mean the opposite of what is said, for humour or emphasis

Wit: using words and ideas in a clever and inventive way to create humour

Pun: a joke made out of the different possible meanings of a word or phrase

Tone: a way of writing which conveys the writer's attitude towards the reader

David Leafe's purpose is to engage the reader through the use of humour, and in this opening paragraph, he achieves this by using several different techniques.

- **Irony:** 'Flash' is an ironic name because this is the exact opposite of how quickly a snail travels.
- **Wit:** 'his personal hygiene could do with some improvement' is witty because it makes it sound like the writer is talking about a man who doesn't wash, rather than a snail that lives in the dirty garden soil.
- **Pun:** 'he really needs to come out of his shell' is a pun because coming out of your shell can be interpreted both literally and metaphorically – to come out of your shell is to be more sociable and in the case of the snail, it actually has a real shell that it needs to come out of in order to race.

Activity 1

With a partner, discuss anything else you think is amusing in the headline or the opening paragraph.

The writer continues the article using the same light-hearted **tone**.

Aintree has the Grand National and Epsom the Derby, but Congham is home to that most thrilling of sports, the World Snail-Racing Championships. Around here, they talk about snails not as garden pests but as revered champions. 'Snails like damp conditions and as Congham is very low lying and surrounded by ponds, it is just right for them,' says churchwarden Hilary Scase, organiser of the event.

It was here, in this most English of villages, that a snail called Archie slid his way into the Guinness Book of Records back in 1995. He completed the 13 inch course in a far from sluggish two minutes and 20 seconds. His achievement stands intact and while I am hoping that Flash can surpass it, we undoubtedly face serious competition. [...]

Some 200 snails are expected to be entered for today's heats, competing for the trophy – a silver tankard filled with lettuce. Each will be identified by a number, written on a bright orange sticker attached to its back, and then placed in the middle of a round, wooden table. The course is dampened with a water-spray between each heat to encourage the snails to glide across it, and the first to reach the finishing line around the outside is the winner. [...]

As the race gets under way [...], Flash slips towards me, horns outstretched. For a few wonderful moments he lives up to his name, but suddenly he loses interest and stops dead.

The winner of Flash's heat, Terri, goes on to win the grand final at a snail's pace of two minutes 49 seconds. His trainer is nursery nurse Claire Hopkins, 27, from nearby Fakenham, whose partner Warren Hammond confides the chilling secret of her success: 'We told him that if he didn't win, we would feed him to the birds.'

Oh dear. I'm not sure I'm up to mollusc menacing, and I say goodbye to Flash, handing him to an enthusiastic young girl with a tub full of snails. He might have run at a snail's pace today, but who knows? With training, and a little intimidation, he might one day win his place in the slime-light.

Activity 2

a. Looking at the rest of the article, note any other examples of irony, wit or puns you find effective.

b. Find some examples where it is the ideas themselves that are funny and add them to your notes.

c. Discuss your notes with a partner. Which examples do you find particularly effective and why?

Stretch

The tone of an article often tells us how the writer feels about his subject. What do you think the humorous tone tells us about David Leafe's attitude to the World Snail-Racing Championships, and even the English as a nation? Do you think Claire and Warren think the same way?

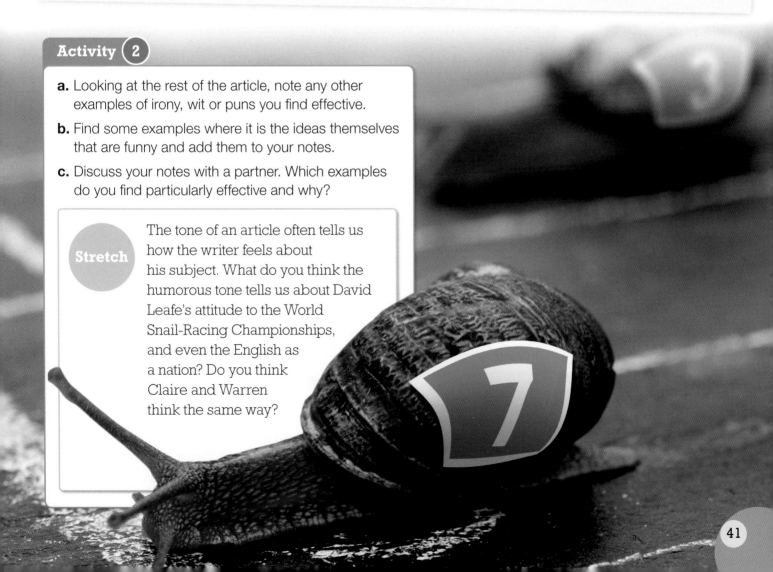

Activity 3

Using all the work you have done so far, write your response to the following question:

To what extent do you think the writer has been successful in creating a humorous article? Give your own opinion and quote from the text to support what you say.

The following extract is also about snail racing. This time seven-year-old Michael and his friend have secretly been collecting snails for weeks, making an adventure of searching through cabbage leaves and under bricks and stones. But on the day they decide to hold their race, the bullies attack.

Tip ✓

The skills you are practising with this text can be applied to any fiction or non-fiction text from any century.

Extract from *Grandad with Snails* by Michael Baldwin

One day we raced our snails on the table where his father sold trousers. I had watched through a door while his father stood with a measure around his neck and chalk in his hands, talking to men with creases; I had watched the blinds drawn up and the cloth folded, and his father go in to tea. Then we pulled the table from the shop into the yard, and started our races. The table was leathery green and the snails moved along it unrolling silver slime. We raced them in twos and fours. A face stood at my shoulder.

Then another, breathing over my head.

Then another.

The *boys* had got in!

One put his hand on a snail and pulled it, plop, from the table. It was Beauty!

He held it high in the air while my partner grabbed at it. Then he bent down and scooped its shell in some sand. Beauty bubbled through the sand and the sand wriggled. We grabbed again. He held us off, and the shell snapped between his thumb and finger. He wiped it off on my partner's coat.

We started to cry.

They did not run in a hurry: they jeered until they heard footsteps. Then they walked through the gate and slammed it shut.

Both the newspaper article and the extract about the bullies deal with the subject of snail racing, but they are written in different centuries and from different perspectives.

Activity 4

In small groups, discuss the similarities and differences of snail racing in the two texts.

In particular, you could analyse:

- who is racing the snails and why
- attitudes shown towards the snails
- the audience of the races .
- the writers' use of tone
- the writers' use of structure and language.

Activity 5

Using both sources and what you have learned from your discussion, write your response to the following:

Compare how the writers convey the subject of snail racing. Use your own words but also quote from both texts to support what you say.

Progress check

Use the chart below to review the skills you have developed in this chapter. For each Assessment Objective, start at the bottom box and work your way up towards the highest achievement in the top box. Use the box above your current achievement as your target for the next chapter. If you're at the top, can you stay there?

I can analyse ideas and synthesize evidence from different texts.	I can analyse a writer's choice of language and structure.	I can make detailed comparisons and analyse how writers' methods convey ideas.	I can evaluate the effect of a variety of writers' choices, using a range of quotations.	I can write convincingly, employing a range of complex linguistic and structural features.	I can use a range of effective sentences and spelling and punctuation are precise.
I can interpret ideas, select evidence and make clear connections between texts.	I can explain clearly the effects of language and structure.	I can compare ideas from different texts and explain how they are conveyed.	I can explain the effect of writers' methods, using relevant quotations.	I can write clearly and effectively, using linguistic and structural features appropriately.	I can use sentences for effect and spelling and punctuation are mostly accurate.
I can understand some ideas, linking evidence from different texts.	I can identify and comment on features of language and structure.	I can make comparisons between texts, commenting on how ideas are conveyed.	I can comment on writers' methods and use some quotations.	I can write with some success, using some linguistic features and paragraphs.	I can use a variety of sentence forms, with some accurate spelling and punctuation.
I can find information and ideas and make references to texts.	I can find examples of language and structure.	I can identify similarities and differences between texts.	I can give my views on texts and support them with evidence from the text.	I can write in a simple way to communicate my ideas.	I can write in sentences, using basic punctuation and some accurate spelling.
AO1	AO2	AO3	AO4	AO5	AO6

Assessment

This unit tests all the reading and writing skills that you have learned in this chapter to see if you are able to apply them to different sources.

Read the article below and then complete the activities that follow.

A bug's life: Bed bugs are back and living under a mattress near you!

THOUSANDS of families across the land are engaged in all-out war. The enemy? That remarkably hardy little beast, the bed bug.

by Rachel Carlyle

A fact of life in Victorian Britain but thought almost extinct by the 1980s, this unwelcome guest is making an alarming comeback. Pest control company Rentokil reports a 70 per cent increase in cases in the past three years, and the epidemic shows no sign of abating.

Bed bugs are small, rust-coloured creatures about the size of an apple pip. They can't fly, or even crawl very fast, but they are incredible survivors. During the day they live in crevices – the wooden frame of your bed or bedside table is ideal. Then at night they crawl out to feed off your blood. They can be difficult to detect because more than half of us don't react to the first bite. Another 10 per cent never react at all. Many people take weeks or even months to notice, and by then they have an infestation on their hands.

Company director Torie Chilcott knows exactly what that feels like. She and her family, from East Molesey in Surrey, had trouble with bugs following a trip to the Philippines. They assumed the problem had been solved after a mammoth spring-clean, but when Torie's nine-year-old son Archie arrived at her bedroom doorway one morning covered in bites, she searched his bed and immediately found the culprits.

'There were loads of them – on the bedding, hidden in the bed frame and even on his teddies. It was absolutely disgusting,' she says. 'I took two days off work and stripped the place. All the bedding went, the curtains went to the cleaners – I was like a woman possessed.' Torie also called in a pest-control team who sprayed chemicals all over the room. 'The bugs never got as far as my daughter Kate's bedroom,' she says. 'We were told they probably couldn't be bothered to go any further because they had everything they wanted in Archie's room – him.'

Contrary to popular opinion, bed bugs are not the result of poor domestic hygiene. If you have them, they probably hitched a lift in your luggage during your last holiday abroad. Hotels are a big source, as are cruise ships, hostels and even airline seats. Pest controllers told Torie Chilcott that her son's bugs had probably migrated from suitcases stored in a cupboard next to his room.

The bugs' resurgence since the 1980s may be because they are developing immunity to certain poisons, or it may simply reflect a more mobile human population. Either way, David Cain of London-based pest controllers Bed Bugs Ltd puts the problem in stark terms: 'I've heard it said that once you have stayed in 20 hotels, theoretically you will have picked them up.'

To remind yourself of how to apply AO1 skills, look back at the work you did in *All creatures great and small* (pages 14–17) and in *Industrious fleas* (pages 28–31).

Activity 1

a. Look at the first paragraph of the article. Find four explicit pieces of information about bed bugs in this paragraph.

b. Now look at the second paragraph. This contains both explicit and implicit ideas. What do you understand about bed bugs from this part of the text?

c. Using your answers to the above and the rest of the article, write your response to the following question:

What do you understand about bed bugs from the article? Use your own words but also quote from the text to support what you say.

To remind yourself of how to apply AO2 skills on structure, look back at the work you did in *The collecting bug* (pages 24–27).

Activity 2

a. Write a summary phrase for each of the six paragraphs.

b. Which text structures apply to this article and what effect does this have on the reader?

c. Select two or three sentences that you find particularly effective because of their structure and explain why they are so effective.

d. Using your answers to the above, and any other structural features you find interesting, write your response to the following question:

How has the writer structured the article to engage the reader?

To remind yourself of how to apply AO2 skills on language, look back at the work you did in *All creatures great and small* (pages 14–17) and *Invasion!* (pages 32–35).

Activity 3

a. The writer uses the words 'epidemic' in the first paragraph and 'infestation' in the second paragraph. What does her choice of language tell us about bed bugs?

b. In the sentence 'Then at night they crawl out to feed off your blood', what effect do the words 'crawl' and 'feed' have on the reader?

c. What is the effect of the metaphors 'all-out war' and 'enemy' in the article's subheading? What do they tell us about the relationship between humans and bed bugs?

d. Find two further examples of metaphors in the article and explain the effect on the reader. How do they add to your understanding of the text?

e. Using your answers to the above and any other examples of language that you find effective, write your response to the following question:

How does the writer use language to engage the reader?

Now read the following extracts from a short story called 'The Feather Pillow', written in 1907 by Horacio Quiroga, a writer known for his supernatural horror stories. Alicia, a beautiful, newly married young woman, inexplicably becomes ill with exhaustion and anaemia. Her husband Jordan and the doctors can do nothing to stop her decline and after being bed-ridden for five days, during which she begins to hallucinate, she dies. Only then does the housemaid discover what was lurking in her pillow and the true danger of bed bugs!

Extracts from 'The Feather Pillow' by Horacio Quiroga

Alicia began to have hallucinations, vague images, at first seeming to float in the air, then descending to floor level. Her eyes excessively wide, she stared continuously at the carpet on either side of the head of her bed. One night she suddenly focused on one spot. Then she opened her mouth to scream, and pearls of sweat suddenly beaded her nose and lips.

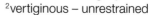

Alicia's life was fading away in the sub-delirium of anemia, a delirium which grew worse throughout the evening hours but which let up somewhat after dawn. The illness never worsened during the daytime, but each morning she awakened pale as death, almost in a swoon. It seemed only at night that her life drained out of her in new waves of blood. Always when she awakened she had the sensation of lying collapsed in the bed with a million-pound weight on top of her. Following the third day of this relapse she never left her bed again. She could scarcely move her head. She did not want her bed to be touched, not even to have her bedcovers arranged. Her crepuscular[1] terrors advanced now in the form of monsters that dragged themselves toward the bed and laboriously climbed upon the bedspread.

*****

Finally, Alicia died. The servant, when she came in afterward to strip the now empty bed, stared wonderingly for a moment at the pillow.

"Sir!" she called to Jordan in a low voice. "There are stains on the pillow that look like blood." [...]

Jordan picked it up; it was extraordinarily heavy. He carried it out of the room, and on the dining room table he ripped open the case and the ticking with a slash. The top feathers floated away, and the servant, her mouth opened wide, gave a scream of horror and covered her face with clenched fists: in the bottom of the pillowcase, among the feathers, slowly moving its hairy legs, was a monstrous animal, a living, viscous ball. It was so swollen one could barely make out its mouth.

Night after night, since Alicia had taken to her bed, this abomination had stealthily applied its mouth – its proboscis one might better say – to the girl's temples, sucking her blood. The puncture was scarcely perceptible. The daily plumping of the pillow had doubtlessly at first impeded its progress, but as soon as the girl could no longer move, the suction became vertiginous[2]. In five days, in five nights, the monster had drained Alicia's life away.

[1] crepuscular – nightly
[2] vertiginous – unrestrained

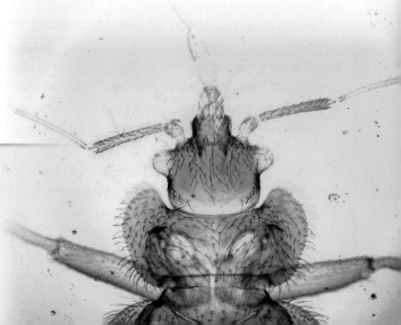

To remind yourself of how to apply AO4 skills, look back at the work you did in *Obsession* (pages 18–21) and *A place in the slime-light* (pages 40–43).

Activity 4

a. Look at the details used in the first extract to describe Alicia's hallucinations – what she does, thinks and feels – and also Quiroga's use of language. What do you find effective and why? How does this extract prepare the reader for what happens at the end?

b. Look at the details and Quiroga's choice of language in the second extract which describes Alicia's decline. What do you find effective and why? How does this extract also prepare the reader for what happens at the end?

c. The final extract reveals what has been happening to Alicia and the ultimate cause of her death. What do you find effective about the details and Quiroga's choice of language, and why?

d. Using your answers to the above and anything else you find interesting, write your response to the following question:

How successful is Quiroga in conveying Alicia's gradual decline and preparing the reader for the story's climax? Give your own opinion and quote from the text to support what you say.

Both the article and the short story extracts deal with the subject of bed bugs, but they are written in different centuries and from different perspectives.

To remind yourself of how to apply AO3 skills, look back at the work you did in *The collecting bug* (pages 24–27) and *A place in the slime-light* (pages 40–43).

Activity 5

a. How do humans and bed bugs interact in both the article and the short story extracts?

b. How do the writers use language and structure in very different ways?

c. Using your answers to the above and any other similarities or differences in the two texts, write your response to the following task:

Compare how the writers convey the subject of bed bugs. Use your own words but also quote from both texts to support what you say.

To remind yourself of how to apply AO5 and AO6 skills, look back at the work you did in *Caught in the spider's web* (pages 22–23) and *Fireflies at dusk* (pages 36–39).

Activity 6

Write either a narrative story or a description suggested by either of the sources used in this unit.

2 Fight for freedom

'Freedom!' is the cry which has echoed throughout history and across continents as people have risen up against their oppressors. It is a cry of protest, of injustice, but also of hope that one day things will be different.

In this chapter, you will hear the voices of people fighting for their freedom – freedom from prejudice, from oppression, from poverty and war. For many of them, writing about their experiences is the only way they can express how they feel and communicate with the wider world. They have written speeches, articles, novels, letters and essays to convey their ideas and demand freedom.

The chapter is divided into four units:

- Prejudice
- Oppression
- War
- Assessment.

The chapter begins with *Prejudice*. We all know how it feels to be treated differently because of the way we look or speak, or because of where we live or who we are. In this first unit, you will read texts about people who have suffered a range of different prejudices, some of which you may have experienced yourself.

At times through history, people's prejudices have hardened, sinking deeper into the minds and attitudes of those in power who use the rule of law to control and persecute the powerless. The second unit will introduce texts written by or about the oppressed.

In the third unit, ordinary people caught up in the extraordinary and often brutal events of war share their fears and hopes through factual and fictional accounts of their experiences.

In these first three units you will learn a number of reading and writing skills, and in the final assessment unit, you will be able to put these skills into practice to make sure you have understood them.

Skills, Assessment Objectives and examination coverage

All the skills covered in this chapter focus on the Assessment Objectives and are directly relevant to the requirements of English Language.

Reading skills include how to:

- identify and interpret ideas
- find and use quotations
- combine quotations from different texts
- explore the effects of language and structure
- compare and evaluate texts.

Writing skills include how to:

- write in different ways for different people
- adapt your style to match your audience
- write effectively and imaginatively
- organize ideas clearly.

For to be free is not merely to cast off one's chains, but to live in a way that respects and enhances the freedom of others.
Nelson Mandela from *Long Walk to Freedom*, 1994

The only real prison is fear, and the only real freedom is freedom from fear.
Aung San Suu Kyi

You can't separate peace from freedom because no one can be at peace unless he has his freedom.
Malcolm X, 1965

Activity

a. Discuss the quotations above with a partner. Which one do you think is the most convincing?

b. What topical news stories can you think of which relate to prejudice, oppression or war? Share your ideas in small groups.

Prejudice

In this unit, you will read texts about people who have suffered and fought against a range of different prejudices, including racial and gender discrimination. You will learn how to read these texts closely and how to **interpret** the different levels of meaning within the texts.

Skills and objectives

- To identify and interpret explicit and implicit ideas **(AO1)**
- To select evidence from texts **(AO1)**

Key terms

Interpret: explain the meaning of something in your own words, showing your understanding

Explicit: stated clearly, exactly and openly

1 Written in black and white

In 1963, Martin Luther King gave a speech against racial prejudice at a civil rights rally in Washington, USA.

Extract from a transcript of a speech by Martin Luther King

I am happy to join with you today in what will go down in history as the greatest demonstration for freedom in the history of our nation [...] There are those who are asking the devotees of civil rights: 'When will you be satisfied?' We can never be satisfied as long as the Negro* is the victim of the unspeakable horrors of police brutality. We can never be satisfied as long as our bodies, heavy with the fatigue of travel, cannot gain lodging in the motels of the highways and the hotels of the cities. We cannot be satisfied as long as the Negro's basic mobility is from a smaller ghetto to a larger one. We can never be satisfied as long as our children are stripped of their selfhood and robbed of their dignity by signs stating 'For Whites Only'. We cannot be satisfied and we will not be satisfied as long as a Negro in Mississippi cannot vote and a Negro in New York believes he has nothing for which to vote. No, no, we are not satisfied, and we will not be satisfied until 'justice rolls down like waters and righteousness like a mighty stream'.

*'Negro' is a term that is considered offensive nowadays and should be avoided, but it wasn't at the time when this speech was delivered.

When writing about texts, you need to provide evidence to support each idea you identify. This evidence should be quotations from the text. The quotations can be a sentence, phrase or a single word. You don't need to write out huge chunks of text for quotations. It is better to choose a word or phrase that relates exactly to what you say.

How you introduce the quotation into your writing is important, too. Try to weave it into your sentence as simply as you can. For example:

> In his speech, King is protesting against racism, as he writes 'we will not be satisfied as long as a Negro in Mississippi cannot vote'.

Activity 1

Look at the grid below. For each **explicit** idea listed, select a quotation from the extract opposite to support it.

Explicit idea	Selected quotation
The police are unfair in their treatment of black people.	'the Negro is the victim of the unspeakable horrors of police brutality'
Some hotels do not allow black people to stay there.	
Children are treated differently depending on the colour of their skin.	
Black people in Mississippi do not have the right to vote.	

Activity 2

a. Share the quotations in your grid with a partner. Discuss whether you could use shorter quotations and whether they would still make sense.

b. Write up the explicit ideas from your grid as a single paragraph. Use the quotations you have selected to support the ideas you have identified.

Tip ✓

Always refer to the writer by their last name, for example, King or Dickens, not Martin or Charles!

Activity 3

Read the second extract from King's speech below. What do you understand from this extract about Martin Luther King's hopes for the future? Remember to use quotations to support your answer.

Extract from a transcript of a speech by Martin Luther King

I have a dream that one day this nation will rise up and live out the true meaning of its creed: 'We hold these truths to be self-evident: that all men are created equal.'

I have a dream that one day on the red hills of Georgia the sons of former slaves and the sons of former slave-owners will be able to sit down together at a table of brotherhood.

I have a dream that one day even the state of Mississippi, a desert state, sweltering with the heat of injustice, sweltering with the heat of oppression, will be transformed into an oasis of freedom and justice.

I have a dream that my four little children will one day live in a nation where they will not be judged by the colour of their skin but by the content of their character.

I have a dream today!

Key terms 🔑

Implicit: implied or suggested but not stated openly; beneath the surface

Infer: reach an opinion from what someone implies, rather than from an explicit statement

To show a more developed understanding of what you read, you need to explore the **implicit** meanings of texts. This means explaining what is suggested or hinted at, rather than openly stated. For example:

This is the explicit idea.

This is the quotation.

This is an implicit meaning of the text.

In his speech, King is protesting against racism, as he writes 'we will not be satisfied as long as a Negro in Mississippi cannot vote', which suggests he is frustrated at the lack of freedom experienced by the black population.

King doesn't use the word 'frustrated' explicitly in the speech; it is something he implies and which the reader can **infer**.

The extract below is from the novel *Small Island* by Andrea Levy, written in 2004. Levy explores how racial prejudice was widespread in London after the Second World War. The narrator, Mrs Bligh, is a white woman who rents out rooms in her house.

Extract from *Small Island* by Andrea Levy

I knew he'd be round, as soon as that woman, Gilbert's wife, left her trunk in the road for all to see. A woman. You don't see many coloured* women. I'd seen old ones with backsides as big as buses but never a young one with a trim waist. His head popped out of his door then darted back in again. Probably went to get his shoes.

I was right. Not five minutes after Gilbert had taken the trunk inside he was on the door step. 'Mr Todd,' I said, 'what can I do for you?'

Another darkie*, that's what the look on his face said. The motley mixture of outrage, shock, fear, even – nostrils flaring, mouth trying to smile but only managing a sneer. 'Yes. I just wanted to have a quick word with you, Mrs Bligh, about your paying guests.'

I bet he did. He'd have told that horrible sister of his that more coloureds had just turned up. How many is it now? They'd have said to each other. Fifty? Sixty? 'You'll have to speak to her, Cyril,' she'd have told him, before bemoaning how respectable this street was before they came. They'd have got all those words out – decent, proper – polished them up and made them shine, before blaming Mrs Queenie Bligh for singlehandedly ruining the country. They were the same during the war, although even they couldn't blame me for that. Too many Poles. Overrun by Czechs. Couldn't move for Belgians. And as for the Jews. They moaned about the Jews even after we knew what the poor beggars had been through. They were all right in their own country, Mr Todd reasoned, but he wanted none of them down our street.

*The words 'coloured' and 'darkie' are considered offensive nowadays and should be avoided, but they were commonly used in the past.

Activity 4

Remember to use quotations to support your answers to the questions below.

a. How do think Mrs Bligh feels about Mr Todd and his sister?

b. Why is Mr Todd only able to manage a sneer rather than a smile?

c. What do you understand about Mr Todd's views on Mrs Bligh's paying guests?

Stretch

Do you think the author, Andrea Levy, shares the narrator's perspective? What clues are there in the text that she might or might not?

The black poet Benjamin Zephaniah is famous for making a stand against the prejudice that many black people have endured – and still do. He wrote the following article after he was told that the Queen wanted to give him an official honour – an OBE (Order of the British Empire).

Me? I thought, OBE me? Up yours, I thought. I get angry when I hear that word 'empire'; it reminds me of slavery, it reminds me of thousands of years of brutality, it reminds me of how my foremothers were raped and my forefathers brutalised. It is because of this concept of empire that my British education led me to believe that the history of black people started with slavery and that we were born slaves, and should therefore be grateful that we were given freedom by our caring white masters. It is because of this idea of empire that black people like myself don't even know our true names or our true historical culture. I am not one of those who are obsessed with their roots, and I'm certainly not suffering from a crisis of identity; my obsession is about the future and the political rights of all people. Benjamin Zephaniah OBE – no way Mr Blair, no way Mrs Queen. I am profoundly anti-empire.

Activity 5

Summarize Zephaniah's views on receiving the offer of an OBE.

In your response:

* identify both implicit and explicit ideas from the text
* select quotations to support your ideas
* interpret the ideas to show your understanding of their meaning.

Support

Which of these adjectives might describe how Zephaniah feels about being offered the OBE?

SPAG

insulted   delighted   embarrassed   angry

surprised   worried   disappointed   contemptuous

Choose three words and look for evidence in the text to support your choice.

Key term

Summarize: to give the main points of something briefly

Skills and objectives

- To interpret explicit and implicit ideas **(AO1)**
- To begin to compare ideas and tone **(AO3)**

2 Sugar and spice

It's easy to take freedom and equality for granted. Look at the people sitting in your classroom today. Boys or girls, you are all entitled to an education. Most of you can choose your career and marry or live with a partner of your choice. When you are 18 you will all have a vote and can even stand for Parliament yourself. It is hard for us to imagine how different life was for girls and women in the past.

In an essay written in 1929, the writer Virginia Woolf explores this issue. She imagines that William Shakespeare had an equally gifted sister called Judith.

Extract from *A Room of One's Own* by Virginia Woolf

She was as adventurous, as imaginative, as agog to see the world as he was. But she was not sent to school. She had no chance of learning grammar and logic, let alone of reading Horace and Virgil. She picked up a book now and then, one of her brother's perhaps, and read a few pages. But then her parents came in and told her to mend the stockings or mind the stew and not moon about with books and papers. They would have spoken sharply but kindly, for they were substantial people who knew the conditions of life for a woman and loved their daughter – indeed, more likely than not she was the apple of her father's eye. Perhaps she scribbled some pages up in an apple loft on the sly, but was careful to hide them or set fire to them.

Soon, however, before she was out of her teens, she was to be betrothed to the son of a neighbouring wool-stapler. She cried out that marriage was hateful to her, and for that she was severely beaten by her father. Then he ceased to scold her. He begged her instead not to hurt him, not to shame him in this matter of her marriage. He would give her a chain of beads or a fine petticoat, he said; and there were tears in his eyes. How could she disobey him? How could she break his heart? The force of her own gift alone drove her to it.

She made up a small parcel of her belongings, let herself down by a rope one summer's night and took the road to London. She was not seventeen. The birds that sang in the hedge were not more musical than she was. She had the quickest fancy, a gift like her brother's, for the tune of words. Like him, she had a taste for the theatre. She stood at the stage door; she wanted to act, she said. Men laughed in her face. The manager – a fat, loose-lipped man – guffawed. He bellowed something about poodles dancing and women acting – no woman, he said, could possibly be an actress. He hinted – you can imagine what. She could get no training in her craft. Could she even seek her dinner in a tavern or roam the streets at midnight? Yet her genius was for fiction and lusted to feed abundantly upon the lives of men and women and the study of their ways.

At last – for she was very young, oddly like Shakespeare the poet in her face, with the same green eyes and rounded brows – at last Nick Greene the actor-manager took pity on her; she found herself with child by that gentleman and so – who shall measure the heat and violence of the poet's heart when caught and tangled in a woman's body? – killed herself one winter's night and lies buried at some cross-roads where the omnibuses now stop outside the Elephant and Castle.

Activity 1

a. Read the extract and then write a list of the **facts** of Judith's life, like the one started below.

> 1. She didn't go to school.
> 2. She wasn't taught about language.

b. What does this tell you about Judith's life?

Key term

Fact: something that can be proved to be true

Virginia Woolf was a novelist as well as a writer of essays, and in this extract she uses a fictional story to express her views about the lack of equality and freedom suffered by girls in the past. Adding fictional details to her narrative increases the reader's sympathy for Judith and makes her message more powerful. There are many implied meanings in the extract which the reader can infer or interpret.

Activity 2

a. Why does Judith's father stop beating her and beg her instead?

b. Why does Woolf compare women acting to poodles dancing?

c. Why does Judith go to the stage door?

 Stretch What do you think Woolf means when she writes about the 'heat and violence of the poet's heart… caught and tangled in a woman's body'?

Activity 3

Using the list you made in Activity 1, and what you have learned from answering the questions in Activity 2, summarize Woolf's ideas about how girls were treated differently to boys in Shakespeare's time.

Perspectives on equality between men and women have changed over the past century. On these pages you will be looking at the perspectives of two different writers – one female and one male – comparing their views on equality. The extracts below are from the BBC's radio programme *Woman's Hour*, broadcast in 1947.

Extracts from a radio script from *Woman's Hour*, 1947

There used to be a time – and it wasn't very long ago – when there were some rather strict ideas about what they considered to be, as they put it, 'a woman's job'. And usually what was 'a woman's job' was certainly 'not a man's job'. Running a house – and all the work that's attached to it – was in this category, and although some men broke the rules and occasionally gave a hand at washing the dishes or even scrubbing a floor, they did it very secretly and no one was supposed to know. It was a disgraceful thing, in other words. Well, thank goodness we've progressed a bit since then. I'm not suggesting that we're reaching the stage when husbands stay at home and run the house while the wives go out and earn the money – even though humorists sometimes say we are. No! But at least there's no disgrace in a man taking the children for a walk or running the vacuum cleaner over the stair carpet nowadays.

* * *

The first thing that men discover when they start helping their wives is how badly women have been treated concerning their working conditions. We only seem to have realised during the past few years that a woman spends a very large part of her life in her kitchen. It therefore follows that the kitchen should be one of the best rooms in the house – bright, sunny and cheery, with as many labour-saving gadgets as possible. But is that the case? [...] Many a man, after helping his wife, has come to the conclusion that the vacuum cleaner or something like that which she's been asking for, perhaps for years, really is necessary after all.

Activity 4

a. With a partner, discuss the views of the writer of the radio script extracts using the questions below.

  i. Do you think the writer is a man or a woman? Why?

  ii. How do you think people's views have changed since this radio broadcast?

  iii. How do you think a woman might respond to these views?

b. Write three statements which summarize this writer's views.

The extract opposite is from the *Independent* newspaper in 2014. The writer is arguing that books and toys should not be labelled specifically for boys or girls.

Sugar and spice and all things nice, that's what little girls are made of. And boys? They're made of trucks and trains and aeroplanes, building blocks, chemistry experiments, sword fights and guns, football, cricket, running and jumping, adventure and ideas, games, farts and snot, and pretty much anything else they can think of.

At least, that's the impression that children are increasingly given by the very books that are supposed to broaden their horizons. [...]

There are those who will say that insisting on gender-neutral books and toys for children is a bizarre experiment in social engineering by radical lefties and paranoid 'femininazis' who won't allow boys to be boys, and girls to be girls. (Because, by the way, seeking equality of rights and opportunities was a key plank of Nazi ideology, was it?) But the 'experiment' is nothing new. When I grew up in the 1970s, and when my parents grew up in the 1950s, brothers and sisters shared the same toys, books and games, which came in many more colours than just pink and blue, and there was no obvious disintegration of society as a result. Publishers and toy companies like to say that they are offering parents more 'choice' these days by billing some of their products as just for boys and others as just for girls. What they're actually doing, by convincing children that boys and girls can't play with each other's stuff, is forcing parents to buy twice as much stuff.

Activity 5

a. What is the writer implying by giving so many examples of boys' interests?

b. Why do you think the writer mentions the colour of toys when she was growing up?

c. What do you think the writer means by the word 'femininazis'?

Both these texts are about gender equality. The writers have different points of view and adopt a very different **tone**. Adopting a particular tone can help writers to achieve their purpose.

Activity 6

a. Choose two adjectives to describe the tone of each text.

| aggressive | gentle | patronizing | frustrated | spiteful |

b. Add a quotation from the text to support your choice of each adjective.

c. Make notes on what effect adopting this tone might have on the reader or listener. Are they positive or negative effects?

Support Try reading parts of the texts aloud to a partner, using different expressions in your voice. Some will sound 'wrong', while others will match the words much better and help you identify the writer's tone.

Key term

Tone: a way of speaking or writing which conveys the speaker's or writer's attitude towards the listener or reader

Activity 7

Compare how equality is presented differently in these two texts. Comment on the ideas as well as the tone in which they are delivered.

3 Speaking out

- To organize information in order to communicate clearly and effectively **(AO5)**

- To check the clarity and accuracy of your work **(AO6)**

There are many different forms of prejudice in our society. People can be victims of prejudice on the grounds of race, colour, religion, gender, sexuality, age, appearance or disability.

Below are the opening paragraphs of an article which highlight the prejudice against gay footballers.

NEWSONLINE

FA and Premier League slammed by fans for failure to tackle anti-gay abuse

The Football Association faces calls for immediate action as authoritative research demonstrates that anti-gay abuse in the sport has been witnessed by seven in ten fans. The new Stonewall research also reveals that fans now expect visible action from the FA.

'Leagues behind – Football's failure to tackle anti-gay abuse' features a YouGov survey of over 2,000 football fans from across Britain and interviews with top football insiders and lesbian and gay players. It finds that:

- Three in five fans believe that anti-gay abuse from fans dissuades gay players from coming out

- Almost two thirds of fans believe football would be a better sport if anti-gay abuse was eradicated

- Two thirds of fans would feel comfortable if a player on their team came out

- Over half of fans think the FA, Premier League and Football League are not doing enough to tackle anti-gay abuse

'Sadly, this survey demonstrates that football is institutionally homophobic*,' says Ben Summerskill, Stonewall's Chief Executive. 'Too little action has been taken about an issue which deters not just gay players and fans from enjoying our national game, but also thousands of other fans too. Football has a firm track record tackling problems such as hooliganism and racism. But anti-gay abuse still almost always goes unchallenged. When England is looking to host and win the 2018 World Cup, football cannot risk this loss of potential talent and supporters.'

*homophobia – an irrational dislike and fear of gay people

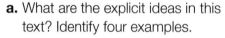

Structure: the organization of the text, how it is introduced, presented and concluded; structure also includes how paragraphs and ideas are grouped or linked together

Activity 1

a. What are the explicit ideas in this text? Identify four examples.

b. Summarize the views of the writer in one or two sentences.

c. What tone does the writer adopt and what is the effect of using it?

d. How does the writer use the following features to **structure** the text: introduction, conclusion, headline, interviews, bullet points?

Support Look at the headline for clues about the writer's tone. What does the word 'slammed' suggest about the writer's attitude?

Activity (2)

Write an article for a magazine to express your views against prejudice. The headline of the article should be:

> ## There is no place for prejudice in 21st-century Britain. We are all equal now.

The purpose of the article you are writing is to argue, so your argument needs to be clear and logical.

Use the steps below to help you plan, write and proofread your article.

Stage 1: Planning

- Decide what sort of prejudice you are interested in writing about. You may need to do some research about your chosen subject and make notes on useful facts and ideas. You may want to use quotations from interviews.
- Think carefully about your point of view. Have you thought about different aspects of your chosen topic? Are your ideas moderate or extreme?
- Share your ideas with a partner and consider any ideas that they suggest.
- Decide how you will structure your argument, and what organizational devices you will use to present your ideas, such as headings, subheadings, paragraphs and bullet points. Sketch out a rough plan showing the 'shape' of your argument.

> **Writing tip** /
>
> Avoid using too many facts or statistics in your writing. They can be useful to support your point of view, but do not overload your reader!

Stage 2: Writing

- Start writing, thinking carefully about the tone that you want to adopt. Remember that the tone can make a big difference to the effect of your article on the reader. Look at the two student texts. Read them aloud with a partner and decide what different effects they have on the reader.
- Complete your magazine article, referring back to your plans to check that you have included everything.

Stage 3: Proofreading

- Proofread your work, checking that what you have written is clear, accurate and includes a range of vocabulary. Use a dictionary to check spellings if necessary.
- Share your article with a partner. Invite them to suggest further changes to improve your work.

Student A

> I don't think anyone should judge someone because of how old they are. It isn't fair to pick on teenagers and young people as if they are all the same. There are lots of examples of teenagers who are not lazy or selfish.

Student B

> What gives anyone the right to judge someone else, just because of their age? It is ridiculous to assume that all people of the same age behave in the same way. Many teenagers are neither lazy nor selfish – take a look at Malala, a Nobel Prize winner and she's a teenager too!

Oppression

In this unit, you will read texts about people who are or have been oppressed, whose freedom has been curtailed by others who are more powerful than themselves. Oppression comes in many forms, including slavery, bullying and poverty.

Skills and objectives

- To analyse how writers use language and structure to achieve effects **(AO2)**

- To compare how writers convey their perspectives using language and structure **(AO3)**

Key term

Contrast: the use of opposing ideas and words in order to emphasize differences

4 Big Brother

People who are oppressed live with fear. They fear the powerful authorities that silence anyone who disagrees with them. They have no freedom.

Read the extracts on pages 60–63 taken from the start of the opening chapter of the novel, *Nineteen Eighty-Four*. The author, George Orwell, wrote the novel to express his fear of government becoming too powerful. Look carefully at how the structure builds up through each stage:

- opening sentence
- setting the scene
- spotlight on character
- first introductions
- shifting focus
- wider perspectives.

Opening sentence

> **Extract from *Nineteen Eighty-Four* by George Orwell**
>
> It was a bright cold day in April, and the clocks were striking thirteen.

The opening sentence in the structure of any text is very important because it needs to immediately capture the interest of the reader. It needs to have impact.

Activity (1)

The first part of Orwell's sentence appears very ordinary, but then it changes. Discuss the sentence with a partner.

a. What effect is created by each of the two clauses?

b. Why do you think the writer has created the **contrast**?

c. What do you think might be happening?

First introductions

> **Extract from *Nineteen Eighty-Four* by George Orwell**
>
> Winston Smith, his chin nuzzled into his breast in an effort to escape the vile wind, slipped quickly through the glass doors of Victory Mansions, though not quickly enough to prevent a swirl of gritty dust from entering along with him.

Having captured the reader's attention, the writer introduces a character, Winston, and where he lives. Structurally, Orwell uses a short paragraph so as not to give too much away and to entice the reader to find out more.

Activity 2

a. Pick out three words or phrases which you find evocative (producing particular feelings, images or memories). Write down the **connotations** of each word or phrase.

b. Compare your ideas with a partner. How and why do they differ?

Support Use a dictionary to look up the meaning of any words you are not sure about. You could also use a thesaurus to find other words with a similar meaning.

Key term

Connotation: an idea or feeling suggested, in addition to the main meaning; for example, the connotations of the word 'beach' might be sunshine or gritty sand, depending on your experience of the beach

Setting the scene

Extract from *Nineteen Eighty-Four* by George Orwell

The hallway smelt of boiled cabbage and old rag mats. At one end of it a coloured poster, too large for indoor display, had been tacked to the wall. It depicted simply an enormous face, more than a metre wide: the face of a man about forty-five, with a heavy black moustache and ruggedly handsome features. Winston made for the stairs. It was no use trying the lift. Even at the best of times it was seldom working, and at present the electric current was cut off during daylight hours. It was part of the economy drive in preparation for Hate Week. The flat was seven flights up, and Winston, who was thirty-nine and had a varicose ulcer above his right ankle, went slowly, resting several times on the way. On each landing, opposite the lift-shaft, the poster with the enormous face gazed from the wall. It was one of those pictures which are so contrived that the eyes follow you about when you move. BIG BROTHER IS WATCHING YOU, the caption beneath it ran.

BIG BROTHER IS WATCHING YOU

For a writer, starting a new paragraph is similar to a film director using the camera to change the perspective so the viewer focuses on something different.

By starting a new paragraph, the writer moves the reader's attention from the character to the setting. A setting may include physical details of places like the landscape, the buildings, the country or city, as well as the weather, the time of day or the season. The setting may also include, as in this extract, the society in which the characters live.

Activity 3

With a partner, find any clues that suggest the society in which the character lives is unlike our own. Be prepared to explain your ideas with close reference to the text.

Shifting focus

Extract from *Nineteen Eighty-Four* by George Orwell

Inside the flat a fruity voice was reading out a list of figures which had something to do with the production of pig-iron. The voice came from an oblong metal plaque like a dulled mirror which formed part of the surface of the right-hand wall. Winston turned a switch and the voice sank somewhat, though the words were still distinguishable. The instrument (the telescreen, it was called) could be dimmed, but there was no way of shutting it off completely.

Here the focus changes again. The first words of this paragraph signal to the reader where the action is moving: from outside to inside, to create a more personal, intimate view of where Winston lives.

Activity 4

Orwell uses a range of vocabulary in this extract and the words combine to create an overall impression. Select words from anywhere in the extracts up to this point which combine to create the effect of greyness and misery.

Spotlight on character

Extract from *Nineteen Eighty-Four* by George Orwell

He moved over to the window: a smallish, frail figure, the meagreness of his body merely emphasized by the blue overalls which were the uniform of the party. His hair was very fair, his face naturally sanguine, his skin roughened by coarse soap and blunt razor blades and the cold of the winter that had just ended.

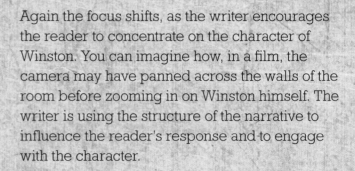

Again the focus shifts, as the writer encourages the reader to concentrate on the character of Winston. You can imagine how, in a film, the camera may have panned across the walls of the room before zooming in on Winston himself. The writer is using the structure of the narrative to influence the reader's response and to engage with the character.

Activity (5)

a. What does the word 'meagreness' suggest about Winston and his life?

b. Why do you think he is wearing 'the uniform of the party'?

c. What is the effect of describing his skin as 'roughened by coarse soap and blunt razor blades'?

Wider perspectives

Extract from *Nineteen Eighty-Four* by George Orwell

Outside, even through the shut window-pane, the world looked cold. Down in the street little eddies of wind were whirling dust and torn paper into spirals, and though the sun was shining and the sky a harsh blue, there seemed to be no colour in anything, except the posters that were plastered everywhere.

Orwell uses the start of the paragraph to shift the reader's focus again and uses the window as an effective structural device to widen the reader's perspective beyond the room where Winston is standing.

Extract from *Nineteen Eighty-Four* by George Orwell

In the far distance a helicopter skimmed down between the roofs, hovered for an instant like a bluebottle, and darted away again with a curving flight. It was the police patrol, snooping into people's windows. The patrols did not matter, however. Only the Thought Police mattered.

The writer has taken us on a journey from the beginning of the extract, introducing the character and the setting, and creating a sense of unease and fear, through both the structure and the language he has used.

Activity (6)

What images and language does the writer use in these final short extracts to convey the impression that Winston lives in a hostile, oppressive society?

With a partner, consider:

• the descriptions of the natural world

• the impression created by 'posters that were plastered everywhere'

• the effect of the word 'snooping'

• the repetition in the final two sentences.

Stretch How does Orwell prepare the reader in this opening section for a novel about the fate of an individual in an authoritarian state?

Halfway across the world and more than half a century later, a young Pakistani girl was protesting against the oppressive regime in her country which meant that only boys were allowed to go to school. Her public protests made her a target. The following extract is from her autobiography *I Am Malala*, written in 2013 when she was just 15 years old.

Extract from *I Am Malala* by Malala Yousafzai

One morning in late summer, when my father was getting ready to go to school he noticed that the painting of me looking at the sky which we had been given by the school in Karachi had shifted in the night. He loved that painting and had hung it over his bed. Seeing it crooked disturbed him. 'Please put it straight,' he asked my mother in an unusually sharp tone.

That same week our maths teacher Miss Shazia arrived at school in a hysterical state. She told my father that she'd had a nightmare in which I came to school with my leg badly burned and she had tried to protect it. She begged him to give some cooked rice to the poor, as we believe that if you give rice, even ants and birds will eat the bits that drop to the floor and will pray for us. My father gave money instead and she was distraught, saying that wasn't the same.

We laughed at Miss Shazia's premonition, but then I started to have bad dreams too. I didn't say anything to my parents but whenever I went out I was afraid that Taliban with guns would leap out at me or throw acid in my face, as they had done to women in Afghanistan. I was particularly scared of the steps leading up to our street where the boys used to hang out. Sometimes I thought I heard footsteps behind me or imagined figures slipping into the shadows.

Unlike my father, I took precautions. At night I would wait until everyone was asleep – my mother, my father, my brothers, the other family in our house and any guests we had from our village – then I'd check every single door and window. I'd go outside and make sure the front gate was locked. Then I would check all the rooms, one by one. My room was at the front with lots of windows and I kept the curtains open. I wanted to be able to see everything, though my father told me not to. 'If they were going to kill me they would have done it in 2009,' I said. But I worried someone would put a ladder against the house, climb over the wall and break in through a window.

Then I'd pray.

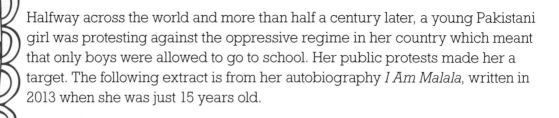

This text is non-fiction (which means the events really happened, unlike the events in the novel), but it is also a narrative. The writer uses structure to achieve similar effects for the reader.

The extract comes at the start of a chapter. The chapter ends with Malala being shot in the head on her way home from school. Structurally, the first paragraph establishes the scene: the characters, the setting and the viewpoint. The focus here is on the characters of Malala's father and mother; the setting is her parents' bedroom, one morning in late summer, and although Malala is writing from her own point of view, she uses the third person, as she is not personally involved in the action.

For the writer to build to a climax, she has to start at a low level. The effect of this opening paragraph is to set the scene for the reader in a calm, domestic way – nothing exciting happens, but there is a hint that things are not right.

Key terms

Symbol: something that is used to represent something else; often a simpler portrayal of something more complex or abstract

Connective: a word that joins phrases or sentences, such as: 'whereas', 'although', 'while', 'despite', 'therefore', 'alternatively', 'because'

Activity 7

a. Each of the three remaining paragraphs in the extract represents a shift in focus. For each of them, make detailed notes on how the structural focus shifts, in terms of character, setting and viewpoint.

b. How does the writer use structural features to emphasize her growing fears?

Stretch The extract offers glimpses of a distorted reality, which foreshadows the violent disfigurement of Malala, shot later in the chapter. Explore the symbolic and structural significance of the crooked picture, the teacher's nightmare and the threat of having acid thrown in her face.

As well as structure, Yousafzai also uses language to help the reader understand and empathize more closely with her experience.

Activity 8

Answer the following questions, where necessary using quotations from the text to support your response.

a. What are the connotations of the words 'crooked,' 'disturbed' and 'unusually sharp' in the first paragraph and what mood or atmosphere do they create?

b. How does the writer use the painting as a **symbol** in this extract?

c. What is the effect of using the **connective** 'but' in the opening sentence of the third paragraph?

d. What effect is created by the use of the phrase 'figures slipping into the shadows'?

e. How does the writer use listing in the last paragraph to have an effect on the reader?

f. There is a range of tenses used in the last paragraph. What effect does this have?

g. What is the impact of the final sentence?

Activity 9

Compare how a similar sense of foreboding is created by the writers in the extracts from *Nineteen Eighty-Four* and *I Am Malala*.

You should analyse the use of both language and structure in your response.

5 A slave's tale

- To select evidence from texts **(AO1)**
- To communicate imaginatively for different purposes, forms and audiences **(AO5)**

Key term 🔒

First-person narrative: story or account told from the point of view of a character or person involved, typically using the pronoun 'I'

Slavery is a means of oppression where people are bought and sold like property. Although slavery is now illegal in every country in the world, it still continues illegally.

In this session you will read a personal account of slavery and write a **first-person narrative** of your own.

The following extract was written in 1861 by Harriet Jacobs.

Extract from *Incidents in the Life of a Slave Girl* by Harriet Jacobs

When I was six years old, my mother died; and then, for the first time, I learned, by the talk around me, that I was a slave. My mother's mistress was the daughter of my grandmother's mistress. She was the foster sister of my mother. They played together as children; and, when they became women, my mother was a most faithful servant to her whiter foster sister. [...] I grieved for her, and my young mind was troubled with the thought who would now take care of me and my little brother. I was told that my home was now to be with her mistress; and I found it a happy one. [...] My mistress was so kind to me that I was always glad to do her bidding, and proud to labor for her as much as my young years would permit. I would sit by her side for hours, sewing diligently, with a heart as free from care as that of any free-born white child. [...] Those were happy days—too happy to last. The slave child had no thought for the morrow; but there came that blight, which too surely waits on every human being born to be a chattel[1].

When I was nearly twelve years old, my kind mistress sickened and died. [...] I was now old enough to begin to think of the future; and again and again I asked myself what they would do with me. I felt sure I should never find another mistress so kind as the one who was gone. [...] After a brief period of suspense, the will of my mistress was read, and we learned that she had bequeathed[2] me to her sister's daughter, a child of five years old.

[1] chattel – possession
[2] bequeathed – left in a will

Activity ①

Imagine that a teacher is producing a worksheet to teach students about slavery. The teacher wants to use evidence from this extract to show how slaves were treated as possessions. Select three quotations from the extract which highlight how the slave girl was treated as a possession and explain what each quotation reveals about slavery.

Activity 2

a. What is the effect of using a first-person narrative, knowing that the narrator is writing about her own life?

> **Stretch**
>
> Why do you think Jacobs chose to use this narrative form for her writing? What alternatives could she have chosen and what difference would it make to the effect on the reader and to achieving her purpose?

b. Write your own first-person narrative, following the steps below. The title should echo the extract opposite: 'Incidents in the Life of _____'.

Stage 1: Planning

Before you start writing, you need to make notes on character and structure.

Character

In a first-person narrative, a writer can either write about their own life or adopt a **persona**. You could choose a persona from any age or culture – for example, a Tudor princess, an American astronaut or an Olympic athlete. Think about the voice of this persona and how you will convey their character through your writing.

> **Key term**
>
> **Persona:** a character that the writer imagines themselves to be

Structure

You will need to structure your writing in paragraphs. Think about how you will move the narrative on by shifting the reader's focus in each paragraph. You could move from what is happening around you to what you are thinking; from small details to a wider perspective; from a viewpoint inside to the view outside.

Write a heading for each of your paragraphs to plan how your writing will develop.

Stage 2: Writing

Write your narrative, using your planning notes. Make sure you include details about your character and setting and that you follow a clear structure of paragraphs.

Stage 3: Proofreading [SPAG]

When you have finished writing, proofread your work. Check that what you have written is clear and well-structured.

6 Soup and crackers

Poverty can be oppressive. Lack of money can weigh people down with worry and fear. Here you will **evaluate** two non-fiction texts in which writers explore the effects of poverty. You will learn how to summarize quotations from both and how to make a comparison of the writers' ideas and methods.

The first extract was written by Henry Mayhew in 1861. Mayhew is writing about the lives of costermongers, whose job was to sell fruit on the streets.

- To synthesize evidence from different texts **(AO1)**

- To compare writers' perspectives and how these are conveyed **(AO3)**

- To evaluate texts critically **(AO4)**

Key term

Evaluate: to judge the value, quality or success of something

---

Extract from *London Labour and the London Poor* by Henry Mayhew

The story of one coster-girl's life may be taken as a type of the many. When quite young she is placed out to nurse with some neighbour. [...] As soon as it is old enough to go alone, the court is its play-ground, the gutter its school-room, and under the care of an elder sister the little one passes the day, among children whose mothers like her own are too busy out in the streets helping to get the food, to be able to mind the family at home. When the girl is strong enough, [...] she is lent out to carry about a baby, and so made to add to the family income by gaining her sixpence weekly. Her time is from the earliest years fully occupied; indeed, her parents cannot afford to keep her without doing and getting *something*. Very few of the children receive the least education. 'The parents,' I am told, 'never give their minds to learning, for they say, "What's the use of it? That won't yarn[1] a gal a living."' [...]

At about seven years of age the girls first go into the streets to sell. A shallow basket is given to them, with about two shillings for stock-money, and they hawk[2], according to the time of year, either oranges, apples, or violets; some begin their street education with the sale of water-cresses. The money earned by this means is strictly given to the parents. Sometimes – though rarely – a girl who has been unfortunate during the day will not dare to return home at night, and then she will sleep under some dry arch or about some market, until the morrow's gains shall ensure her a safe reception and shelter in her father's room.

The life of the coster-girls is as severe as that of the boys. Between four and five in the morning they have to leave home for the markets, and sell in the streets until about nine. Those that have more kindly parents, return then to breakfast, but many are obliged to earn the morning's meal for themselves. After breakfast, they generally remain in the streets until about ten o'clock at night; many having nothing during all that time but one meal of bread and butter and coffee, to enable them to support the fatigue of walking from street to street with the heavy basket on their heads. [...]There are many poor families that, without the aid of these girls, would be forced into the workhouse[3].

[1]yarn – earn
[2]hawk – carry and sell things
[3]workhouse – place where poor people could work for very basic food and accommodation

Over 150 years later, a single mum from the North East wrote about her own life of poverty in a newspaper article.

Maria lives in a bungalow she can't afford to rent and suspects that she and her two-year-old son, Taiu, will be evicted soon

I survive on food from food banks, and by selling things I own. I often go without meals, but always ensure Taiu eats. I'm told that families like mine normally spend £35 a week on food. I have that for a month to buy things in Iceland. We eat a lot of soup and crackers. Taiu loves that. I prefer fresh vegetables, but the price of them is so high. At Christmas my dad sent me a little hamper from America and also someone from church sent me a shop round from Tesco. I think they found out by accident that I was really struggling because I try and keep quite private about that – I think that's pride.

I'm struggling at the moment and it's like, "Right, what can I pay today?" And that's it; it's the bills and everyone's had their gas and electric bills go up. When mine went up they said to me "Sorry, we haven't been charging you enough for the last year, so you now owe us". I mean, they just sent me a bill for £423 because I was paying my gas and electric bills at £38 a month and they turned around and said "We should have been charging you over £70 a month". Their mistake, but now they're expecting it all. [...]

There's no public transport in this town between eight and nine in the morning, on Sundays, and after six o'clock. My work as a care co-ordinator started at nine. I was working in town but there were no buses. I could get in for about quarter past nine and then try to make the time up in my break. My work said no. You can start at half nine, but you've got to work to half five. I told them if I work until then the next bus is at a quarter past six, by the time I've picked my son up and got home its going to be gone seven. I said I couldn't do that, plus they wanted me to be on call one week per month, which means if anyone got sick or couldn't do a care call I'd have to do it. I just couldn't do it.

I've got a lot of stuff off Freecycle, toys for my son and charity shops or eBay. For Christmas I go on to eBay – you can get good toys on there and if you can watch things you can get a £20 toy for a couple of pounds.

Shoes for him are always second hand. He hasn't had a brand new pair of shoes for a long time. My sister gives me some of her son's shoes but Taiu is a narrow fitting [...] I know you have to be careful with their feet as they're growing.

Taiu misses out on activities and going out and doing things, other than just going to the park. One of my friends said, "Let's go on holiday – let's do the 10 pound holiday". I can't afford that. It's 10 pound each, plus you've then got to pay your electric, then you've got to buy your food when you're there, then you've got to pay for your transport, then you've got to pay for your excursions. It's too much.

There are similarities and differences between these two accounts. You are going to explore these by using quotations from both texts and synthesizing them. Synthesis means bringing together ideas and quotations from different sources and making connections between them.

Activity 1

a. Discuss the similarities and differences between the parents in these two texts. Think about:

- how they feed their children
- how they care for their children
- what work they do
- what effect poverty has on them and the children.

Choose four ideas from each text about the parents and select quotations to support these ideas.

 Support Lay out your ideas and quotations in a grid like the one started below.

Explicit idea	Quotation from text 1	Quotation from text 2
Parents feed children	'after breakfast'	'soup and crackers'

Tip ✓

Use words such as 'whereas', 'although', 'equally', 'in contrast', 'however', 'likewise' and 'similarly' when writing about the ideas in two different texts.

b. What is implied by each of the quotations about the writer's perspective on parents?

c. Summarize the similarities and differences between the ideas about parents in these two texts, using the quotations you have selected to support what you have written, including any inferences you have made.

Comparing texts is not just about the ideas and perspectives the writers present. It is also about comparing how they convey or put across their ideas to the reader. The first step is to identify what the writers' ideas and perspectives are.

Activity 2

a. Read both extracts again and select four ideas about poverty from each text, with quotations to support them, as in the previous activity.

b. What can you infer about poverty from these quotations?

Once you have identified the writers' points of view, you need to consider how they express those points of view.

When writing about how ideas of poverty are presented you need to focus on:

● language – what features are used to create an effect on the reader

● structure – how ideas are organized to engage the reader's interest

● tone – what attitude or feeling the writer wants to convey to the reader.

Activity 3

a. Make notes on the language, structure and tone of these two texts. Are the methods used by the writers similar or different?

b. What is the effect on the reader of using these methods? Analyse the effects in both texts.

c. Using all the work you have done so far, write a response to the task below:

Compare the writers' ideas on poverty in these two texts and how they are presented.

Having explored the ideas and methods the two writers presented, you are in a good position to be able to evaluate their success.

Activity 4

Read the extract from the article about Maria and answer the question below, using quotations to support your **opinions**.

How successful do you think the writer has been in engaging the reader's sympathy for her situation?

 Stretch Write a response to the editor of the newspaper, regarding the article about Maria and her son, offering your own views on poverty and parenting. Consider carefully how to structure your response and what tone and **register** would be most appropriate.

> ### Key terms
>
> **Opinion:** a view or judgement not necessarily based on fact or knowledge
>
> **Register:** the kind of words (for example, formal, informal, literary) and the manner of speaking or writing used; varies according to the situation and the relationship of the people involved

> ### Tip ✓
>
> The focus of this question is on 'engaging the reader's sympathy', so all your comments should be directed towards evaluating the success of that particular aspect. You need to judge how well the writer has used ideas, language, structure and tone to engage the reader's sympathy.

War

The fight for freedom can lead to war. Two world wars have dominated European history in the last 100 years, but as time moves on, living memories fade and we rely more and more on people's written accounts of their experiences during those war years.

7 Fighting talk

Skills and objectives

- To analyse how writers use language to achieve effects and influence readers **(AO2)**
- To compare how writers convey ideas through language and tone **(AO3)**

The extract below is an autobiographical account of a soldier arriving in the trenches, in France, during the First World War.

Extract from *Goodbye to All That* by Robert Graves

Collecting the draft of forty men we had with us, we followed [the man] through the unlit suburbs of the town – all intensely excited by the noise and flashes of the guns in the distance. None of the draft had been out before, except the sergeant in charge. They began singing. Instead of the usual music-hall songs, they sang Welsh hymns, each man taking a part. The Welsh always sang when pretending not to be scared; it kept them steady. And they never sang out of tune.

We marched towards the flashes, and could soon see the flare-lights curving across the distant trenches. The noise of the guns grew louder and louder. [...] From about two hundred yards behind us, on the left of the road, a salvo of four shells whizzed suddenly over our heads. This broke up *Aberystwyth* in the middle of a verse, and sent us off our balance for a few seconds; the column of fours tangled up. The shells went hissing away eastward; we saw the red flash and heard the hollow bang where they landed in German territory […]

The roadside cottages were now showing more and more signs of dilapidation. A German shell came over and then whoo – oo – ooo – oooOOO – bump – CRASH! landed twenty yards short of us. We threw ourselves flat on our faces. Presently we heard a curious singing noise in the air, and then flop! flop! little pieces of shell-casing came buzzing down all around. 'They call them the musical instruments,' said the sergeant. 'Damn them,' said my friend Frank Jones-Bateman, cut across the hand by a jagged little piece, 'the devils have started on me early.' 'Aye, they'll have a lot of fun with you before they're done, sir,' grinned the sergeant. Another shell came over. Everyone threw himself down again, but it burst two hundred yards behind us. Only Sergeant Jones had remained on his feet. [...]

After a meal of bread, bacon, rum, and bitter stewed tea sickly with sugar, we went through the broken trees to the east of the village and up a long trench to battalion headquarters. The wet and slippery trench ran through dull red clay. I had a torch with me, and saw that hundreds of field mice and frogs had fallen into the trench but found no way out. The light dazzled them, and because I could not help treading on them, I put the torch back in my pocket.

Activity 1

a. With a partner, group the words and phrases below according to whether they are examples of **alliteration**, onomatopeia, verbs, noun phrases or repetition.

louder and louder   broken trees   buzzing   dull red clay   flop! flop!

jagged little piece   CRASH   red flash   flare-lights   hollow bang

flat on our faces   unlit suburb   hissing   burst   dazzled   bump   whizzed

b. Choose three examples and discuss the effect they have on you as a reader.

Key term

Alliteration: repetition of the same letter or sound at the beginning of several words

Activity 2

Read the following examples of students writing about the effects of language. Decide which you think is the best of the three responses and discuss why with your partner.

Consider whether the student:

- uses an appropriate quotation
- uses the correct term to identify the language feature
- offers a general comment on the effect of the language on the reader
- develops their response to analyse the effect in this specific text.

Student A

The writer uses repetition to describe how lots of shell casings fell on them: 'flop! flop!' This makes the reader think about how small they were because the words are small. But although the shell casings were small, the 'jagged little pieces' still hurt.

Student B

The writer describes the shell casings falling. He uses the words 'flop! flop!' to describe the noise they make when they land on the soldiers. The language makes the reader feel as if they were really there. It makes the description come alive.

Student C

The writer uses onomatopoeia with the words 'flop! flop!' to create an impression of how the shell casings fell, small and harmless, more like raindrops than weapons, in contrast to the 'bang' and 'crash' of the shells. The flopping sound is juxtaposed to the sound of singing, as if the shells too were musical instruments, but deadly.

Reading tip 📖

When analysing language, focus on the effect the language has on the reader – how the words make the reader think, feel, imagine or respond.

Key term 🔑

Symbolism: the use of symbols to represent something else; often a simpler portrayal of something more complicated or abstract

Activity

a. What do you think the dialogue (speech) in this extract adds to the overall effect of the description?

b. How does Graves use contrast in the extract to enhance the overall effect? Think about the way he writes about light and dark, ignorance and experience.

c. How does Graves use language to give readers a vivid impression of the sights and sounds of the battlefield?

Stretch Graves uses the idea of the soldiers singing as a symbol of their bravery and describes how their song, and also their courage, falters under fire. How does he use **symbolism** in his description of the field mice and frogs?

One of Robert Graves' comrades was a poet, Siegfried Sassoon. While on leave, Sassoon wrote a letter to his Commanding Officer refusing to return to fight in France. The letter was published in *The Times* in 1917.

Extract from 'Finished with War – A Soldier's Declaration' by Siegfried Sassoon

I am making this statement as an act of wilful defiance of military authority because I believe that the war is being deliberately prolonged by those who have the power to end it. I am a soldier, convinced that I am acting on behalf of soldiers. I believe that the war upon which I entered as a war of defence and liberation has now become a war of aggression and conquest. I believe that the purposes for which I and my fellow soldiers entered upon this war should have been so clearly stated as to have made it impossible to change them and that had this been done the objects which actuated us[1] would now be attainable by negotiation.

I have seen and endured the sufferings of the troops and I can no longer be a party[2] to prolong these sufferings for ends which I believe to be evil and unjust. I am not protesting against the conduct of the war, but against the political errors and insincerities for which the fighting men are being sacrificed.

On behalf of those who are suffering now, I make this protest against the deception[3] which is being practised on them; also I believe it may help to destroy the callous complacency[4] with which the majority of those at home regard the continuance of agonies which they do not share and which they have not enough imagination to realise.

[1] the objects which actuated us – the aims that motivated us
[2] be a party – agree
[3] deception – lying and secrecy
[4] callous complacency – unfeeling smugness

Activity 4

a. What do you think is the purpose of each of these texts?

b. Discuss with a partner what the major difference is between the ideas and perspectives in these two texts. What impact do you think two years of fighting has made on the soldiers? Does that explain their differences?

c. Both writers use the first person, but very differently. Discuss the differences in the writers' choices and their impact on the reader.

Activity 5

a. Consider the way Sassoon uses language in his *Declaration*. The register he uses is very formal. Why do you think he uses such formal language?

b. The tone of these two texts is very different. Discuss how you would describe the tone each writer uses, for example, sentimental, apologetic, assertive, humorous, detached, passionate, indifferent, determined.

c. What is the effect on the reader of adopting a particular tone?

Activity 6

Using all the work you have done so far, complete the following task:

Compare how the writers' perspectives on war are presented differently in the two texts.

 Support

When comparing texts, you are often given a particular aspect to compare. In this case, how the writers present their views on war. Therefore, your focus needs to be on the writers' methods. You have explored a range of methods so far in this section:

- language
- dialogue
- contrast
- register
- tone
- point of view.

To write your answer, choose four of these methods to explore in more detail. Structure your answer by using a separate paragraph to analyse how each writer uses each method, giving you a total of eight paragraphs.

Conclude your answer by explaining which text you think is the most effective.

> **Tip** ✓
>
> Remember that whether you are writing about ideas, language, register or tone, you always need to provide evidence (quotations) from the texts to support what you have written.

8 Operation Dynamo

Skills and objectives

- To analyse how writers use structure to achieve effects **(AO2)**

- To evaluate texts critically and use appropriate evidence from texts **(AO4)**

Operation Dynamo was the codename for the massive rescue operation of British soldiers stranded at the port of Dunkirk in France during the Second World War.

The extract below is from an eyewitness account of one of the men who sailed to the rescue. After reading it, you will consider how the structure of his account achieves particular effects. You will also have the opportunity to evaluate the success of the account.

Extract from 'Miracle at Dunkirk' by Arthur D. Devine

It was the queerest, most nondescript flotilla* that ever was, and it was manned by every kind of Englishman, never more than two men, often only one, to each small boat. There were bankers and dentists, taxi drivers and yachtsmen, longshoremen, boys, engineers, fishermen and civil servants […]

It was dark before we were well clear of the English coast. […] Soon, in the dark, the big boats began to overtake us. We were in a sort of dark traffic lane, full of strange ghosts and weird, unaccountable waves from the wash of the larger vessels. When destroyers went by, full tilt, the wash was a serious matter to us little fellows. We could only spin the wheel to try to head into the waves, hang on, and hope for the best […]

Even before it was fully dark we had picked up the glow of the Dunkirk flames, and now as we drew nearer the sailing got better, for we could steer by them and see silhouetted the shapes of other ships, of boats coming home already loaded, and of low dark shadows that might be enemy motor torpedo boats.

Then aircraft started dropping parachute flares. We saw them hanging all about us in the night, like young moons. The sound of the firing and the bombing was with us always, growing steadily louder as we got nearer and nearer. The flames grew, too. From a glow they rose up to enormous plumes of fire that roared high into the everlasting pall of smoke. As we approached Dunkirk there was an air attack on the destroyers and for a little the night was brilliant with bursting bombs and the fountain sprays of tracer bullets.

The beach, black with men, illumined by the fires, seemed a perfect target, but no doubt the thick clouds of smoke were a useful screen […]

The picture will always remain sharp-etched in my memory – the lines of men wearily and sleepily staggering across the beach from the dunes to the shallows, falling into little boats, great columns of men thrust out into the water among bomb and shell splashes. The foremost ranks were shoulder deep […] As the front ranks were dragged aboard the boats, the rear ranks moved up, from ankle deep to knee deep, from knee deep to waist deep, until they, too, came to shoulder depth and their turn. […]

There was always the red background, the red of Dunkirk burning. There was no water to check the fires and there were no men to be spared to fight them. Red, too, were the shell bursts, the flash of guns, the fountains of tracer bullets.

*flotilla – small fleet of boats

The account is a factual narrative – it is telling a story, but a true story. The narrative is structured in a traditional way. It is **chronological** and takes the reader on a journey from one place to another; the text begins on the English coast and travels across the sea to the French coast.

Activity 1

Imagine you are a film director who is making a film of this account. Design a storyboard to show the different shots you will film. For each paragraph of the text, identify the writer's viewpoint and describe how you would show the shift in focus. You could draw pictures but also describe in words what should be in each shot.

Read each paragraph carefully to consider where the writer's focus is, such as looking forward or looking back; up or down; detailed or distant; inside or outside, happening in reality or as thoughts in his head.

> For example: Picture/Paragraph 1 – close-up shot of the men in their boats leaving England which is visible behind them. Showing details of the men to see that they are different, e.g. fishermen, boys.
>
> Picture/Paragraph 2 – long shot, taken from the boat, maybe with movement to show the waves, looking towards France, taking in the returning boats and the destroyers passing by.

Having identified some of the structural features the writer uses, you need to ask why the writer has chosen to organize their ideas like this. A structural feature is a tool, just like a language feature, and each one can be used to create different effects. For example, the purpose of narrowing the focus is to concentrate the reader's attention on details. The effect of that could be to create a feeling of intrigue, or a sense of disgust, or to engage the reader's sympathy, depending on the context. So when writing about structure, you need to analyse:

- which structural feature is used
- why it is used
- what effect it creates in this specific text.

Activity 2

Use the diagram on page 78 to explore some of the possible effects of a range of structural features and answer the following question:

How has the writer used structure in this extract to capture the interest of the reader?

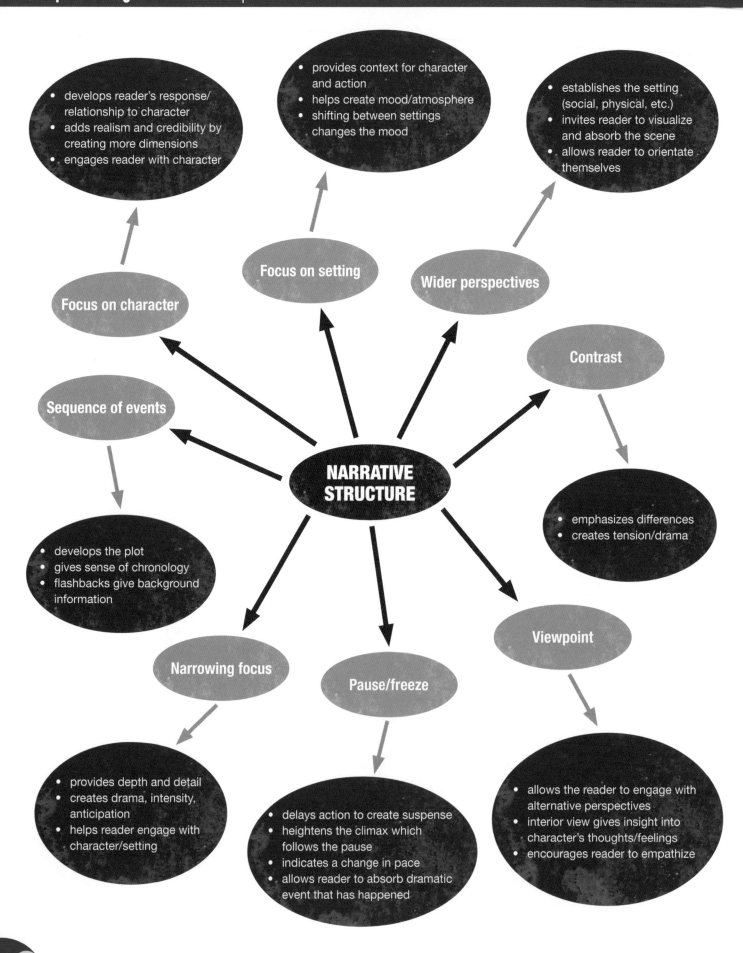

NARRATIVE STRUCTURE

Focus on character
- develops reader's response/ relationship to character
- adds realism and credibility by creating more dimensions
- engages reader with character

Focus on setting
- provides context for character and action
- helps create mood/atmosphere
- shifting between settings changes the mood

Wider perspectives
- establishes the setting (social, physical, etc.)
- invites reader to visualize and absorb the scene
- allows reader to orientate themselves

Contrast
- emphasizes differences
- creates tension/drama

Sequence of events
- develops the plot
- gives sense of chronology
- flashbacks give background information

Narrowing focus
- provides depth and detail
- creates drama, intensity, anticipation
- helps reader engage with character/setting

Pause/freeze
- delays action to create suspense
- heightens the climax which follows the pause
- indicates a change in pace
- allows reader to absorb dramatic event that has happened

Viewpoint
- allows the reader to engage with alternative perspectives
- interior view gives insight into character's thoughts/feelings
- encourages reader to empathize

Evaluating texts means judging how well you think the writer has succeeded in achieving their purpose and the effects they wanted to create. This means writing about ideas, language and structure in just the same way as you have been practising already and bringing them all together in one essay.

Writing an evaluation may seem a daunting task, but it helps to break it down into separate steps.

Activity 3

One student wrote the following about 'Miracle at Dunkirk':

'It really brings alive what it was like to be there that night. You can almost see the "plumes of fire" he describes.'

How far do you agree with this student?

Step one: Choose three or four elements from the text which you find interesting. It could be the language, mood and setting; or the characters, structure and tone.

Step two: For each of these elements, you need to provide three or four examples from the text and explain in detail how and why the writer has used them, how well you think the writer has succeeded and what effect they have on you as the reader.

Step three: Every example you choose has to be supported with an appropriate, accurate quotation from the text.

Step four: Conclude your response with one or two sentences to summarize your view of the writer's overall success.

Progress check

Use the chart below to review the skills you have developed in this chapter. For each Assessment Objective, start at the bottom box and work your way up towards the highest achievement in the top box. Use the box above your current achievement as your target for the next chapter. If you're at the top, can you stay there?

AO1	AO2	AO3	AO4	AO5	AO6
I can analyse ideas and synthesize evidence from different texts.	I can analyse a writer's choice of language and structure.	I can make detailed comparisons and analyse how writers' methods convey ideas.	I can evaluate the effect of a variety of writers' choices, using a range of quotations.	I can write convincingly, employing a range of complex linguistic and structural features.	I can use a range of effective sentences and spelling and punctuation are precise.
I can interpret ideas, select evidence and make clear connections between texts.	I can explain clearly the effects of language and structure.	I can compare ideas from different texts and explain how they are conveyed.	I can explain the effect of writers' methods, using relevant quotations.	I can write clearly and effectively, using linguistic and structural features appropriately.	I can use sentences for effect and spelling and punctuation are mostly accurate.
I can understand some ideas, linking evidence from different texts.	I can identify and comment on features of language and structure.	I can make comparisons between texts, commenting on how ideas are conveyed.	I can comment on writers' methods and use some quotations.	I can write with some success, using some linguistic features and paragraphs.	I can use a variety of sentence forms, with some accurate spelling and punctuation.
I can find information and ideas and make references to texts.	I can find examples of language and structure.	I can identify similarities and differences between texts.	I can give my views on texts and support them with evidence from the text.	I can write in a simple way to communicate my ideas.	I can write in sentences, using basic punctuation and some accurate spelling.

Assessment

This unit tests all the reading and writing skills that you have learned in this chapter to see if you are now able to apply them to different sources.

Read the extract below and complete the activities that follow. The extract is from an autobiography called *Coming to England* by Floella Benjamin. The writer describes her first experience of school in England, having moved from Trinidad in 1960.

Extract from *Coming to England* by Floella Benjamin

When I arrived at the school, many of the children rushed over and touched me then ran away giggling. I thought they were being nice to me. At that time I didn't realize it was because I was different, a novelty, something to be made a fool of and to be laughed at. The dingy Victorian building squatted in the large grey playground like a bulldog ready to attack. It was surrounded by high wire fencing, a hopscotch game was marked out on the ground and on one of the walls a bull's-eye pattern was painted.

Above the school's main door were some letters engraved in the stone; they were Latin words and I never did find out what they meant. Inside the school the walls of the long corridors were tiled halfway up, making the building feel cold. The tiles had been painted a mushy green, some of it flaking off where it had been scratched over the years by passing children. The ceilings and upper half of the walls were a dull beige colour and the floors were covered with worn and splintering wooden parquet. Off the corridors were separate, unwelcoming classrooms, each one with its own door, not partitions like the ones in Trinidad. But the desks and the blackboards were the same. I felt a little comforted when I saw them. At least there was something I'd seen before.

The structure of the day was also a familiar routine: lessons, playtime, more lessons, lunch and play, then ending the day with more lessons. The work the teacher gave us was so easy and simple compared to the work I was used to. Yet the teacher treated me like an idiot because she couldn't understand my Trinidadian accent even though I could understand her. I felt like a fish out of water. [...]

There was one game, however, which I didn't understand at first but in no time at all I began to hate. The first time I saw the children play it, I knew it was wrong and cruel. I was standing next to the wall with the painted bull's-eye when some boys came up and spat strange words at me, words that I had never heard before but from their faces I knew they were not nice. They were words which told me that I was different from them and that they felt my kind shouldn't be in their country. I looked at them, confused and baffled like a trapped and helpless creature. What was 'my kind' and why shouldn't I be in the country I was brought up to love? The land of hope and glory, mother of the free. I began to feel angry and violent as I stood and watched their ugly faces jeering at me. But they might as well have been talking in a foreign language because I didn't understand the words they were shouting. I didn't let them make me cry though. I had learnt how to be tough during the time Marmie had left us in Trinidad. When I got home and asked Marmie what the words meant, she looked sad and sat us all down and slowly explained that because of the colour of our skin some people were going to be cruel and nasty to us. But we must be strong, make something of ourselves and never let them get the better of us. That was the day I realized that in the eyes of some people in this world I was not a person but a colour.

To remind yourself of how to apply AO1 skills, look back at the work you did in *Written in black and white* (pages 50–53) and *Sugar and spice* (pages 54–57).

Activity 1

a. Find four pieces of information in the first paragraph about the English school Benjamin attended.

b. The second and third paragraphs contain both explicit and implicit ideas. What do you understand about how Benjamin felt about her new school from this part of the text?

c. Using your answers to the questions above and the rest of the extract, write your response to the following question:

What do you understand about how Floella Benjamin was treated at school? Use your own words and quotations from the text to support what you say.

To remind yourself of how to apply AO2 skills on structure, look back at the work you did in *Big Brother* (pages 60–65) and *Operation Dynamo* (pages 76–79).

Activity 2

a. Write a summarizing sentence for each of the four paragraphs.

b. How does the writer shift the narrative from one paragraph to the next?

c. What is the effect of these structural shifts?

d. Using your answers to the questions above, write your response to the following question:

How has the writer structured the narrative to engage the interest of the reader?

To remind yourself of how to apply AO2 skills on language, look back at the work you did in *Big Brother* (pages 60–65) and *Fighting talk* (pages 72–75).

Activity 3

a. The writer uses the words 'mushy green' to describe the colour of the paint on the walls. What does her choice of language tell you about how she feels about the school?

b. She describes the school as a building which 'squatted in the large grey playground like a bulldog ready to attack'. What effect does this description have on the reader?

c. The writer uses the words 'the land of hope and glory, mother of the free' in the fourth paragraph. What is the effect of using these particular words?

d. Find an example of a rhetorical question in the extract and explain its effect on the reader.

e. Using your answers to the above and any other examples of language that you find effective, write your response to the following question:

How does the writer use language to describe her experience to the reader?

To remind yourself of how to apply AO4 skills, look back at the work you did in *Soup and crackers* (pages 68–71) and *Operation Dynamo* (pages 76–79).

Activity 4

a. Look again at the description of the school buildings and playground. What details does the writer use to convey how she feels?

b. Consider the tone Benjamin uses in this extract. How would you describe the tone she adopts and what effect do you think it has on the reader?

c. Read the final sentence again. Why do you think this is an effective way to end the extract?

d. Using your answers to the questions above, write your response to the following question:

How successful do you think Benjamin is in conveying her sense of isolation? Give your opinion and use quotations from the text to support what you write.

Tip ✓

The skills you are practising with this text can be applied to any fiction text from any century.

Read the following extract from *Wuthering Heights*, a novel written by Emily Brontë in 1847. Mr Earnshaw has been to Liverpool on business and had promised to bring back gifts for his children, Hindley and Cathy, as well as something for the servant Nelly, who is the narrator in this extract.

Extract from *Wuthering Heights* by Emily Brontë

Mrs Earnshaw expected him by supper-time, on the third evening, and she put the meal off hour after hour; there were no signs of his coming, however, and at last the children got tired of running down to the gate to look. Then it grew dark; [...] just about eleven o'clock, the door-latch was raised quietly, and in stepped the master. He threw himself into a chair, laughing and groaning, and bid them all stand off, for he was nearly killed – he would not have such another walk for the three kingdoms.

'And at the end of it, to be flighted to death!' he said, opening his great-coat, which he held bundled up in his arms. 'See here, wife! I was never so beaten with anything in my life: but you must e'en take it as a gift of God; though it's as dark almost as if it came from the devil.'

We crowded round, and over Miss Cathy's head I had a peep at a dirty, ragged, black-haired child; big enough both to walk and talk: indeed, its face looked older than Catherine's; yet when it was set on its feet, it only stared round, and repeated over and over again some gibberish, that nobody could understand. I was frightened, and Mrs Earnshaw was ready to fling it out of doors: she did fly up, asking how he could fashion to bring that gipsy brat into the house, when they had their own bairns to feed and fend for? What he meant to do with it, and whether he were mad? The master tried to explain the matter; but he was really half dead with fatigue, and all that I could make out, amongst her scolding, was a tale of his seeing it starving, and houseless, and as good as dumb, in the streets of Liverpool, where he picked it up and inquired for its owner. Not a soul knew to whom it belonged, he said; and his money and time being both limited, he thought it better to take it home with him at once, than run into vain expenses there: because he was determined he would not leave it as he found it. Well, the conclusion was that my mistress grumbled herself calm; and Mr Earnshaw told me to wash it, and give it clean things, and let it sleep with the children.

Hindley and Cathy [...] entirely refused to have it in bed with them, or even in their room; and I had no more sense, so I put it on the landing of the stairs, hoping it might be gone on the morrow.

To remind yourself of how to apply AO1 skills, look back at the work you did in *Soup and crackers* (pages 68–71).

Activity 5

a. The rescued child is called Heathcliff, and he becomes one of the main characters in the novel. What do we learn about Heathcliff from this extract?

b. What words and phrases does the writer use to describe how different Heathcliff is to the members of the Earnshaw family?

c. Using your answers to the questions above, complete the following task:

Using details from both texts, summarize the similarities between the way Floella Benjamin and Heathcliff are presented.

To remind yourself of how to apply AO3 skills, look back at the work you did in *Soup and crackers* (pages 68–71) and *Fighting talk* (pages 72–75).

Activity 6

a. What sort of narrative perspective is used in each of the two texts?

b. What is the effect of using these different narrative perspectives on the reader's understanding of the characters' thoughts and feelings?

c. Using your answers to the above, write your response to the following task:

Compare how the different narrative perspectives in these two texts influence the reader's response to the writers' ideas about prejudice.

To remind yourself of how to apply AO5 and AO6 skills, look back at the work you did in *Speaking out* (pages 58–59) and *A slave's tale* (pages 66–67).

Activity 7

Think about a time when you felt isolated or different to other people around you.

Write a first-person account describing what happened and how you felt.

3 Trapped

To be trapped is to be stuck, caught in a situation that is beyond your control. It may be an ongoing situation; something that you are forced to come to terms with because there is no way out and no hope of rescue. Or it may be that, with time and effort, and perhaps a bit of luck, you can escape.

Some people find themselves physically trapped. Anne Frank and her family, for example, spent over two years hiding in a secret annex during the German occupation of the Netherlands in the Second World War. Although she was only 13, Anne knew that discovery by the Nazis meant certain death.

Other people find themselves metaphorically trapped, either mentally because of illness, trauma or emotional breakdown, or because of poverty or other restrictions beyond their control.

In this chapter you will encounter many different examples of being trapped by reading a range of writing from different genres and across different centuries.

The chapter is divided into three units:

- External fences
- Internal walls
- Assessment.

External fences represents the obstacles that we have to overcome. It focuses on people or creatures that are physically trapped and, through sheer determination and endurance, manage to survive. *Internal walls* symbolizes the barriers we have to break down. It deals with those who are metaphorically trapped: in their minds, in poverty, in time or in a situation in which they feel completely powerless.

In these first two units you will learn a number of reading and writing skills, and in the final unit, *Assessment*, you will be able to put these skills into practice to make sure you have understood them.

By the end of the chapter you may have not only empathized with the people or creatures that are trapped but also learned some ways to overcome entrapments of your own.

Skills, Assessment Objectives and examination coverage

All the skills covered in this chapter focus on the Assessment Objectives and are directly relevant to the requirements of English Language.

Reading skills include how to:

- identify and interpret information and ideas
- select and summarize evidence from the text(s) to support your views
- examine how the writer's word choice influences the reader
- examine how the writer uses structure to influence the reader, in particular key sentences and phrases, as well as discourse markers
- compare writers' ideas and perspectives
- evaluate what the writer does to make their writing successful, in particular the creation of tension and the use of contrast.

Writing skills include how to:

- communicate imaginatively, in particular through dialogue
- communicate discursively, in particular by explaining a point of view
- organize your ideas so that your writing is shaped and accurate.

Activity

a. With a partner, discuss any experiences you have had of being trapped, either physically or metaphorically. These may be real situations where you felt you had no power, or in virtual situations such as playing a character in an electronic game.

You might like to consider:

- any situation, real or virtual, when you were physically trapped
- how you reacted and how you escaped
- any situation where you felt metaphorically trapped
- how you reacted and how you escaped.

b. Join with another pair to share your experiences. Do you think you react well in such circumstances? Are real-life feelings of being trapped replicated in the virtual world?

External fences

This unit focuses on people or creatures that are physically trapped and, through sheer determination and endurance, manage to survive.

Skills and objectives

- To identify and interpret ideas and information (**AO1**)
- To select and synthesize evidence from different texts (**AO1**)

1 Survival of the fittest

Aron Ralston may not be a name that you recognize, but if you have seen the movie *127 Hours*, then his story may well be familiar to you. Aron Ralston was a mountain climber who became trapped under a boulder while hiking alone in the canyons of Utah, USA. In the opening of a newspaper article below, the scene is set for an act of courage that is almost unbelievable, as Aron is forced to resort to desperate measures in order to survive.

127 Hours:
Aron Ralston's story of survival

When the sun starts to go down on the canyonlands of south-eastern Utah in the American west, it bathes the vast rock formations and caverns in a deep red glow. It's beautiful.

But at night, if you're alone, it can be a cold and frightening place. Particularly if you find yourself trapped in one of the deep ravines that split the sandstone monoliths* in two. It would be difficult for anyone to hear you during the day – but in the dark, a cry for help would be met with only silence.

No one knows that more than 35-year-old Aron Ralston. In 2003, he had gone hiking, alone, near Robbers Roost – an old outlaw hideout used in the dying days of the Wild West by Butch Cassidy. But while Ralston was climbing down a narrow slot in Bluejohn Canyon, a boulder became dislodged, crushing Ralston's right forearm and pinning it against the wall.

For five and a half days, he struggled to get free until he was forced to do the unthinkable. Using a blunt knife from his multi-tool, he began amputating his arm.

*monolith – huge upright block of stone

Key term 🔑

Interpret: explain the meaning of something in your own words, showing your understanding

The information and ideas contained in this article are both explicit and implicit. If something is explicit it is clearly stated, but when something is implicit it is just suggested and you have to **interpret** the text to work it out for yourself. To show you understand a text, you are expected to interpret as well as identify the ideas and information.

Activity 1

Which of the following explicit pieces of information and ideas are found in these opening paragraphs?

- Aron Ralston is 35 years old.
- His left arm was crushed by a rock.
- The area is beautiful when the sun sets.
- He was hiking in the east of America.
- Aron struggled to free himself for five and a half days.
- The area is cold at night but not frightening.
- Aron was climbing in Blackjohn Canyon when the accident happened.
- Robbers Roost was used as a hideout by Butch Cassidy.

Now you are going to look beneath the surface at the implicit ideas and information contained in the article. To show your understanding you have to interpret using your own words, but also select supporting quotations from the text to show how you have come to this understanding.

Activity 2

Read the interpretations below and on page 88 written by three students in response to the opening of this article. They are ranked in order, with Student A's comment being the weakest and Student C's the best. With a partner, discuss what makes Student B's response better than Student A's. What does Student C do that Student A and Student B do not?

Support — Look at the amount of detail each student has included and the quality of the interpretation they have made. Also look at the use of supporting quotations.

Reading tip 📖

The word 'suggests' shows that Student B is beginning to interpret the implicit information and ideas. Other useful phrases include: 'This means…', 'This lets us know…', 'This indicates…', 'This implies…' and 'This makes me think…'.

Student A

When Aron Ralston becomes trapped and cannot get free, even after struggling for five and a half days, he has to amputate his own arm. He says he was 'forced to do the unthinkable'.

Student B

When Aron Ralston becomes trapped and cannot get free, even after struggling for five and a half days, he has to amputate his own arm. He says he was 'forced to do the unthinkable'. This suggests he is desperate to escape and can see no other way out if he wants to live. We understand that he is a really brave person to go through with such an extreme plan.

Student C

When Aron Ralston becomes trapped and cannot get free, even after struggling for five and a half days, he has to amputate his own arm. He says he was 'forced to do the unthinkable'. This suggests he is desperate to escape and can see no other way out if he wants to live. We understand that he is a really brave person to go through with such an extreme plan. We know the environment is hostile and unforgiving, 'a cold and frightening place', and most people would have lost hope and surrendered to inevitable death, but Aron showed true resilience and unbelievable resourcefulness. When he set off on the trip, he could never have anticipated the unimaginable act he would have to undertake in order to survive.

Although Aron was an experienced climber, he made a costly mistake by not telling anyone where he was going that day, and therefore he knew there was no hope of rescue. The following extract from the same article shows his thoughts during the time he was trapped and how he finally managed to free himself.

'I realised early on that I was going to have to cut my arm off to get free but there was also resistance: I didn't want to do it,' he says. 'But by the second day I was already figuring out how I could do it, so in the film you see that progression: trying to cut into the arm like a saw, finding the tourniquet, then the realisation that the knife was too dull to get through the bone. That despair was followed by a kind of peace; a realisation that I was going to die there and there was nothing I could do. It was no longer up to me. All I could do was see it through to the end.'

After five and a half days inside the canyon, out of water, delirious and hallucinating, Ralston had an epiphany*. 'I felt my bone bend and I realised I could use the boulder to break it. It was like fireworks going off – I was going to get out of there.'

Ralston managed to use his body weight to violently bend his arm until the boulder snapped his forearm. He then ingeniously used the attachment from his hydration pack – a bendy rubber hose that you use to suck water out of the pack – as a makeshift tourniquet, and began sawing and cutting through the remaining cartilage, skin and tendons with his multi-tool.

*epiphany – sudden realization

Activity 3

Using both extracts, write your response to the following question:

What do you understand about Aron Ralston's experience of being trapped? Use your own words but also include quotations from the text to support what you say.

The following extract from a newspaper article is also about being trapped, but the circumstances are very different. This time, the person involved is a young girl who worked in an industrial cotton mill in the 1860s.

A shocking accident, which will probably prove fatal, occurred at the Mechanics Mill, this forenoon. Annie McNeal, a girl about 15 years old [...] in some unknown manner, got her hair caught in the 'back shaft' of a fine speeder* and was drawn into the machine. The speeder was stopped as soon as possible but it was some time before the girl could be extracted, her hair and portions of her scalp having become wound around the machine. She was immediately removed to her home on North Main Street, and Dr A.M. Jackson was summoned. Dr Jackson found four scalp wounds, the one behind the left ear being five inches long. A piece of the skull two inches long by an inch and a quarter wide was also missing and the brain was laid bare though uninjured. It is barely possible that the child will recover, but it is more probable that inflammation will set in with fatal results.

*speeder – large factory machine that makes cloth

Some of the information and ideas are similar in both sources, although the outcomes for Aron Ralston and Annie McNeal are very different. When **synthesizing**, you need to select evidence from both texts and interpret and make connections between the information and ideas.

Key terms

Synthesize: to combine information and ideas from different texts and produce new material

Summarize: to give the main points of something briefly

Activity 4

With a partner, discuss the similarities and differences between what happened to Aron Ralston and Annie McNeal.

In particular, you could analyse:

- the environment in which they became trapped
- any control they had over the situation
- the efforts made to free them
- the involvement of others
- the eventual outcome.

Activity 5

Using the work you have done so far, write your response to the following question:

Summarize the similarities and differences between what happens to Aron Ralston and Annie McNeal. Use your own words but also quote from both texts to support what you say.

2 Turtle trap

When analysing language it is important to select an appropriate example from the text on which to comment. Selection is an important skill because if you do not choose wisely you will have very little to say. In the following piece of travel writing, Liz Cleere recalls a time when she and her husband Jamie were sailing in the Indian Ocean and stopped to rescue two turtles trapped in a fisherman's net. In this paragraph, she uses descriptive language to set the scene.

> **Extract from travel writing competition entry by Liz Cleere**
>
> I clung to the guard rail while I looped a rope round the broken sail. A wave rose, then fell back before it reached me. We were adrift in an Indian Ocean the colour of dishwater. A platoon of grey clouds marched across the sky, softening us up before the storm.

Key term 🔖

Metaphor: a comparison showing the similarity between two quite different things, stating that one actually *is* the other

A poor choice of language to analyse would be 'A wave rose, then fell back' because this tells us something about the movement of the ocean, but little else. A better choice of language to analyse is the **metaphor** 'a platoon of grey clouds marched across the sky'. By describing the clouds as a 'platoon' that is 'marching', Liz Cleere is preparing the reader for the approaching storm. The comparison with an army of soldiers makes it sound as if the storm is inevitable: there are lots of clouds forming one large unit, just like a platoon, and they are advancing purposefully, as if they are 'marching' to battle, intent on attacking with their weapons of wind and rain.

Activity ①

Stretch

a. Which other words in Cleere's paragraph add to the negative, rather ominous atmosphere?

b. What is the effect of the phrase 'softening us up'?

It is not just metaphors that create an effect on the reader but also the choice of individual words and phrases. The choice of one word rather than another can completely alter the meaning of a piece of writing.

Activity 2

a. Look at the next few sentences that describe Jamie attempting to rescue the trapped turtles. There are four gaps, each with a choice of words to insert. Decide which word best fits into each gap.

> He _____ [1] over the side and _____ [2] bare hands through the mesh. The nylon line which trapped and was strangling the animals now cut into his fingers. Spidery crabs _____ [3] everywhere, sharpening their claws in anticipation of the _____ [4] to follow.

[1] leaned/lunged/hung
[2] put/thrust/pushed
[3] ran/climbed/clambered
[4] food/meal/feast

b. Compare your choice of words with a partner. Do you agree? How does the meaning change depending on which word is chosen? Is the effect on the reader different?

The rest of the account explains the difficulties Liz and Jamie encountered before they finally succeed in rescuing the turtles.

Extract from travel writing competition entry by Liz Cleere

Fins circled in the shadows beneath. To have any chance of freeing the turtles, we would have to haul them on board. I tried to hook a rope through the tangle, but the clip jumped from my grip and the line swung away from the boat. Jamie stood to catch it while I held the unbreakable web with gloved hands. But he missed and the rope flew away again, out over the waves.

Cursing the fishermen for dumping their net, I tugged at the heavy load and pulled it clear of the water. Crabs crawled up my arms. Jamie, his hands now bleeding, scrambled next to me and together we heaved the whole stinking mess into the cockpit.

The first rain pellets began to pepper the deck. We worked in silence. Cutting the turtles free was quick with our sharp sailing knives. Their shells were smooth, glossy and serrated towards the back, and creamy underneath. They peered into our eyes. Afterwards we wondered what they had been thinking. As the clouds darkened, we slipped them back into the water.

Activity 3

Look at the highlighted words in the extract. With a partner, discuss the effect of using these particular words. How would the effect on the reader be different if other words were used instead?

Activity 4

Using all the work you have done so far and any other examples of language in the text that you find effective, write your response to the following:

Analyse Liz Cleere's use of language and its effect on the reader.

3 Let's talk about it

Skills and objectives

- To communicate imaginatively, in particular through dialogue **(AO5)**
- To write clearly and accurately **(AO6)**

Dialogue is a conversation between two or more people. There are many reasons why writers feature dialogue in their stories, including:

- to reveal more about the characters to the reader
- to establish how different characters interact
- to drive the plot forward
- to break up the action of the story.

In the most successful imaginative writing, every line of the dialogue should advance the story or the character in a meaningful way.

The dialogue below is taken from a novel called *Eleven Hours*. This title represents the amount of time the central character, Didi, is forced to spend with an unknown man who hijacks her car while she is shopping at a mall in Texas. The extract shows the conversation Didi has with the man as he drives away with her trapped in the car.

Extract from *Eleven Hours* by Paullina Simons

'You could let me out.' She looked at him with hope. 'There's no harm done –'

'There is already.'

'No, not really,' she said quickly, wanting to wipe her mouth. 'I think you've made a mistake. You must think I'm rich, but I'm not really –'

'I don't think that, ma'am,' he said.

She pressed on, 'But if you continue, then you know, this will be a... a...' She couldn't get the awful word out.

'Kidnapping?'

'Yes,' she said. 'All you have to do is let me out right here. Please,' she added. 'Stop and think, think. Don't you know that kidnapping is a capital crime? In Texas, I think you get life for it.'

'They'd have to catch me first,' the man said.

'But they always catch the –' Didi wanted to say *the bad guy*.

'Not always,' he said. 'Let them try to find us.'

Activity ①

a. Consider what could happen next and make a note of your ideas.

b. Discuss your notes with a partner. See if there are any further ideas that could be added to improve your work.

When including dialogue in stories, there are punctuation rules that have to be followed to make it clear for the reader who is talking and what they are saying.

Punctuation of dialogue

There are six main rules for punctuating direct speech.

1 Speech marks, also known as inverted commas, always enclose the actual words spoken, for example, *'I don't think that, ma'am,' he said.* Here the actual words spoken by the man are *'I don't think that, ma'am.'* You can use single or double speech marks, as long as you are consistent.

2 The words that are said must be separated from the person saying them, for example, *'Please,' she added.* Here a comma divides what is being said (*'Please'*) from who is saying it (*she added*). A question mark or exclamation mark can also be used to separate the two parts of the sentence if appropriate. A comma would also be required to separate the two parts if the word order were reversed, for example, *She added, 'Please.'*

3 All punctuation goes inside the speech marks, for example, *'No, not really,' she said quickly.* Here the comma comes after the word *'really'* but before the closing speech mark.

4 The first word spoken always begins with a capital letter, for example, *'You could let me out.'* Here the first word spoken is *'You'.* This happens even when the first word spoken comes in the middle of a sentence, for example, *She pressed on, 'But if you continue…'* Here the word *'But'* has a capital letter.

5 The first word after the speech in the same sentence does not begin with a capital letter, for example, *'Not always,' he said.* Here the word *'he'* begins with a lower-case letter.

6 Every time a new speaker begins to speak, a new paragraph must be started, for example, *'Kidnapping?'* spoken by the man is on one line and the *'Yes'* that follows is on the next line because it is spoken by Didi.

> **Writing tip**
>
> The writer can show what a character has said in two ways, either using direct speech, which is dialogue where the actual words are quoted directly, or reported speech, where the words are just summarized within the narrative, for example, 'She told him to go home'. The most successful imaginative writing is a balance between the two.

Activity 2

a. Write a continuation of the dialogue opposite between Didi and her kidnapper, making sure you punctuate your work correctly.

> **Support** Note that you do not always have to name the person who is speaking. Sometimes it is obvious from the flow of the conversation, especially if there are just two people involved.

b. When you have finished your dialogue, proofread your work. Check that what you have written is clear, correctly spelled and accurately punctuated. Make any changes that would improve your demonstration of AO6 skills.

c. Share your dialogue with a partner. Ask them to suggest any further changes that could be made to improve your work.

4 Fighting back

- To evaluate how effectively the writer creates tension **(AO4)**
- To compare writers' ideas and perspectives **(AO3)**

You're sitting in the cinema watching a scary movie. The whole audience knows something terrible is about to happen – they are collectively holding their breath. The music becomes more sinister; the light on the screen is fading, creating shadows of something unspeakable in the corner of the graveyard; and the camera zooms in to show a little boy's face, paralysed with fear.

Suddenly he screams. And so do you, followed by several members of the audience, who then start to giggle to cover their embarrassment. The moment of tension has passed, and the director's work is done.

It's not quite the same for a writer. There's no music available, no sound effects, no lighting, no clever camera angles. The writer has to build anticipation and a sense of uncertainty using the only tools available to him: words on the page. This can be done through *what* he says, the content, and *how* he says it, the style.

Content can include:

- setting – locating the action in a particular place and time
- events – devising conflict that is potentially dangerous for the character and adding details to make us fear for their safety
- character reaction – making the character recognize the threat of danger and therefore experience a range of heightened emotions.

Style can include:

- descriptive language – creating a tense atmosphere through the use of dramatic words, phrases or language features
- **structure** – manipulating the reader through the order in which things are revealed, including plot twists and withholding information
- sentence forms – engaging the reader by varying the length or construction of sentences for effect.

The following extract is the opening of a short story called 'The Waste Land' by Alan Paton, in which a man finds himself trapped in a remote area by a gang of men. Despite having no idea who the man is, we are plunged into a tense situation from the very first sentence.

> **Key term** 🔑
>
> **Structure:** the organization of the text, how it is introduced, presented and concluded; structure also includes how paragraphs and ideas are grouped or linked together

Extract from 'The Waste Land' by Alan Paton

The moment that the bus moved on he knew he was in danger, for by the lights of it he saw the figures of the young men waiting under the tree. That was the thing feared by all, to be waited for by young men. It was a thing he had talked about, now he was to see it for himself.

It was too late to run after the bus; it went down the dark street like an island of safety in a sea of perils. Though he had known of his danger only for a second, his mouth was already dry, his heart was pounding in his breast, something within him was crying out in protest against the coming event.

His wages were in his purse; he could feel them weighing heavily against his thigh. That was what they wanted from him. Nothing counted against that. His wife could be made a widow, his children made fatherless, nothing counted against that. Mercy was the unknown word.

While he stood there irresolute he heard the young men walking towards him, not only from the side where he had seen them, but from the other also. They did not speak, their intention was unspeakable. The sound of their feet came on the wind to him. The place was well chosen, for behind him was the high wall of the Convent, and the barred door that would not open before a man was dead. On the other side of the road was the waste land, full of wire and iron and the bodies of old cars. It was his only hope, and he moved towards it; as he did so he knew from the whistle that the young men were there too.

His fear was great and instant, and the smell of it went from his body to his nostrils. At that very moment one of them spoke, giving directions. So trapped was he that he was filled suddenly with strength and anger, and he ran towards the waste land swinging his heavy stick. In the darkness a form loomed up at him, and he swung the stick at it, and heard it give a cry of pain. Then he plunged blindly into the wilderness of wire and iron and the bodies of old cars.

Key term 🔑

Connotation:
an idea or feeling suggested, in addition to the main meaning; for example, the connotations of the word 'beach' might be sunshine or gritty sand, depending on your experience of the beach

Content

The title of the story tells us that the events are set near a waste land, a bleak and neglected part of town. We learn that it is 'full of wire and iron and the bodies of old cars'. One way this helps to create tension is because it suggests that the area is abandoned, a place where car 'bodies' are dumped (which carries the **connotations** of death), with no one around to help the man if he encounters anything threatening. It might also imply that there are instruments that would be used as weapons against him.

Activity ①

a. Other details of the setting are gradually revealed to us as the story progresses. Find some further details that tell us where and when the story takes place.

b. Compare your details with a partner. How does the setting add tension to the story?

What happens to the man and how he reacts to the danger posed by the gang is also revealed throughout the text.

Activity ②

a. Look at the events that happen to the man and how he reacts. Record these events and the man's reactions in a grid like the one started below. Add some quotations to support your points.

What happens	Man's reaction	Supporting quotation
He thinks about running after the bus but it's too late.	He realizes he can't now easily escape and his body starts to react physically to the danger.	'his mouth was already dry, his heart was pounding on his breast, something within him was crying out in protest'

b. Compare your grid with a partner's. How do the events and the man's reactions add tension to the story?

Style

The writer not only creates tension through the content of a story but also the style in which it is written. One of the reasons we can relate to the man's growing anxiety and fear is because of the writer's choice of words, phrases and language features.

Key term 🔑

Simile: a comparison showing the similarity between two quite different things, stating that one is *like* the other

Activity ③

a. The departing bus is described as being 'like an island of safety in a sea of perils'. What does this **simile** tell us about the man's fear at that moment?

 Support Consider which two things are being compared and why. What does the bus represent to the man? What effect is the writer trying to achieve by using this simile?

b. The writer describes how the man hears the approaching footsteps: 'The sound of their feet came on the wind to him.' Why has the writer chosen this description? What effect does it have on the reader?

c. Look at the final two sentences. What do the verbs 'loomed' and 'plunged' tell us?

d. With a partner, discuss these and any other examples of language that you find effective. How does the writer's choice of language add tension to the story?

Stretch Read the full story of 'The Waste Land' by Alan Paton.
    a. How is tension maintained beyond the opening extract?
    b. What effect does the twist at the end have on the reader?

Tension is also created through structure. In the cinema the camera would make this obvious: the opening panoramic landscape would zoom in to the man and his purse, followed by a panning shot of the approaching gang, a close-up of the man trapped behind the wall, and finally back to a wide shot as he bursts out into the wilderness in an attempt to escape. The writer has to convey this by the way he structures his writing, in both the whole text and at a sentence level.

Key term

Chronological: arranged in the order that things happened

Activity 4

a. The extract consists of five paragraphs in **chronological** order with each one shifting the focus of the story. How does the focus of each paragraph gradually build up the tension?

b. The second paragraph contains a long complex sentence to describe what is happening to the man. What effect does this have on the reader? Which phrase in this sentence warns the reader of what is to come?

c. The third paragraph contains several short statements. Why do you think the writer has chosen to include them at this point? How do they add to the tension?

Stretch

Sometimes writers withhold information from the reader. An example of this comes in the first paragraph: 'That was the thing feared by all, to be waited for by young men.' How does this add to the tension of the story, even though we do not yet understand the significance of the line?

Activity 5

Using all the work you have done so far, write your response to the following question:

How successful is Alan Paton in creating tension in the opening of 'The Waste Land'? Give your own opinion and quote from the text to support what you say.

What happens in the following extract is very similar to the situation in 'The Waste Land', except this time it is a true story. A young woman, Samantha Barlow, is walking to work in a notorious area of Sydney, Australia.

Extract from *Left for Dead* by Samantha & Laurence Barlow

The woman is walking fast; she doesn't like being around these deserted streets on her own in the dark. Suddenly, she hears a soft footfall approaching from behind, pulls her left headphone off her ear and immediately quickens her pace. But she's too late.

Before she realises what's happening, two strong arms grab her from behind, a hand is clamped over her mouth and she smells the rancid breath of her attacker close to her face, hears his ragged breathing in her ear. 'Hey baby, don't you want to…' she hears him whisper. She twists and tries to push his arms off her face to wrest herself free but is simply not strong enough to break his grip. Instead, she falls heavily to the ground in a desperate attempt to duck away. She cuts one knee badly but has no time to try to stem the flowing blood. 'Give me the money!' he barks at her. 'Give me the money!'

Instead, she lashes out at him, thrashing wildly with the bags she's carrying, tries to kick him, to punch him, to scratch him. She wants to hurt him before he can hurt her. And she knows, in this dark and lonely street, she may well be fighting for her life.

Activity 6

In small groups, discuss the similarities and differences between the two texts. Analyse both content and style.

Activity 7

Using both sources and what you have learned from your discussion, write your response to the following question:

Compare how a person in danger is conveyed by the two writers. Use your own words but support your ideas with quotations from both texts.

Internal walls

This unit deals with those who are metaphorically trapped: in their minds, in poverty, in time or in a situation in which they feel completely powerless. They have to fight to break down the barriers they encounter.

Skills and objectives

- To examine how the writer uses key sentences, phrases and discourse markers to influence the reader **(AO2)**

- To select evidence from the text to support your views **(AO2)**

5 A giant in science

Professor Stephen Hawking is a genius. His scientific achievements would be outstanding for any man, let alone one who has had to overcome the physical challenges of Motor Neurone Disease for much of his life. In the following article, the journalist Lawrence McGinty recalls interviewing Stephen Hawking.

Stephen Hawking: 'I'm a scientist not a celebrity'

by Lawrence McGinty

Interviewing Stephen Hawking is a very strange experience for a journalist. Even meeting him is a little daunting. He is, of course, a giant in science. So you know that behind those spectacles is a very sharp brain. But the Motor Neurone Disease that has afflicted him for 50 years and left him unable to move means that there are no outward signs of that.

I say 'hello'. He cannot respond. He's just arrived in the lift at his office in the Department of Mathematical Sciences at Cambridge University. One of the two carers who accompany him all the time leans across his motorised wheelchair and holds Stephen's hand out, offering a handshake for him. I shake the limp hand and say hi again. No response.

When it comes to the interview, we have submitted our questions days before so he can prepare his answers in advance. He does this with a gadget in his spectacles which sends out a beam that controls his computer. He builds up sentences word by word, sometimes letter by letter and then sends it to the voice synthesiser that has now become his trademark almost. The robotic voice speaks his answers with a long gap between sentences. My problem is that I can't see his computer screen during the interview and I don't know when he's finished.

But it's sorted – everything seems to be sorted with Stephen. His carer who can see the screen gives me a nod when he reaches the end of an answer.

So yes, the stereotype of a giant intellect trapped in a twisted body is true. Stephen is very aware that's why he has become such a celebrity – his office is decorated with photographs of him with Barack Obama, Nelson Mandela and the Queen.

But he is above all a scientist. His place in scientific history is guaranteed by his discoveries in cosmology – for example, that Black Holes don't suck in everything

– they give OUT thermal radiation – heat. And whatever question you ask him, his answer is rooted in science. Is there a God? We are only intelligent monkeys on one planet among probably many in the Universe that might support life. A Creator is unnecessary to explaining our existence. Fracking? We will need the gas when the lights start to go out.

Hawking is now 71 – when he was diagnosed with ALS (a type of Motor Neurone Disease) he was given two years to live. That was 50 years ago. He's still confounding the doctors. He says he knows every day could be his last and he's dedicated to passing on his love of science – not just to his graduate students, but to everyone.

We leave Cambridge feeling that we've been in the presence of a unique, great man. Uplifted. And happy to have met a hero.

Lawrence McGinty's impression of Stephen Hawking develops throughout the article, and in his concluding paragraph he sums up by saying he is 'happy to have met a hero.' How he comes to this final opinion can be traced through the structure of the article and the changing focus of each paragraph. Key sentences and phrases, along with **discourse markers**, are used as structural devices to show the reader when his opinion is about to be shifted, moderated, contradicted or confirmed.

Activity 1

SPAG

a. Look at the first two paragraphs. What positive impression of Stephen Hawking is given in the first paragraph? Which sentence in the first paragraph lets us know that the second paragraph is about to qualify the first?

b. The third paragraph conveys the difficulties Stephen Hawking encounters when communicating verbally. How does the discourse marker 'But it's sorted' at the beginning of the fourth paragraph effectively link these two paragraphs together?

c. Which sentence in the fifth paragraph is used to sum up Lawrence McGinty's impressions so far?

d. The title of the article tells us that Stephen Hawking considers himself a scientist rather than a celebrity. Which sentence linking the fifth and sixth paragraphs shows Lawrence McGinty agrees with this point of view?

e. The whole text follows a cyclical shape, shifting focus through a series of time frames, and ending with the same positive impression of Stephen Hawking with which it started. How does this structure help to influence our own impression of Stephen Hawking?

Key term

Discourse markers: words or phrases used as organizational tools to link ideas, such as 'but', 'although', 'on the other hand', 'however', 'nevertheless'

Activity 2

Using all the work you have done so far, write your response to the following question:

How has Lawrence McGinty structured his article to convince us that Stephen Hawking is a 'hero'?

Skills and objectives

6 The shackles of poverty

You are going to write an article for a broadsheet newspaper in which you explain your point of view on the following statement:

> **'People who beg on the streets are a disgrace to society. They should get a job and stop expecting us to support them.'**

When explaining a point of view, there are a number of things you need to consider:

- purpose, audience and form
- structure
- a strong opening
- strategies to engage the reader
- effective vocabulary choices and language features.

Before you start to write, it is important to spend time planning what you are going to say and the order in which you are going to say it.

Stage 1: Planning

Purpose, audience and form

The *purpose* is the reason why you are writing: it may be to argue, to persuade or to offer a point of view. The *audience* is the person (or people) you are writing for, for example, readers of a magazine, listeners of a radio programme or your Head Teacher. The *form* is the type of writing that you are producing, for example, an article, a letter or a speech.

In the above task, the purpose of your writing is to explain a point of view on the statement about begging; the audience is the readers of the broadsheet newspaper and the form is an article.

Structure

First, you need to decide on your point of view. Do you agree or disagree with the statement about begging, or do you agree with some aspects but not others? It is important to have a clearly defined point of view so that you can explain it convincingly, and it should be included in your opening paragraph.

Next you need to list two or three reasons why you hold this point of view. There may be many reasons but it is best to concentrate on the most important ones that you can discuss in detail. You should also consider any alternative viewpoint at this stage. If you include counter-arguments in your response and dismiss them effectively, it will make your point of view seem stronger.

There are many ways to structure your article. One effective way is to discuss each of your reasons in a separate paragraph, making sure your point of view is developed and sustained, and that the paragraphs are linked together in a logical order.

The **Skills and objectives** are:

- To communicate discursively, in particular by explaining a point of view **(AO5)**
- To write clearly and accurately **(AO6)**

Activity 1

a. Decide on your point of view on the statement about begging.

b. Complete a plan like the one below. It consists of five paragraphs: an introduction, three reasons for holding your point of view and a conclusion. This is just an example – you can decide on your own point of view and your own reasons.

1. Introduction: I mostly disagree with this statement about begging.
2. Reason 1: Beggars are in genuine need and many of us can afford to spare a little money. It is an act of human kindness.
3. Reason 2:
4. Reason 3:
5. Conclusion:

Key term

Tone: a way of writing which conveys the writer's attitude

Strong opening

It is important to make the opening paragraph of your article as effective as possible so that your audience is immediately engaged. It is a good idea to consider **tone** at this stage. Your tone makes it obvious what you think about the subject or even what you think about the reader.

Activity 2

a. Look at the example below of an opening paragraph. With a partner, discuss what makes it engaging for the reader.

> Have you ever seen a beggar sitting on the pavement, asking passersby for any spare change? What do you do, hand over a couple of pounds or avert your eyes and cross to the other side of the road? Some people are trapped in a cycle of poverty and however hard they try, they are unable to escape. If you're the person deliberately looking the other way then you should be ashamed of yourself.

 Support Look at both what is being said, the content, and how it is being said, the style.

b. Write the opening paragraph for your article. Include your clearly defined point of view and remember to keep in mind the purpose, audience and form, plus any tone you have decided to adopt.

Writing tip

There are many tones you could adopt, for example, light-hearted, witty, mocking, bitter, reassuring or angry. You may vary your tone throughout your response. The tone you choose is up to you, as long as it is appropriate to your subject, purpose and audience.

An effective conclusion is as important as a strong opening. In your conclusion you need to sum up your points, refer back to the title and re-state your point of view.

Strategies to engage the reader

When offering a point of view, the aim is to convince your reader to think the same way as you. The best way to do this is to discuss your reasons fully and present them with conviction and a strong personal voice. Sometimes it is helpful to provide evidence to support what you are saying. Evidence can include:

- the **opinions** of others, for example, 'My father always ignores beggars as a matter of principle but I believe we have a moral obligation to help people in need.'

- **facts**, for example, 'Beggars can be found in all large cities in the UK.'

- **anecdotes**, for example, 'When I gave some money to the beggar in Cheriton Park, I could see the gratitude in his eyes.'

Activity 3

a. Think about how you are going to develop each of your reasons and then list some evidence you can include in your article that will support your point of view.

b. Discuss your list with a partner. See if there are any further examples that could be added to improve your work.

Key terms

Opinion: a view or judgement not necessarily based on fact or knowledge

Fact: something that can be proved to be true

Anecdote: a short, relevant story about an apparently real incident or person

Writing tip

Evidence should only be used if it supports your own point of view. It needs to be carefully woven into your argument, not included just for the sake of it.

Effective vocabulary choices and language features

Another way to convince your reader of your point of view is to include effective vocabulary choices and occasional language features. These can include:

- **language for emotive effect**, for example, 'If you're the person deliberately looking the other way then you should be ashamed of yourself.'
- **rhetorical questions**, for example, 'Have you ever seen a beggar sitting on the pavement, asking passersby for any spare change?'
- **imagery**, for example, 'Some people are trapped in a cycle of poverty and however hard they try, they are unable to escape.'
- repetition, for example, 'Beggars are human beings. They deserve a hot meal; they deserve a roof over their heads; they deserve a life.'

Activity 4

a. List some effective vocabulary choices and language features you can include in your article that will support your point of view.

b. Discuss your list with a partner. See if there are any further examples that could be added to improve your work.

Stage 2: Writing

Activity 5

Using all the work you have done so far, including your opening paragraph, write your response to the following task:

'People who beg on the streets are a disgrace to society. They should get a job and stop expecting us to support them.'

Write an article for a broadsheet newspaper in which you explain your point of view on this statement.

Stage 3: Proofreading

Activity 6

a. When you have finished your article you need to proofread your work. Check that what you have written is clear, accurate and includes a range of vocabulary. Make any changes that would improve your demonstration of AO6 skills.

b. Share your article with a partner. Ask them to suggest any further changes that could be made to improve your work.

Key terms

Language for emotive effect: words and phrases that are deliberately used to provoke an emotional reaction

Rhetorical question: a question asked for dramatic effect and not intended to get an answer

Imagery: the use of figurative or other special language to convey an idea and create a particular effect on the reader

Writing tip

Remember to consider any counter-arguments in your response and effectively dismiss them, as this will make your point of view seem stronger, for example, 'Although we work hard for our money and beggars don't, these people are obviously in genuine need and many of us can afford to spare a little of what we earn'.

Skills and objectives

- To evaluate how effectively the writer uses contrast **(AO4)**

- To select evidence from the text to support your views **(AO4)**

Tip ✓

The skills you are practising with this text can be applied to any fiction or non-fiction text from any century.

Key term 🔑

Contrast: the use of opposing ideas and words in order to emphasize differences

7 Time warp

In 1860, Charles Dickens created the character of Miss Havisham in his novel *Great Expectations*. A wealthy woman, Miss Havisham was left humiliated and heartbroken when her fiancé abandoned her on their wedding day. From that moment on she was trapped in time, so traumatized by the experience that 50 years later she still sits in her decaying mansion, surrounded by debris from the unattended wedding reception and still wearing the same wedding dress.

In the following paragraph, Pip, a young orphan, visits the mansion and describes his impressions of Miss Havisham and her surroundings.

Extract from *Great Expectations* by Charles Dickens

She was dressed in rich materials – satins, and lace, and silks – all of white. Her shoes were white. And she had a long white veil dependent from her hair, and she had bridal flowers in her hair, but her hair was white. Some bright jewels sparkled on her neck and on her hands, and some other jewels lay sparkling on the table. Dresses, less splendid than the dress she wore, and half-packed trunks, were scattered about. She had not quite finished dressing, for she had but one shoe on – the other was on the table near her hand – her veil was but half arranged, her watch and chain were not put on, and some lace for her bosom lay with those trinkets, and with her handkerchief, and gloves, and some flowers, and a prayer-book, all confusedly heaped about the looking-glass.

It was not in the first few moments that I saw all these things, though I saw more of them in the first moments than might be supposed. But, I saw that everything within my view which ought to be white, had been white long ago, and had lost its lustre, and was faded and yellow. I saw that the bride within the bridal dress had withered like the dress, and like the flowers, and had no brightness left but the brightness of her sunken eyes. I saw that the dress had been put upon the rounded figure of a young woman, and that the figure upon which it now hung loose, had shrunk to skin and bone. Once, I had been taken to see some ghastly waxwork at the Fair, representing I know not what impossible personage lying in state. Once, I had been taken to one of our old marsh churches to see a skeleton in the ashes of a rich dress that had been dug out of a vault under the church pavement. Now, waxwork and skeleton seemed to have dark eyes that moved and looked at me. I should have cried out, if I could.

When Pip first glimpses Miss Havisham he thinks she is a beautiful and grand lady. It is only on closer inspection that he realizes all is not as it first appears. Dickens uses **contrast** to convey Pip's initial impressions of both Miss Havisham and her surroundings, and then what he actually sees when he is closer.

Activity

a. Dickens originally describes Miss Havisham as being 'dressed in rich materials – satins, and lace, and silks – all of white'. What other positive impressions does Pip initially have of Miss Havisham and her surroundings?

> **Support**
>
> All Pip's positive impressions are found in the first paragraph. Look at the words Dickens uses to describe Miss Havisham and her surroundings, as well as the ideas connected with her.

b. Pip soon realizes that Miss Havisham now lives in a world of decay. He says 'Everything within my view which ought to be white, had been white long ago, and had lost its lustre, and was faded and yellow'. What other examples does Dickens include that describe the true condition of Miss Havisham and her surroundings?

c. Now look in particular at the use of contrasting language. Find some examples of positive language that show how Miss Havisham first appeared and negative language that conveys the reality. Which words and phrases do you find the most effective and why?

> **Stretch**
>
> Look in particular at the images of death and decay. What does this tell us about Miss Havisham's state of mind?

d. Compare your work with a partner. Consider any alternative contrasting ideas and words and add them to your list.

e. Why do you think Dickens uses contrast to emphasize the difference between Pip's initial impressions of both Miss Havisham and her surroundings, and then what he actually sees on closer inspection? What does it tell us about the character of Miss Havisham?

Activity

Using all the work you have done so far, write your response to the following question:

How effective do you find Dickens's use of contrast in describing Miss Havisham and her surroundings? Use your own words but support your ideas with quotations from the text.

> **Stretch**
>
> Read the full story of *Great Expectations* by Charles Dickens, or any of his other works. Do you think his themes are still relevant today?

Skills and objectives

- To identify and interpret information and ideas **(AO1)**
- To compare writers' ideas and perspectives **(AO3)**

8 For better or worse?

We like to think that we live in a modern society with freedom of speech and the ability to make our own choices and dictate our own lives. Unfortunately, this is not always the case. In the following true life account from 2013, Sara Batuk recalls being forced into marriage in Turkey when she was still a teenager, despite being born and raised in Britain.

The marriage was supposed to protect me from the ways of the western world I was born into. Dad remained deeply suspicious of those ways, despite having lived in London by then for 25 years himself. [...]

It was about adherence to old customs and the protection of family honour that my father had unreasonably convinced himself I was on course to disgrace. Six months earlier, Dad discovered I had a boyfriend, a stranger my parents knew nothing of or about, and he panicked. He saw this as the start of an inevitable rebellion against my cultural heritage and his strong moral values. And so his knee-jerk reaction was to get me out of Britain and married off to a Turkish boy as quickly as possible.

He and my mother tricked me into thinking we were going to Turkey just for a holiday, something we had done every summer throughout my life. On the final day, Dad took me to one side and firmly explained that I wasn't going back with them. 'You're staying here with your uncle and he's going to find you someone to marry. If you want to get married then it will be to someone we choose rather than a stranger you bring home.'

Terrified, I pleaded with my father to take me back. I was a good girl. I didn't drink alcohol or go clubbing and had mutely accepted all the restrictions he had put on my life that saw me spend most of my time outside college helping run the family home. Taking my first boyfriend at 17 didn't mean I wanted marriage. Dad was unmoved, and drove away with my younger brother and sister sobbing in the car just as hysterically as I was. My mother swallowed any upset she must have felt through total loyalty to my father, which compounded my sense of betrayal.

In this account we discover Sara's attitude towards being forced into marriage. Some ideas and information are explicitly told to us but others we have to interpret to work out for ourselves.

Activity 1

a. List four explicit things you learn about Sara in the final paragraph.

b. Sara says she had 'mutely accepted all the restrictions [her father] had put on my life'. What can you interpret from this about her character?

c. Sara takes her first boyfriend at the age of 17. What does this tell us about her expectations of the future and how they might conflict with what her parents expect?

d. What sort of relationship do you think Sara has with her mother?

Sara finds herself being forced into marriage because of her father. The following extracts from the 1991 novel *The Buddha of Suburbia* by Hanif Kureishi also focuses on the issue of forced marriage, but this time the approach of Jamila's father, Anwar, to getting his own way is very different. The novel is narrated by Karim, Jamila's cousin and best friend, and in the extracts below he visits his Uncle Anwar and finds him ill in bed.

Extracts from *The Buddha of Suburbia* by Hanif Kureishi

'Why didn't you tell me he's sick?' I whispered to Jamila.

But I wasn't convinced he was simply sick, since the pity in her face was overlaid with fury. She was glaring at her old man, but he wouldn't meet her eyes, nor mine after I'd walked in. He stared straight in front of him as he always did at the television screen, except that it wasn't on.

'He's not ill,' she said.

'No?' I said, and then, to him, 'Hallo, Uncle Anwar. How are you, boss?'

His voice was changed: it was reedy and weak now. 'Take that damn kebab out of my nose,' he said. 'And take that damn girl with you.'

Jamila touched my arm. 'Watch.' She sat down on the edge of the bed and leaned towards him. 'Please, please stop all this.'

'Get lost!' he croaked at her. 'You're not my daughter. I don't know who you are.'

* * *

'What's going on here?' I asked her.

'Look at him, Karim, he hasn't eaten or drunk anything for eight days! He'll die, Karim, won't he, if he doesn't eat anything!'

'Yes. You'll cop it, boss, if you don't eat your grub like everyone else.'

'I won't eat. I will die. If Gandhi could shove out the English from India by not eating, I can get my family to obey me by exactly the same.'

'What do you want her to do?'

'To marry the boy I have selected with my brother.'

'But it's old-fashioned, Uncle, out of date,' I explained. 'No one does that kind of thing now. They just marry the person they're into, if they bother to get married at all.'

This homily* on contemporary morals didn't exactly blow his mind.

'That is not our way, boy. Our way is firm. She must do what I say or I will die. She will kill me.'

*homily – a lecture-like speech

Tip ✓

The skills you are practising with this text can be applied to any fiction or non-fiction text from any century.

Although the first text is a true account and the second is a fictional story, both fathers want to force their daughters into a marriage against their will.

Activity 2

In a small group, discuss the similarities and differences between Sara's father and Jamila's father.

In particular, you could analyse:

- why the fathers want their daughters to marry
- how each father behaves in order to get what he wants
- what the father/daughter relationship is like in each text
- how other family members react to the fathers' behaviour and attitude
- who the narrator of each text is and if this affects your view of the fathers
- when the texts were written and if this affects the fathers' behaviour
- the tone of each text in relation to its genre (the type of text it is)
- the writers' use of language and structure.

Support When comparing two texts, you need to consider both what is being said, the content, and how the writers say it, the style.

Activity 3

Using both sources and what you have learned from your discussion, write your response to the following question:

Compare how the writers convey the two fathers differently. Use your own words but support your ideas with quotations from both texts.

Stretch Read the full story of *The Buddha of Suburbia* by Hanif Kureishi. How effective do you find it to deal with such a serious topic in a humorous way?

Progress check

Use the chart below to review the skills you have developed in this chapter. For each Assessment Objective, start at the bottom box and work your way up towards the highest achievement in the top box. Use the box above your current achievement as your target for the next chapter. If you're at the top, can you stay there?

AO1	AO2	AO3	AO4	AO5	AO6
I can analyse ideas and synthesize evidence from different texts.	I can analyse a writer's choice of language and structure.	I can make detailed comparisons and analyse how writers' methods convey ideas.	I can evaluate the effect of a variety of writers' choices, using a range of quotations.	I can write convincingly, employing a range of complex linguistic and structural features.	I can use a range of effective sentences and spelling and punctuation are precise.
I can interpret ideas, select evidence and make clear connections between texts.	I can explain clearly the effects of language and structure.	I can compare ideas from different texts and explain how they are conveyed.	I can explain the effect of writers' methods, using relevant quotations.	I can write clearly and effectively, using linguistic and structural features appropriately.	I can use sentences for effect and spelling and punctuation are mostly accurate.
I can understand some ideas, linking evidence from different texts.	I can identify and comment on features of language and structure.	I can make comparisons between texts, commenting on how ideas are conveyed.	I can comment on writers' methods and use some quotations.	I can write with some success, using some linguistic features and paragraphs.	I can use a variety of sentence forms, with some accurate spelling and punctuation.
I can find information and ideas and make references to texts.	I can find examples of language and structure.	I can identify similarities and differences between texts.	I can give my views on texts and support them with evidence from the text.	I can write in a simple way to communicate my ideas.	I can write in sentences, using basic punctuation and some accurate spelling.

Assessment

This unit tests all the reading and writing skills that you have learned in this chapter to see if you are able to apply them to different sources.

Read the newspaper article from 2013 below and then complete the activities that follow.

'I've got it nice,' says killer as he brags of easy life in jail

Eugene Henderson reports on a new TV documentary about prisons.

A SMIRKING killer has revealed the cushy time he and fellow 'lifers' enjoy behind bars in a controversial TV documentary that is certain to infuriate taxpayers. Callous Lance Rudge smiles as he tells of how enjoyable prison is for him, with his widescreen television, stereo and three meals a day. The unrepentant 24-year-old is puzzled why anyone would want to leave jail where he 'has it nice' and does not need to get a job.

Rudge was sentenced for the murder of disabled Gregory Baker at his home in 2007. He will not be released until 2025 at the earliest, but during the Channel 4 documentary filmed at Gartree prison, in Leicestershire, he makes it clear he is in no hurry. Last night, friends of his victim attacked the system that allows a cold-hearted killer to see out his sentence in 'holiday camp' surroundings. [...]

Sitting in his cell in a Stoke City shirt, Rudge tells viewers: 'In here you've got everything. You've got a stereo, a TV. You've got three meals a day. I've got it nice. I don't want it to change.' When asked what he thinks life is like outside, he says: 'Horrible. A nightmare to get a job. I wouldn't like to be out there at all now. I'd prefer to stay inside for a while, and wait until it calms down.' In the documentary, Rudge [...] tells the interviewer that being on trial for murder had been 'boring'. Rudge says: 'I fell asleep five times. It wasn't really the best impression to make but I couldn't help it. When I got sentenced I almost collapsed. But now I don't even think about it. Time flies by.'

Last night Staffordshire University lecturer Ken Raper, who as a former detective investigated the case, said: 'Rudge's words show there is no honour or loyalty among these people and just how little thought they give to others.' Alton parish councillor Tony Moult, who knew

Mr Baker, said: 'Rudge is lucky. If he had been tried before the Sixties he might have been hanged. It seems that prison is like a holiday camp. It is terrible for Gregory's family for it all to be raked up again.'

Last night the Tax Payers' Alliance called on the Government to tackle the issue of the easy life Britain's boasting lags have behind bars. Jonathan Isaby, the campaign group's political director, said: 'Any right-thinking person will find Rudge's attitude appalling and beyond contempt. Taxpayers expect to see prisoners being punished for their crimes, not given luxuries that many of us cannot afford in the outside world. Part of the regime should be about rehabilitation, such as instilling a work ethic in prisoners, something which appears to be lacking.'

A Channel 4 spokesman said: '"Lifers" provides insight into the realities of long-term imprisonment and the rehabilitative efforts of prison authorities.'

To remind yourself of how to apply AO1 skills, look back at the work you did in *Survival of the fittest* (pages 86–89) and *For better or worse?* (pages 108–111).

Activity 1

a. Look at the first paragraph of the article. Find four explicit pieces of information about Lance Rudge's life in prison.

b. Now look at the second and third paragraphs. These contain both explicit and implicit ideas. What do you understand about Lance Rudge's attitude to prison life from this part of the text?

c. Using your answers to questions **a** and **b** and the rest of the article, write your response to the following question:

What do you understand about Lance Rudge's experience of prison from the article? Use your own words but support your ideas with quotations from the text.

To remind yourself of how to apply AO2 skills on structure, look back at the work you did in *A giant in science* (pages 100–101).

Activity 2

a. What time shift occurs in the first three paragraphs? Why do you think the writer has used this structure and how effective do you find it?

b. Several significant people are introduced in the fourth and fifth paragraphs. How does this structure strengthen the argument against Lance Rudge's views?

c. The idea of prisoners having a TV, a stereo and three meals a day is repeated in the text. Which other ideas are repeated? What effect does this structural feature have on the reader?

d. Using your answers to the above and any other structural features you find interesting, write your response to the following question:

How has the writer structured the article to engage the reader?

To remind yourself of how to apply AO2 skills on language, look back at the work you did in *Turtle trap* (pages 90–91).

Activity 3

a. In the first paragraph the writer uses the adjectives 'smirking', 'callous' and 'unrepentant' to describe Lance Rudge. How does this choice of words influence our initial impressions of him? Which phrase in the second paragraph reinforces this impression?

b. What is the effect of the simile 'like a holiday camp'? What does it tell us about how prison life is viewed by some people in society?

c. In the sentence 'Any right-thinking person will find Rudge's attitude appalling and beyond contempt', what effect do the words 'appalling' and 'contempt' have on the reader?

d. Using your answers to the above and any other examples of language that you find effective, write your response to the following question:

How does the writer use language to engage the reader?

Now read the following account of Charles Dickens's visit to Newgate Prison in 1836. This recalls an experience of prison that is very different from the modern-day scenario on page 112 as he encounters a man who is due to be hanged the next day for his crimes.

Extract from 'A Visit to Newgate' by Charles Dickens

We entered the first cell. It was a stone dungeon, eight feet long by six wide, with a bench at the further end, under which were a common horse-rug, a bible, and prayer-book. An iron candlestick was fixed into the wall at the side; and a small high window in the back admitted as much air and light as could struggle in, between a double row of heavy, crossed iron bars. It contained no other furniture of any description.

Conceive the situation of a man, spending his last night on earth in this cell. Buoyed up with some vague and undefined hope of reprieve, he knew not why – indulging in some wild and visionary idea of escaping, he knew not how – hour after hour of the three preceding days allowed him for preparation, has fled with a speed which no man living would deem possible, for none but this dying man can know. [...] and now that the illusion is at last dispelled, now that eternity is before him, and guilt behind: now that his fears of death amount almost to madness, and an overwhelming sense of his helpless, hopeless state rushes upon him, he is lost and stupefied, and has neither thoughts to turn to, nor power to call upon, the Almighty Being, from whom alone he can seek mercy and forgiveness. [...]

Hours have glided by, and still he sits upon the same stone bench with folded arms, heedless alike of the fast decreasing time before him [...] The feeble light is wasting gradually, and the deathlike stillness of the street without, broken only by the rumbling of some passing vehicle which echoes mournfully through the empty yards, warns him that the night is waning fast away.

The deep bell of St. Paul's strikes – one! He heard it; it has roused him. Seven hours left! He paces the narrow limits of his cell with rapid strides, cold drops of terror starting on his forehead, and every muscle of his frame quivering with agony. Seven hours!

To remind yourself of how to apply AO4 skills, look back at the work you did in *Fighting back* (pages 94–99) and *Time warp* (pages 106–107).

Activity 4

a. Look at the details used to describe the cell in Newgate Prison and also Dickens's use of language in the first paragraph. How appropriate is this setting for a man who is about to be hanged?

b. In the rest of the extract, the man is completely focused on his imminent death. How do his thoughts and feelings convey his increasing despair?

c. Look at the use of language and structure in the rest of the extract. How does Dickens's choice of words and phrases show the man's increasing despair? How is his increasing despair also reflected in the whole text structure and the sentence forms?

d. Using your answers to the above, write your response to the following question:

How successful is Dickens in conveying the increasing despair of the condemned man? Give your own opinion and support your ideas with quotations from the text.

Both the article and the account deal with the subject of people in prison, but they are written in different centuries and from different perspectives.

To remind yourself of how to apply AO3 skills, look back at the work you did in *Fighting back* (pages 94–99) and *For better or worse?* (pages 108–111).

Activity 5

a. How do the prison experiences of Lance Rudge and the man in Newgate Prison differ?

b. How do the writers use language and structure in very different ways?

c. Using your answers to the above, write your response to the following:

Compare how the writers convey the experience of prison differently in the two texts. Use your own words but also support your ideas with quotations from both texts.

To remind yourself of how to apply AO5 and AO6 skills, look back at the work you did in *The shackles of poverty* (pages 102–105).

Activity 6

'Prisons are a soft option these days. Prisoners should endure hardship; they are not there to have a good time.'

Write a letter to a national newspaper in which you explain your point of view on this statement.

4 All in the mind

Your mind is immensely and amazingly powerful. You have the potential to store huge amounts of information, retain thousands of memories and process millions of thoughts over a lifetime.

The human brain is the command centre for your entire nervous system and controls your response to all that you see, hear, touch, taste and smell. It is also your mind, rather than your heart, which feels, stores and processes emotions.

Your imagination is the creative part of your mind. William Blake was an 18th-century poet who wrote highly imaginative poems, creating new landscapes, mythical creatures and amazing gods. He describes the power of the imagination in one of his poems, 'Auguries of Innocence'.

To see a World in a grain of sand,
And a Heaven in a wild flower,
Hold Infinity in the palm of your hand,
And Eternity in an hour.

We all perceive the world around us in different ways. To 'perceive' means to process the information we get from our senses and to give it meaning. The same event may be experienced by a number of people, all of whom perceive it differently.

In this chapter you will explore different ideas and concepts linked to the theme of the mind through a range of writing from different genres and across different centuries.

The chapter is divided into three units:

- Phantasmagoria
- A fine line
- Assessment.

Phantasmagoria focuses on the power of the imagination and explores issues around fact, fiction, fantasy and realism. *A fine line* focuses on the sometimes fragile boundary between what an individual mind perceives and what the rest of the world perceives. It includes some writers' experiences of losing control of their minds and how it has affected their lives.

In the first two units you will develop a number of reading and writing skills and in the final unit, *Assessment,* you will be able to put these skills into practice to make sure you have understood them.

By the end of the chapter, you will have been on a journey through the minds of many different people.

Skills, Assessment Objectives and examination coverage

All the skills covered in this chapter focus on the Assessment Objectives and are directly relevant to the requirements of English Language.

Reading skills include how to:

- identify and interpret explicit and implicit ideas
- select and summarize evidence from texts
- analyse how writers use language and structure to create effects
- compare writers' ideas across different texts
- compare how writers present their ideas
- evaluate how successful writers have been.

Writing skills include how to:

- write for different purposes
- communicate clearly
- choose the right tone and style for your writing
- organize your ideas and use structural features.

Activity

a. Try to imagine at least two of the following in detail:

the highest building	the loudest explosion
the fastest vehicle	the brightest colour
the tastiest food	the roughest sea
a zero-gravity world	your greatest fear
the smelliest cheese	a profound thought

b. Jot down some words and phrases to describe your ideas (thinking about all your senses, not just what you see) and then explain your ideas to a partner.

c. Writers, artists, musicians, chefs, architects, designers, engineers, film directors, inventors and many others are all engaged in the challenging but fabulous process of transforming their imagination into reality. How easy or difficult is it to find the right language to communicate what you imagine?

Phantasmagoria

This unit focuses on the fictional world of fantasy, where writers draw readers into settings and characters created purely in their imaginations.

Skills and objectives

1 Talking cats

From the Hare and the Tortoise in *Aesop's Fables* to the rabbits in *Watership Down*, from Aslan in the Narnia stories to the Cowardly Lion in *The Wizard of Oz*, there are many fabulous examples of talking animals in literature. One of the most famous appears in *Alice's Adventures in Wonderland*, a children's story published in 1866, in which a girl falls down a rabbit hole and finds herself in a strange imaginary world.

- To identify and interpret explicit and implicit ideas **(AO1)**

- To select and synthesize evidence from different texts **(AO1)**

> **Extract from *Alice's Adventures in Wonderland* by Lewis Carroll**
>
> She was a little startled by seeing the Cheshire Cat sitting on a bough of a tree a few yards off.
>
> The Cat only grinned when it saw Alice. It looked good-natured, she thought: still it had very long claws and a great many teeth, so she felt that it ought to be treated with respect.
>
> 'Cheshire-Puss', she began, rather timidly, as she did not at all know whether it would like the name: however it only grinned a little wider.

The writer, Lewis Carroll, introduces the Cat as a character in the story. He gives us **explicit** information about the Cat.

Key terms 🔑

Explicit: stated clearly, exactly and openly

Implicit: implied or suggested but not stated openly; beneath the surface

Interpret: explain the meaning of something in your own words, showing your understanding

Activity 1

a. List four things you find out about the Cat from this short extract. You could write the four things either in your own words or as quotations taken from the text.

b. Share your list with a partner. Check your answers are all:
- true and accurate
- from the extract
- about the Cat.

Writers of stories also include **implicit** meanings. These are for the reader to **interpret** for themselves. For example, read the next section of the story and think about what you learn about the Cat.

Extract from *Alice's Adventures in Wonderland* by Lewis Carroll

'Come, it's pleased so far,' thought Alice, and she went on. 'Would you tell me, please, which way I ought to go from here?'

'That depends a good deal on where you want to get to,' said the Cat.

'I don't much care where – ' said Alice.

'Then it doesn't matter which way you go,' said the Cat.

' – so long as I get somewhere,' Alice added as an explanation.

'Oh, you're sure to do that,' said the Cat, 'if you only walk long enough.'

From this extract, the reader learns that the Cat is clever and confident. This information is not stated explicitly but is shown by the way he answers her question in riddles. To show your understanding of implicit meanings, it is helpful to use quotations. For example, a good quotation to use here to support the idea that the Cat is clever might be: 'Then it doesn't matter which way you go', which shows that the Cat is quick to think of a logical answer to Alice's question.

Extract from *Alice's Adventures in Wonderland* by Lewis Carroll

She tried another question: 'What sort of people live about here?'

'In that direction,' the Cat said, waving its right paw round, 'lives a Hatter: and in that direction,' waving the other paw, 'lives a March Hare. Visit either you like: they're both mad.'

'But I don't want to go among mad people,' Alice remarked.

'Oh, you can't help that,' said the Cat: 'we're all mad here. I'm mad. You're mad.'

'How do you know that I'm mad?' said Alice.

'You must be,' said the Cat, 'or you wouldn't have come here.'

Alice didn't think that proved it at all: however, she went on: 'And how do you know that you're mad?'

'To begin with,' said the Cat, 'a dog's not mad. You grant that?'

'I suppose so,' said Alice.

'Well, then,' the Cat went on, 'you see a dog growls when it's angry, and wags its tail when it's pleased. Now *I* growl when I'm pleased, and wag my tail when I'm angry. Therefore I'm mad.'

'*I* call it purring, not growling,' said Alice.

'Call it what you like,' said the Cat.

Activity 2

a. What do you learn about Alice from this extract? Select explicit information and implicit ideas from the text and use quotations to support what you have written.

b. Share what you have written with a partner and discuss whether there are any differences in the way you have interpreted ideas about the character of Alice.

c. What else is implied in the text to suggest this is not the real world?

Tip ✓

The skills you are practising with this text can be applied to any fiction or non-fiction text from any century.

The following extract is from a 21st-century novel for children called *Coraline*, by Neil Gaiman. A girl walks through a door into another world and meets a cat. Sound familiar?

Extract from *Coraline* by Neil Gaiman

It was a sunny, cold day, exactly like the one she'd left.

There was a polite noise from behind her.

She turned round. Standing on the wall next to her was a large black cat, identical to the large black cat she'd seen in the grounds at home.

'Good afternoon,' said the cat.

Its voice sounded like the voice at the back of Coraline's head, the voice she thought words in, but a man's voice, not a girl's.

'Hello,' said Coraline. 'I saw a cat like you in the garden at home. You must be the other cat.'

The cat shook its head. 'No,' it said. 'I'm not the other anything. I'm me.' It tipped its head on one side; green eyes glinted. 'You people are spread all over the place. Cats, on the other hand, keep ourselves together. If you see what I mean.'

'I suppose. But if you're the same cat I saw at home, how can you talk?'

Cats don't have shoulders, not like people do. But the cat shrugged, in one smooth movement that started at the tip of its tail and ended in a raised movement of its whiskers. 'I can talk.'

'Cats don't talk at home.'

'No?' said the cat

'No,' said Coraline.

The cat leapt smoothly from the wall to the grass, near Coraline's feet. It stared up at her.

'Well, you're the expert on these things,' said the cat drily. 'After all, what would I know? I'm only a cat.'

It began to walk away, head and tail held high and proud.

'Come back,' said Coraline. 'Please. I'm sorry. I really am.'

The cat stopped walking, and sat down, and began to wash itself, thoughtfully, apparently unaware of Coraline's existence.

'We … we could be friends, you know,' said Coraline.'

'We *could* be rare specimens of an exotic breed of African dancing elephants,' said the cat. 'But we're not. At least,' it added cattily, after darting a brief look at Coraline, '*I'm* not.'

Coraline sighed.

'Please. What's your name?' Coraline asked the cat. 'Look, I'm Coraline. Okay?'

The cat yawned slowly, carefully, revealing a mouth and tongue of astounding pinkness. 'Cats don't have names,' it said.

'No?' said Coraline.

'No,' said the cat. 'Now, *you* people have names. That's because you don't know who you are. We know who we are, so we don't need names.'

The writer uses a lot of dialogue in this extract, but he also includes a range of adverbs to describe how the cat speaks or moves which gives the reader additional ideas about the character of the cat.

Activity 3

a. What clues do the following adverbs from the extract give you about the character of the cat?

smoothly   drily   **SPAG**

carefully   thoughtfully

cattily   slowly

b. Discuss with a partner what adverbs you might use if you were describing a dog talking and moving, or a lion, or a crocodile. Are they very different to those used to describe the cat?

Support Now try writing your own imaginary conversation between a child and an animal, using mostly dialogue to show what the characters are like.

Writing tip

Use adverbs to add detail to your dialogue, describing how the child and the animal speak and behave.

There are clearly similarities between Carroll's Cat and Gaiman's cat, even though the stories were written 150 years apart. To **summarize** those similarities means you are expected to show your understanding of both texts by interpreting the ideas and making connections between them. You also need to use quotations to support what you have written. For example, you could make a point about the cats' attitudes towards humans.

Key term

Summarize: to give the main points of something, briefly

Implicit idea from text 1	Alice's Cat is indifferent to what she thinks. The Cat says, "Call it what you like," as if it doesn't care whether Alice calls the noise it makes growling or purring. The cat in the other text is very similar in that it doesn't seem to care about not having a name. In the dialogue, the cat says: "We know who we are, so we don't need names," as if Coraline was somehow inferior to a cat because she had a name. This demonstrates how smug and arrogant the cat characters are in both texts.	Quotation from text 1
Interpretation of text 1		Implicit idea from text 2
		Interpretation of text 2
Quotation from text 2		Synthesis of ideas

Activity 4

Write a summary of the similarities between the cats in these two texts.

Stretch Within the genre of children's fiction, how would you explain the enduring appeal of talking animals, for both writers and readers? Refer to the texts here as well as any others you may have read.

2 Masters of the macabre

- To analyse how writers use language to create effects **(AO2)**
- To compare how writers' ideas are conveyed across two texts **(AO3)**

Key term 🔑

Gothic: sensational and horrifying, designed to thrill and terrify; gothic fiction was particularly popular in the 19th century

Tip ✓

The skills you are practising with this text can be applied to any fiction text from any century.

One of the 'masters' referred to in the heading is Edgar Allan Poe, an American writer, who created short stories full of mystery and the macabre in the 1830s. His **gothic** imagination is evident in everything he wrote.

In *The Masque of the Red Death*, Poe describes an abbey, inside which a Prince has sealed himself and his thousand guests to escape from the plague. He holds a masquerade (a masked party) to entertain the guests and decorates each of the first six rooms in a different colour.

Extract from *The Masque of the Red Death* by Edgar Allan Poe

The seventh apartment was closely shrouded in black velvet tapestries that hung all over the ceiling and down the walls, falling in heavy folds upon a carpet of the same material and hue. But in this chamber only, the colour of the windows failed to correspond with the decorations. The panes here were scarlet — a deep blood colour. Now in no one of the seven apartments was there any lamp or candelabrum, amid the profusion of golden ornaments that lay scattered to and fro or depended from the roof. There was no light of any kind emanating from lamp or candle within the suite of chambers. But in the corridors that followed the suite there stood, opposite to each window, a heavy tripod, bearing a brazier* of fire, that projected its rays through the tinted glass and so glaringly illumined the room. And thus were produced a multitude of gaudy and fantastic appearances. But in the western or black chamber the effect of the fire-light that streamed upon the dark hangings through the blood-tinted panes was ghastly in the extreme, and produced so wild a look upon the countenances of those who entered, that there were few of the company bold enough to set foot within its precincts at all.

It was in this apartment, also, that there stood against the western wall, a gigantic clock of ebony. Its pendulum swung to and fro with a dull, heavy, monotonous clang; and when the minute-hand made the circuit of the face, and the hour was to be stricken, there came from the brazen lungs of the clock a sound which was clear and loud and deep and exceedingly musical, but of so peculiar a note and emphasis that, at each lapse of an hour, the musicians of the orchestra were constrained to pause, momentarily, in their performance, to harken to the sound; and thus the waltzers perforce ceased their evolutions; and there was a brief disconcert of the whole gay company.

*brazier – a metal framework for holding burning coals

Poe chose not to use lots of **similes** and **metaphors** in his writing, but the words and phrases he selected are vivid and evocative, creating dramatic effects for the reader to visualize. When writing about language in texts, you need to select an appropriate example, identify the **connotations** of the words or phrases and explore the effects they might have. For example, you could choose to write about the word 'chamber'.

> The word 'chamber' has connotations of fairy tales where princesses are held captive or of medieval times where banquets are held. Using the word 'chamber' creates an impression of somewhere grand, dark, luxurious, secret or exciting, or possibly a place of torture, captivity and punishment.

Activity 1

Write about the connotations and effects of the following words and phrases from the text. The first one has been done for you.

- 'shrouded in black velvet'
- 'scarlet'
- 'profusion of golden ornaments'
- 'multitude of gaudy and fantastic appearances'
- 'blood-tinted panes'

> 'shrouded in black velvet': this evokes a feeling of death and mourning. The word 'shroud' sounds soft and sad, suggesting a lingering sense of loss, whereas the 'black velvet' creates a contrasting impression of subtle luxury. The textures too are juxtaposed: the shroud suggesting something thin, like cobwebs or gossamer, unlike the velvet which is thick and sensuous.

Reading tip

Use adjectives, adverbs and abstract nouns to help you describe the effects of language. For example:

> The writer describes the chamber vividly, with words like 'brazier of fire' used to create a sense of brightness and dazzling light.

vividly ← adverb
brightness ← abstract noun
dazzling ← adjective

SPAG

Activity 2

Support Make a collage of the colours, images and atmosphere created by Poe's description, using pictures cut out of magazines or printed from the Internet. Select words from the text and label your collage with quotations to match the images you have chosen.

Poe goes on to describe the grotesque and feverish excitement of the party.

Extract from *The Masque of the Red Death* by Edgar Allan Poe

There were much glare and glitter and piquancy and phantasm – much of what has been seen since *Hernani*. There were arabesque figures with unsuited limbs and appointments. There were delirious fancies such as the madman fashions. There were much of the beautiful, much of the wanton, much of the *bizarre*, something of the terrible, and not a little of that which might have excited disgust. To and fro in the seven chambers there stalked, in fact, a multitude of dreams. And these — the dreams — writhed in and about, taking hue from the rooms, and causing the wild music of the orchestra to seem as the echo of their steps. And, anon, there strikes the ebony clock which stands in the hall of velvet. And then, for a moment, all is still, and all is silent save the voice of the clock. The dreams are stiff-frozen as they stand. But the echoes of the chime die away — they have endured but an instant — and a light, half-subdued laughter floats after them as they depart. And now again the music swells, and the dreams live, and writhe to and fro more merrily than ever, taking hue from the many-tinted windows through which stream the rays from the tripods.

Activity (3)

a. There is a wide range of language features used here. Find examples of **(SPAG)** quotations that include each of these features in the text:

- repetition – using the same words or phrases again to create an effect
- personification – an object or thing described as having human qualities
- juxtaposition – two ideas put together, often contrasting, side by side
- symbolism – using something visual to represent something abstract
- change in tenses – shifting the action from past to present, for example
- varied sentence forms – sometimes shorter, sometimes much longer, divided by commas.

b. Write about each of these features, using your selected quotations, and analyse the effects of the language on the reader.

Stretch

a. How does Poe use language in these two extracts to create a gothic effect?

b. Continue the story of *The Masque of Red Death,* writing in the style of Edgar Allan Poe.

Another writer in the gothic tradition of the 1800s was Mary Shelley. She was on holiday in Switzerland with three other writers when they decided to hold a competition to write a ghost story, a story 'which would speak to the mysterious fears of our nature and awaken thrilling horror – one to make the reader dread to look around, to curdle the blood, and quicken the beatings of the heart.' Those are Mary Shelley's own words, written in the introduction to the story she wrote for that competition, explaining how she came to write such a 'hideous' story at the age of just 20.

Extract from the introduction to a novel by Mary Shelley

As a child I scribbled; and my favourite pastime, during the hours given me for recreation, was to "write stories." Still I had a dearer pleasure than this, which was the formation of castles in the air—the indulging in waking dreams—the following up trains of thought, which had for their subject the formation of a succession of imaginary incidents. My dreams were at once more fantastic and agreeable than my writings. In the latter I was a close imitator—rather doing as others had done, than putting down the suggestions of my own mind. What I wrote was intended at least for one other eye—my childhood's companion and friend; but my dreams were all my own; I accounted for them to nobody; they were my refuge when annoyed—my dearest pleasure when free.

Activity 4

a. What does the phrase 'castles in the air' suggest about Shelley's imagination?

b. What do you think Shelley means when she describes herself as a 'close imitator'?

c. Why do you think Shelley describes her dreams as her 'refuge' and her 'dearest pleasure' rather than her writings?

d. What three words or phrases would you select from this extract as evidence that Shelley was an imaginative child?

Mary Shelley goes on to explain how she struggled to think of a brilliant idea for her story, until the night the writers spent discussing new scientific advances. Remember when you are reading the next extract that this is a non-fiction text. See if you can identify the well-known story she went on to write.

Extract from the introduction to a novel by Mary Shelley

Night waned upon this talk, and even the witching hour had gone by, before we retired to rest. When I placed my head on my pillow, I did not sleep, nor could I be said to think. My imagination, unbidden, possessed and guided me, gifting the successive images that arose in my mind with a vividness far beyond the usual bounds of reverie[1]. I saw—with shut eyes, but acute mental vision,—I saw the pale student of unhallowed arts[2] kneeling beside the thing he had put together. I saw the hideous phantasm of a man stretched out, and then, on the working of some powerful engine, show signs of life, and stir with an uneasy, half vital motion. Frightful must it be; for supremely frightful would be the effect of any human endeavour to mock the stupendous mechanism of the Creator of the world. His success would terrify the artist; he would rush away from his odious handywork, horror-stricken. He would hope that, left to itself, the slight spark of life which he had communicated would fade; that this thing, which had received such imperfect animation, would subside into dead matter; and he might sleep in the belief that the silence of the grave would quench for ever the transient[3] existence of the hideous corpse which he had looked upon as the cradle of life. He sleeps; but he is awakened; he opens his eyes; behold the horrid thing stands at his bedside, opening his curtains, and looking on him with yellow, watery, but speculative eyes.

I opened mine in terror. The idea so possessed my mind that a thrill of fear ran through me, and I wished to exchange the ghastly image of my fancy for the realities around. I see them still; the very room, the dark *parquet*, the closed shutters with the moonlight struggling through, and the sense I had that the glassy lake and white high Alps were beyond. I could not so easily get rid of my hideous phantom; still it haunted me. I must try to think of something else. I recurred to my ghost story – my tiresome unlucky ghost story! O! If I could only contrive one which would frighten my reader as I myself had been frightened that night!

Swift as light and as cheering was the idea that broke in upon me. 'I have found it! What terrified me will terrify others [...]'

[1] reverie – daydream
[2] unhallowed arts – dark arts, implying evil
[3] transient – lasting only a short time

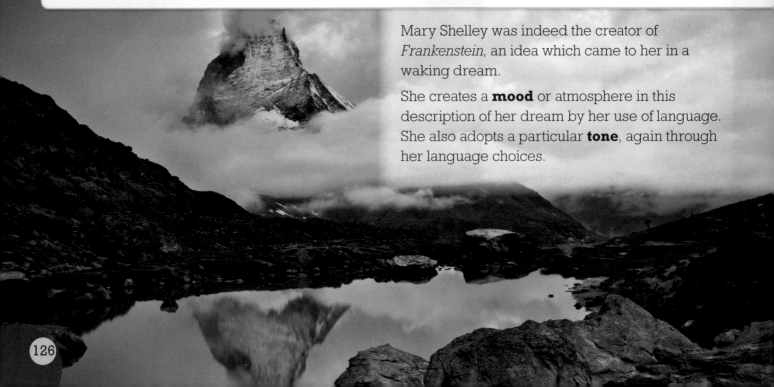

Mary Shelley was indeed the creator of *Frankenstein*, an idea which came to her in a waking dream.

She creates a **mood** or atmosphere in this description of her dream by her use of language. She also adopts a particular **tone**, again through her language choices.

Activity 5

a. With a partner, discuss and make notes on how Shelley creates the mood in this text. You might want to consider:

- vocabulary, such as adjectives, adverbs, verbs
- language features such as repetition, **personification**, **oxymoron**
- sentence forms, look at how Shelley uses punctuation to divide up sentences for effect.

Stretch Read Chapter 5 of *Frankenstein* and compare it to Shelley's introduction to the novel. What similarities can you find in terms of language, tone and style?

b. Read aloud the extract with your partner and experiment with reading it in different ways. This should help you identify the tone of the text. How does it sound best? Try doing the same with the Poe text. Do you think they have a similar tone? What words would you use to describe the tone: dramatic, terrified, excited, mystified, horrified, disgusted, appalled?

Key terms

Mood: the feeling or atmosphere conveyed by a piece of writing

Tone: a way of writing which conveys the writer's attitude towards the reader

Personification: the representation of a quality or idea as a person

Oxymoron: putting words together which seem to contradict each other

Activity 6

Compare the similarities and differences between the methods these two writers use to thrill their readers. You should analyse their use of language, mood and tone in your answer.

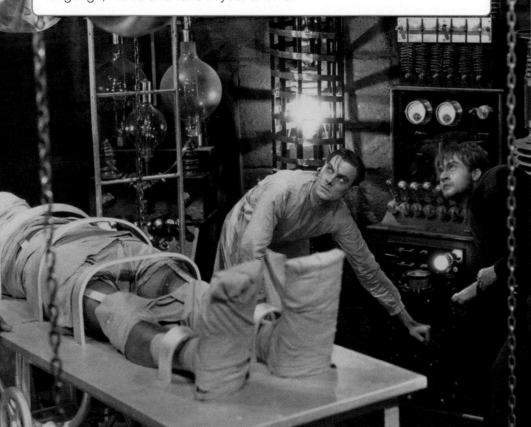

Reading tip

When texts are similar, it is important to identify and analyse the differences between them, even though they may be small. For example, the purpose of both these texts is to thrill the reader, but while one writer uses language to excite, the other might use language to horrify. The language features might be similar, but the effects are very different.

3 Tales of enchantment

Fantasy stories demand that readers suspend their disbelief. This means that readers pretend, just while they are reading, that things which they know can't or don't happen in real life, can and do happen in the world of the story.

- To communicate imaginatively, adapting tone and style for a specific form **(AO5)**

- To use a range of vocabulary for effect and with accuracy **(AO6)**

Extract from *The Night Circus* by Erin Morgenstern

You walk down a hallway papered in playing cards, row upon row of clubs and spades. Lanterns fashioned from additional cards hang above, swinging gently as you pass by.

A door at the end of the hall leads to a spiraling iron staircase.

The stairs go both up and down. You go up, finding a trapdoor in the ceiling.

The room it opens into is full of feathers that flutter downward. When you walk through them, they fall like snow over the door in the floor, obscuring it from sight.

There are six identical doors. You choose one at random, trailing a few feathers with you.

The scent of pine is overwhelming as you enter the next room to find yourself in a forest full of evergreen trees. Only these trees are not green but bright and white, luminous in the darkness surrounding them.

They are difficult to navigate. As soon as you begin walking the walls are lost in shadows and branches.

There is a sound like a woman laughing nearby, or perhaps it is only the rustling of the trees as you push your way forward, searching for the next door, the next room.

You feel the warmth of breath on your neck, but when you turn there is no one there.

Key term

Alliteration: repetition of the same letter or sound at the beginning of several words

Activity ①

Discuss the text with a partner. Consider the following points:

- The writer uses an unusual narrative voice in the extract. What effect does it have on the reader?
- The writer uses **alliteration** in the fourth paragraph. Discuss what effect this sound has on the mood of the text.
- The same paragraph includes a simile. Identify which two things are being compared and what they have in common. What effect does this have?
- The writer has chosen an unusual tense for a narrative. Identify which tense is used and what effect it has on the reader's experience.

You are now going to write your own description. This can be an enchanted piece in the style of *The Night Circus*, or a gothic description in the style of Edgar Allan Poe or Mary Shelley.

Before you start writing, there are several choices you need to make:

- Tone: The tone of your description will depend to some extent on the style, but you still have choices to make. For example, a gothic style might have a gloomy, funereal tone or an extravagant, exuberant tone. A magical descriptive style might have a dreamy, soft tone or a sensuous, exotic tone.

- Language: the words and phrases you use in your description will need to be linked to the style and tone you have chosen. More than anything else, your choice of vocabulary will convey the mood and tone of your writing to the reader.

- Narrative voice: Decide whether to write a **first-**, **second-** or **third-person narrative**. Each has a different effect: first person is intimate and engaging; second person is unusual and draws the reader right into the text; third person is more objective and distant.

Key terms

First-person narrative: story or account told from the point of view of a character or person involved, typically using the pronoun 'I'

Second-person narrative: story or account told from the point of view of the reader, typically using the pronoun 'you'

Third-person narrative: story or account told from the point of view of an 'outsider', a narrator who is not directly involved, typically using the pronouns 'he', 'she', 'it' and 'they'

Activity 2

Develop a word web to help expand your vocabulary. Take a word which links to your ideas for a description, such as 'red', and write down all the connotations and synonyms (words with similar meaning) you can think of.

Do the same for other key descriptive words or ideas.

RED: scarlet, crimson, wine, blood, strawberry, ruby, cherries, blush, flushed, throbbing, vermilion, heart, lips, rose

Word webs are useful when you are creating similes and metaphors. For example, you could use words from the web to describe a flower as 'a ruby rich bed of crimson pleasure'.

Activity 3

Try writing one or two sentences of your description. Then rewrite them using a different narrative voice. Which feels the most effective to you?

Activity 4

a. Now, using all your preparation, write your description. If a word or idea or the narrative voice doesn't work, don't be afraid to try a different approach.

SPAG

b. When you have finished, share your work with a partner. Invite suggestions for improving your description. Finally, proofread your work, checking that you have included a range of vocabulary and that your punctuation and spelling are accurate.

4 A bizarre start

Skills and objectives

- To analyse how writers use structure to achieve effects **(AO2)**

- To evaluate texts critically and select evidence **(AO4)**

The extracts on pages 130–131 are from the first paragraph of a book entitled *The Enchantress of Florence*.

Activity 1

Discuss with a partner what you think the book might be about. Is it likely to be fiction or non-fiction? What genre might it be? What might the themes be?

Once a title has enticed a reader into a book, the writer has to ensure that the structure draws the reader further into the story. Structure is about how the writer organizes their ideas: how they sequence the information.

In *The Enchantress of Florence*, the first sentence sets the scene for the reader.

Extract from *The Enchantress of Florence* by Salman Rushdie

In the day's last light the glowing lake below the palace-city looked like a sea of molten gold. A traveller coming this way at sunset – this traveller, coming this way, now, along the lakeshore road – might believe himself to be approaching the throne of a monarch so fabulously wealthy that he could allow a portion of his treasure to be poured into a giant hollow in the earth to dazzle and awe his guests.

The vision of the 'palace-city' and the 'glowing lake' are described as if seen from a distance. Right from the start, the reader knows it is evening time and the story is set in a landscape which might be from a fantasy or fairy tale.

The second sentence introduces a character to the scene. He has no name; to start with he is just called 'a traveller', suggesting he could be anyone, even you. But then the writer makes the traveller very specific, 'this traveller, coming this way, now,' and changes the tense to the present to create an effect of immediacy and drama, intriguing the reader about the character.

Extract from *The Enchantress of Florence* by Salman Rushdie

And as big as the lake of gold was, it must be only a drop drawn from the sea of the larger fortune – the traveller's imagination could not begin to grasp the size of that mother-ocean!

Here, the writer takes the reader from the real setting to the imagined scene inside the mind of the traveller, so you can appreciate the enormous wealth of the king. By leading the reader into the mind of the character, the writer is encouraging you to engage and empathize with him.

Extract from *The Enchantress of Florence* by Salman Rushdie

Nor were there guards at the golden water's edge; was the king so generous, then, that he allowed all his subjects, and perhaps even strangers and visitors like the traveller himself, without hindrance to draw up liquid bounty from the lake? That would indeed be a prince among men, a veritable Prester John*, whose lost kingdom of song and fable contained impossible wonders. Perhaps (the traveller surmised) the fountain of eternal youth lay within the city walls – perhaps even the legendary doorway to Paradise on Earth was somewhere close at hand?

*Prester John – a wealthy ruler of medieval legend

Now the ideas build up with more exaggerated and extravagant speculation about the king. The writer builds to a climax, taking the reader on a breathless journey of anticipation. The **rhetorical questions** add to the dramatic effect, causing the reader to wonder too.

Extract from *The Enchantress of Florence* by Salman Rushdie

But then the sun fell below the horizon, the gold sank beneath the water's surface, and was lost. Mermaids and serpents would guard it until the return of daylight. Until then, water itself would be the only treasure on offer, a gift the thirsty traveller gratefully accepted.

With the word 'But' the writer shifts back from the imaginary world of the traveller's mind to the real world. The magic drains from the scene, although the reference to the 'mermaids and serpents' gives a hint that the fantasy might return later in the story. The paragraph ends with 'water', one of the basic realities of life, and a return to the character of the traveller drinking.

Key terms

Rhetorical question: a question asked for dramatic effect and not intended to get an answer

Modal verbs: auxiliary (helping) verbs that express possibility, ability, necessity or the future, for example, 'can', 'could',' will', 'would', 'may', 'might', 'shall', 'should', 'must', 'ought to'

Evaluate: to judge the value, quality or success of something

Activity 2

For each of the extracts above and on page 130, make notes on the structural features used by the writer. You might want to comment on:

- viewpoint: where does the reader see the action from?
- narrative voice: who is telling the story?
- tense: when is each event taking place?
- shifts: how have things changed since the last section?
- climax: are the drama and pace rising or falling, speeding or slowing?

Stretch

Consider also the use of **modal verbs** in these extracts. How do they work as structural indicators to show the change in focus?

Activity 3

These four extracts together form the first paragraph of the novel. How effective do you think the writer is in capturing your interest here? **Evaluate** the effect of the structure and language used, selecting quotations to support your response.

Reading tip

When evaluating texts, try to find positive points to make, even if you don't really like the text!

A fine line

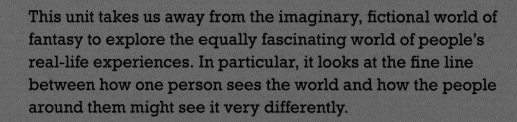

This unit takes us away from the imaginary, fictional world of fantasy to explore the equally fascinating world of people's real-life experiences. In particular, it looks at the fine line between how one person sees the world and how the people around them might see it very differently.

Skills and objectives

- To identify and interpret implicit ideas **(AO1)**
- To select evidence from texts **(AO1)**

5 Tough at the top

Jonny Wilkinson is widely considered to have been one of the best rugby players in the world. Like many other high-achieving sports men and women, he found the pressure to be the best had a profound psychological impact on him. In the extracts below, Wilkinson describes how he reacted to being left out of the team, to have 'a proper rest', while the other players were on tour.

Extracts from *My Autobiography* by Jonny Wilkinson

The England team are out there working hard and facing challenges head on, and with all the attention on them, I am at home not doing anything. And without rugby, without pushing myself as far as I can go, without working on my path towards being the best, who am I? This is all I have ever known. I didn't realise just how attached to it all I had become, and now it's not there, I am no longer sure.

My entire values system has been created around being the best rugby player in the world and doing whatever is required to get there, but away from rugby, where does that leave me? Under the scrutiny of my own harsh judgement, I don't fare too well.

* * *

A sense of helplessness dominates my summer days. Everything feels pointless, and my natural reaction is to treat the problem as I do my kicking – right, work it out and stay here working it out until you have done so. But by focusing so intensely, I just make it worse. My obsessive side has truly kicked in. I simply won't let it go until I find an answer, but I can't find an answer that's satisfactory to me because the real answer is to move on, and to do that I need an off switch and I don't have one. I want to go with the flow, chill, relax, let it go, whatever it is that people say I should do, but I just can't live like that.

I get back from training one day with this darkness inhabiting my brain. I go up to the Slaley Hall Hotel, which is close by and where they are really nice to me, allowing me to use their spa facilities. Usually, I use their pool to relax physically. This time, I make sure that no-one else is around, lower myself into the water until I'm completely submerged, and then I let out a scream of total frustration. I come up for air and then submerge myself again and scream again. No words, just pure desperation. I carry on screaming as long and as loud as I can and I don't stop until I am hoarse. I cannot find any other way of dealing with this non-stop barrage of thoughts and negativity.

Activity 1

For each of the following quotations, explore what you understand about Jonny Wilkinson. The first one has been done for you.

a. 'And without rugby… who am I?'

> Wilkinson is questioning how important rugby is to him and whether there is anything in his life more central to his sense of identity than the game he loves. He suggests that playing rugby is so crucial to him that, 'without rugby', he barely exists. Being left out of the team, even for a rest, has left him uncertain of his purpose and lacking in confidence.

b. 'Under the scrutiny of my own harsh judgement, I don't fare too well.'

c. 'My obsessive side has truly kicked in.'

d. 'I need an off switch and I don't have one.'

e. 'No words, just pure desperation.'

Key term

Infer: reach an opinion from what someone implies, rather than from an explicit statement

Jonny Wilkinson writes very honestly about how he felt and describes as clearly as he can what he was experiencing. However, it is still possible to read between the lines and **infer** more about him than he explicitly tells us.

Activity 2

a. Complete the grid below by selecting quotations from the text as evidence to support these descriptions of Jonny Wilkinson.

Description	Quotation
Unsettled	
Self-critical	
Depressed	
Perfectionist	
Out of control	

b. Discuss your quotations with a partner. Do you think you could have made a better selection? The best quotations are short, with the fewest number of words necessary, and they need to link precisely to the idea you are interpreting from the text.

c. Using all the ideas and quotations from the activities above, write a summary of how Jonny Wilkinson was feeling that summer.

6 Mind blowing

Skills and objectives

- To compare writers' perspectives and how these are conveyed **(AO3)**
- To write for different purposes, forms and audiences, organizing ideas **(AO5)**

People have been experimenting with the effects of drugs on their minds and bodies for centuries. Two hundred years ago, opium (a powerful drug like heroin) was widely available in London. Thomas de Quincey wrote about his experience of being addicted to opium to warn people of the dangers of taking drugs. In his *Confessions of an English Opium-Eater,* he writes about the pain he felt as a result of drug taking.

Extract from *Confessions of an English Opium-Eater* by Thomas de Quincey

In the middle of 1817, I think it was, [...] a change took place in my dreams; a theatre seemed suddenly opened and lighted up within my brain, which presented nightly spectacles of more than earthly splendour. [...] Changes in my dreams were accompanied by deep-seated anxiety and funereal melancholy, such as are wholly incommunicable by words. I seemed every night to descend – not metaphorically, but literally to descend – into chasms and sunless abysses, depths below depths, from which it seemed hopeless that I could ever re-ascend. Nor did I, by waking, feel that I had re-ascended. Why should I dwell on this? For indeed the state of gloom which attended these gorgeous spectacles, amounting at last to utter darkness, [...] cannot be approached by words.

The sense of space, and in the end the sense of time, were both powerfully affected. Buildings, landscapes, etc., were exhibited in proportions so vast as the bodily eye is not fitted to receive. Space swelled, and was amplified to an extent of unutterable and self-repeating infinity. This disturbed me very much less than the vast expansion of time. Sometimes I seemed to have lived for seventy or a hundred years in one night; nay, sometimes had feelings representative of a millennium passed in that time, or, however, of a duration far beyond the limits of any human experience.

Activity 1

a. Choose three words or phrases from the first paragraph which relate to darkness. Write about their connotations and effects.

b. What tone does the writer use? Is it dreamlike or nightmarish? What effect does it have? Use quotations to support your answer.

c. How does the writer use language in the quotations below to describe something few of his readers have experienced?

- 'an extent of unutterable infinity'
- 'the vast expansion of time'
- 'a millennium passed in that time'

In the 21st century, some people are still taking drugs and others are still trying to persuade them of the dangers. One drugs advice group has published an online article on the risks of so called 'legal highs'.

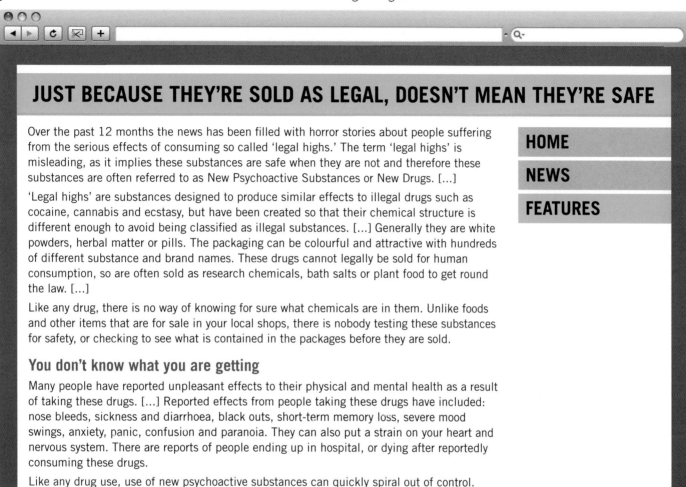

JUST BECAUSE THEY'RE SOLD AS LEGAL, DOESN'T MEAN THEY'RE SAFE

Over the past 12 months the news has been filled with horror stories about people suffering from the serious effects of consuming so called 'legal highs.' The term 'legal highs' is misleading, as it implies these substances are safe when they are not and therefore these substances are often referred to as New Psychoactive Substances or New Drugs. [...]

'Legal highs' are substances designed to produce similar effects to illegal drugs such as cocaine, cannabis and ecstasy, but have been created so that their chemical structure is different enough to avoid being classified as illegal substances. [...] Generally they are white powders, herbal matter or pills. The packaging can be colourful and attractive with hundreds of different substance and brand names. These drugs cannot legally be sold for human consumption, so are often sold as research chemicals, bath salts or plant food to get round the law. [...]

Like any drug, there is no way of knowing for sure what chemicals are in them. Unlike foods and other items that are for sale in your local shops, there is nobody testing these substances for safety, or checking to see what is contained in the packages before they are sold.

You don't know what you are getting

Many people have reported unpleasant effects to their physical and mental health as a result of taking these drugs. [...] Reported effects from people taking these drugs have included: nose bleeds, sickness and diarrhoea, black outs, short-term memory loss, severe mood swings, anxiety, panic, confusion and paranoia. They can also put a strain on your heart and nervous system. There are reports of people ending up in hospital, or dying after reportedly consuming these drugs.

Like any drug use, use of new psychoactive substances can quickly spiral out of control. The long term effects can be serious, similar to other drugs and are not just physical. Your life can be affected in all sorts of negative ways – everything from losing your job to hurting friends and family or even worse. It's just not worth the risk.

HOME

NEWS

FEATURES

This non-fiction article is structured in a way that guides the reader through the ideas. Each paragraph represents a separate stage in the development of the writer's argument.

There are a number of different ways the writer can move between paragraphs to develop the argument:

General information	Detailed information
Identifying an idea	Presenting a contrasting idea
Identifying a cause	Describing the effect
What's happening now	What might happen in the future

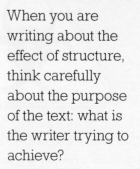

Reading tip

When you are writing about the effect of structure, think carefully about the purpose of the text: what is the writer trying to achieve?

Activity 2

The article has five main paragraphs, with a two-sentence paragraph in the middle.

a. Working in pairs, use the diagram on page 135 to see how the writer has moved from each paragraph to the next.

b. What effect do you think it has on the reader for the ideas to be structured this way? Write about each paragraph in turn and explore the effect of the shift in viewpoint.

Key term

Synthesize: to combine information and ideas from different texts and produce new material

---

Both writers have similar ideas and perspectives on the dangers of drugs, but they adopt different approaches.

When you are comparing writers' ideas and perspectives, you need to summarize and **synthesize** them, highlighting the similarities and/or differences between them and making clear connections between them. For example:

> Thomas de Quincey writes about his own experience of taking drugs so his approach is very subjective. He knows for himself the 'deep-seated anxiety and funereal melancholy' which are the result of taking drugs. However, the writer of the article takes a different approach and advises the reader based on the facts rather than personal experience: 'these drugs... can put a strain on your heart.' Both writers identify the physical impact of drugs, but while one focuses on the effect on the body, 'a strain on your heart', the other concentrates on the effect on the mind: 'deep-seated anxiety'.

Having summarized the writers' ideas and perspectives, you need to explore *how* they present these ideas. Writers have a range of methods they use to present ideas:

- language
- structure
- tone.

There are two ways of comparing methods. One is to focus on each *text* in turn and write about how the first writer uses these methods, then focus on the second writer.

The alternative way is to focus on each *method* in turn and write about how both writers deal with language, then structure, then tone.

Activity 3

Discuss with a partner which way you think is best to approach this comparison task. Using all the work you have done so far on these texts, complete the following task:

Compare how the dangers of drug taking are presented differently in these two texts.

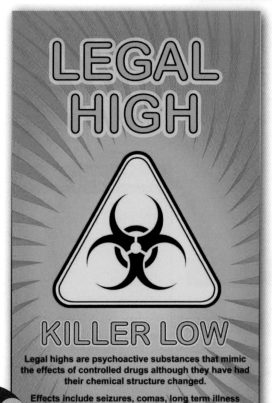

LEGAL HIGH

KILLER LOW

Legal highs are psychoactive substances that mimic the effects of controlled drugs although they have had their chemical structure changed.

Effects include seizures, comas, long term illness and in some cases death.

Don't take chances.

Now you are going to write an article of your own about the dangers of taking drugs. The article will be for a school or college newspaper. Follow the steps below to help you plan, write and proofread your article.

There are several decisions you need to make at the planning stage:

Ideas – where will you do your research for information and ideas?

The Internet is always a useful source of information, but you might find leaflets at the library too. Decide if you want to use **facts** and statistics. Make some notes.

Perspective – will you choose to write personally or impersonally?

If you have some experience, you may want to take a **subjective** approach to the theme of drugs. Or perhaps you feel more comfortable writing from an **objective** standpoint. Think about what the effect of each might be on the reader.

Purpose – do you intend to argue with, persuade or advise the reader?

You need to be clear what your intentions are as this will help you decide on the tone of your article. Advising is usually done calmly; persuading is perhaps more engaging; and arguing is often more passionate.

Register – will your article need to be formal or informal to suit the reader?

You will have to decide if the student readers would respond best to being addressed formally or more casually in the article.

Language – will you use slang, technical terms or other features?

The purpose and register of the article will determine what sort of language you use. Think about using rhetorical devices, repetition, direct address and **anecdotes** to help you achieve your purpose.

Structure – how will you link paragraphs to influence the reader?

Finally, you need to consider how you will sequence the ideas in your article. Try writing a summary of what will be in each paragraph before you start writing.

Activity 4

Write an article for a student newsletter about the dangers of taking drugs.

When you have finished, share what you have written with a partner and discuss if there are any changes you could make to improve your article.

Key terms

Fact: something that can be proved to be true

Subjective: a perspective influenced by personal feelings or opinions

Objective: a perspective *not* influenced by personal feelings or opinions

Register: the kind of words (e.g. formal, informal, literary) and the manner of speaking or writing used; varies according to the situation and the relationship of the people involved

Anecdote: a short, relevant story about an apparently real incident or person

Writing tip

Make sure your final sentence has maximum impact. You need to leave the reader in no doubt about your point of view.

7 Crossing the line

- To identify explicit information and interpret implicit ideas, and to synthesize evidence from different texts **(AO1)**

- To analyse how writers use language to achieve effects **(AO2)**

There isn't much in today's society which is taboo or just not talked about. However, issues to do with mental illness are still largely hidden. As a society, we find it too awkward, too embarrassing, too difficult to discuss openly.

Here, you will read two texts which deal with mental illness. The first is a news article about a woman who suffered from amnesia, which is a medical condition affecting memory.

Rare amnesia leaves mother with 17-year memory gap

Naomi Jacobs, 34, woke up in 2008 but believed she was just about to sit her GCSE exams in the summer of 1992.

The last thing she could remember was falling asleep in her bunk bed as a schoolgirl. She was horrified to learn she was living in the 21st century, and was even mother to an 11-year-old boy she did not recognise.

Doctors revealed that Naomi had been under so much stress that part of her brain had simply closed down, erasing many memories of her life.

She was left baffled by the internet, and flummoxed by her mobile phone as she struggled to get to grips with modern life. Today, three years after waking up in the future, Naomi has finally regained most of her memory, and has written a book about her experiences.

She said: "I fell asleep in 1992 as a bold, brassy, very confident know-it-all 15-year-old, and woke up a 32-year-old single mum living in a council house. The last thing I remember was falling asleep in my lower bunk bed, dreaming about a boy in my class. When I woke up, I looked in the mirror and had the fright of my life when I saw an old woman with wrinkles staring back at me. Then this little boy appeared and started calling me mum. That's when I started to scream.

"I didn't know who he was. I didn't think he was much younger than I was, and I certainly didn't remember giving birth to him. I began sobbing uncontrollably. To say I was petrified was an understatement. I just wanted my mum. I couldn't get my head around going to bed one night and waking up in a different century."

Naomi, who was a psychology student before her memory loss, was told by doctors that she was suffering from Transient Global Amnesia, a form of memory loss brought on by stress. [...]

Slowly she began the difficult task of piecing her life back together by ploughing through years of her diaries and journals.

Naomi added: "At 15, I thought I would have conquered half the planet by the time I was 32. It was a massive shock to discover I was just an ordinary, single mum, living in Manchester and driving a battered old Fiat Brava. At first, I struggled to leave my home, and venture out into the world – but slowly, with the help of my family, I started to get used to the world again. Although it was traumatic, I'm really grateful for being thrown forward through time now. I've been able to follow my childhood dream of becoming a writer – and am currently writing my story."

Activity 1

Read through the following statements and work in pairs to decide, according to the article, which four statements are true:

A The last thing Naomi remembers doing is her GCSEs.

B She couldn't remember how to use the Internet or a mobile phone.

C It has taken 17 years to regain her memory.

D Naomi is disappointed to find that her life is very ordinary.

E Her amnesia was caused by the stress of doing her exams.

F Naomi is a single mum living in a council house with her son.

G Naomi used her diaries to help her remember what had happened in her life.

H She didn't recognise her own mum when she looked in the mirror.

Another young woman who suffered mental illness was Sylvia Plath, an American poet and writer. She suffered from depression at times throughout her life and wrote about her thoughts and feelings in a journal. In 1957 she started work as a teacher and was finding life very hard.

Extracts from *Journals of Sylvia Plath* 1950–1962

Letter to a demon:

Last night I felt the sensation I have been reading about to no avail in James: the sick, soul-annihilating flux of fear in my blood switching its current to defiant fight. I could not sleep, although tired, and lay feeling my nerves shaved to pain & the groaning inner voice: oh, you can't teach, can't do anything. Can't write, can't think. And I lay under the negative icy flood of denial, thinking that voice was all my own, a part of me, and it must somehow conquer me & leave me with my worst visions: having had the chance to battle it & win day by day, and having failed.

* * *

I have a good self, that loves skies, hills, ideas, tasty meals, bright colors. My demon would murder this self by demanding it be a paragon*, and saying it should run away if it is being anything less. I shall doggedly do my best and know it for that, no matter what other people say. I can learn to be a better teacher. But only by painful trial and error. Life is painful trial and error. I instinctively gave myself this job because I knew I needed the confidence it would give me as I needed food: it would be my first active facing of life & responsibility: something thousands of people face every day, with groans, maybe, or with dogged determination, or with joy. But they face it. I have this demon who wants me to run away screaming if I am going to be flawed, fallible. It wants me to think I'm so good I must be perfect. Or nothing. I am, on the contrary, something: a being who gets tired, has shyness to fight, has more trouble than most facing people easily. If I get through this year, kicking my demon down when it comes up, realising I'll be tired after a day's work, and tired after correcting papers, and it's natural tiredness, not something to be ranted about in horror, I'll be able, piece by piece, to face the field of life, instead of running from it the minute it hurts.

*paragon – a person or thing that seems to be perfect

Activity ②

a. What do you learn about Sylvia Plath from each of the quotations below?

- 'the groaning inner voice'
- 'I have a good self, that loves skies, hills, ideas, tasty meals, bright colors'
- 'It wants me to think I'm so good I must be perfect'
- 'kicking my demon down when it comes up'

b. Select quotations from the text which you could use to support the following points:

- Sylvia Plath feels negative about herself as a teacher.
- She is determined to fight the voice which tells her she isn't good enough.
- She lacks confidence in social situations.

Key terms 🔖

Imagery: the use of figurative or other special language to convey an idea and create a particular effect on the reader

Extended metaphor: a metaphor that is continued and developed through a text

Sylvia Plath wrote a lot about her perception of the world and the experience of being mentally ill, including an autobiographical novel about her treatment in a psychiatric hospital. She uses unusual and stimulating **imagery** to try to explain abstract ideas, such as negativity and lack of confidence.

❝ I needed the confidence it would give me as I needed food ❞

In this simile, Plath compares her feeling of a lack of confidence to feeling hungry; she needs to have confidence like she needs food. By this she is suggesting that having confidence is a basic need in life, like eating food, and therefore explains to the reader how important it is to her. Feeling hungry is something everyone can understand, so it helps the reader to appreciate what it might be like to have no confidence.

❝ the negative icy flood of denial ❞

In the metaphor above, Plath compares her feeling of negativity with an 'icy flood' which gives the reader a sense of how cold and overpowering the feeling is, how frozen and stiff she feels. Again, an abstract idea is brought to life by comparing it to something visual which the reader will recognize and understand.

❝ it must somehow conquer me… had the chance to battle it & win ❞

Sometimes writers create a metaphor and then continue to use it throughout the article or paragraph they are writing. Using an **extended metaphor** like this, the writer widens its meaning and makes the comparison more intense. The word 'conquer' illustrates Plath's fear of being defeated and taken over by her depression. She uses the metaphor of a battle to describe how she feels she must fight against the negative voices in her head, almost like a battle between good and evil.

' Letter to a demon '

In the text above, Plath uses personification to convey her negative feelings as a demon which gives the reader a sense of how much she hates these feelings. She writes about the demon murdering her good self, which links to the metaphor of a battle. She also writes about 'kicking my demon down' as if the fight were a physical one.

Reading tip

Choose no more than five or six examples of language to explore in detail or your work will lose focus.

Activity 3

Using what you have understood about the imagery Plath uses and including what you understand about other language features, such as alliteration, repetition and lists, answer the following question:

How does Sylvia Plath use language to give readers a vivid sense of how she is feeling?

Activity 4

In these texts, both women offer the reader a glimpse of what it is like to have a mental illness. Discuss with a partner the similarities and differences between their experiences.

You might like to consider and analyse:

• what impact the illness has on their lives

• how they describe their feelings

• how they deal with their difficulties

• how important writing is to them.

Using quotations from both writers, summarize the similarities and differences between their experiences, as far as you can tell from these texts.

Stretch

Research background information about Sylvia Plath: her life, her relationships and her writing.

Present your findings, in your own words, to the rest of the class or group.

8 Looking past the mirror

- To analyse how writers use language and structure to create effects **(AO2)**
- To evaluate texts and support with evidence **(AO4)**

As we live longer, more elderly people are suffering from a condition called dementia, which causes the memory to gradually fail. Terry Pratchett, the fantasy writer, suffers from dementia and writes here to support a campaign to help fellow sufferers.

Dementia. The word itself describes shrinkage of the brain, the process of abnormal proteins clinging to the spongy masses of our cranium that we rely on to think and speak. However, the real and tangible meaning of the word will be different to everyone living with the condition. For some, they might struggle in a supermarket with finding the right change. That nagging voice in their head willing them to understand the difference between a 5p piece and £1 and yet their brain refusing to help them. Or they might lose patience with friends or family, struggling to follow conversations.

For me, living with posterior cortical atrophy began when I noticed the precision of my touch-typing getting progressively worse and my spelling starting to slip. For an author, what could be worse? And so I sought help, and will always be the loud and proud type to speak my mind and admit I'm having trouble. But there are many people with dementia too worried about failing with simple tasks in public to even step out of the house. I believe this is because simple displays of kindness often elude the best of us in these manic modern days of ours.

Ultimately, research is the answer. While talented scientists beaver away at finding a cure, this campaign holds a mirror up to us all – forcing us to realise we can do more in our everyday lives to help. Look past that mirror, maybe even through the wall, to the house of your next-door neighbour. Maybe it's an older lady, albeit only in her 60s, who you haven't recently seen popping to the shops as usual. You notice that she's forgotten to collect her milk from the doorstep, and that when you last stopped to chat she seemed confused and couldn't follow what you were saying. Think of how you might be able to help her – there are little things you could do to support her and let her know she's not alone. There are hundreds of thousands of us out there living with dementia who – to paraphrase the song in the advert – every now and again really could do with a little help from a friend.

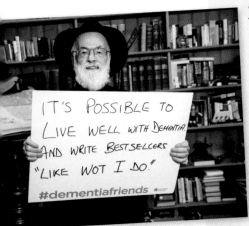

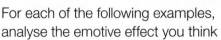
IT'S POSSIBLE TO LIVE WELL WITH DEMENTIA AND WRITE BESTSELLERS "LIKE WOT I DO." #dementiafriends

Key term

Language for emotive effect: words and phrases that are deliberately used to provoke an emotional reaction

Terry Pratchett's purpose here is clearly to persuade readers. He uses **language for emotive effect** to make the reader feel strongly about his subject, hoping to persuade them to do something to help.

Activity 1

For each of the following examples, analyse the emotive effect you think the writer wants the reader to feel:

- 'struggling to follow conversations'
- 'manic modern days of ours'
- 'talented scientists beaver away'
- 'hundreds of thousands of us out there'.

Activity 2

a. Pratchett begins with a definition of dementia, using technical terms. What is the effect of using this sort of language?

b. The writer uses a metaphor of a mirror in the third paragraph. Explain how the metaphor works and its effect on the reader.

Terry Pratchett uses a very simple structure in this article:

The sequence of ideas moves from the subject of dementia (the cause) to how it impacts on older people (the effect). Then the writer identifies how those people struggle (the problem), before explaining how scientists and friends can help (the solution). These are links you will often find in articles where the writer's purpose is to argue or persuade.

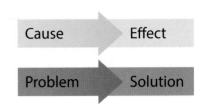

Activity 3

a. With a partner, think of a suitable subheading for each of the three paragraphs.

b. How does the narrative perspective differ in each paragraph, and what is the effect on the reader?

c. How successful is Terry Pratchett in persuading readers that people with dementia need 'a little help from a friend'?

Remember to comment on the writer's use of language, structure and tone.

Progress check

Use the chart below to review the skills you have developed in this chapter. For each Assessment Objective, start at the bottom box and work your way up towards the highest achievement in the top box. Use the box above your current achievement as your target for the next chapter. If you're at the top, can you stay there?

AO1	AO2	AO3	AO4	AO5	AO6
I can analyse ideas and synthesize evidence from different texts.	I can analyse a writer's choice of language and structure.	I can make detailed comparisons and analyse how writers' methods convey ideas.	I can evaluate the effect of a variety of writers' choices, using a range of quotations.	I can write convincingly, employing a range of complex linguistic and structural features.	I can use a range of effective sentences and spelling and punctuation are precise.
I can interpret ideas, select evidence and make clear connections between texts.	I can explain clearly the effects of language and structure.	I can compare ideas from different texts and explain how they are conveyed.	I can explain the effect of writers' methods, using relevant quotations.	I can write clearly and effectively, using linguistic and structural features appropriately.	I can use sentences for effect and spelling and punctuation are mostly accurate.
I can understand some ideas, linking evidence from different texts.	I can identify and comment on features of language and structure.	I can make comparisons between texts, commenting on how ideas are conveyed.	I can comment on writers' methods and use some quotations.	I can write with some success, using some linguistic features and paragraphs.	I can use a variety of sentence forms, with some accurate spelling and punctuation.
I can find information and ideas and make references to texts.	I can find examples of language and structure.	I can identify similarities and differences between texts.	I can give my views on texts and support them with evidence from the text.	I can write in a simple way to communicate my ideas.	I can write in sentences, using basic punctuation and some accurate spelling.

Assessment

This unit tests all the reading and writing skills that you have learned in this chapter to see if you are able to apply them to different sources.

Read the extract below and complete the activities that follow.

The extract is from a non-fiction book called *The Psychopath Test* by journalist Jon Ronson. Jon is taken by Brian, his guide, to meet a man called Tony, who is being held in a psychiatric hospital (for mentally-ill patients) at Broadmoor.

Extract from *The Psychopath Test* by Jon Ronson

The Broadmoor visitors' centre was painted in the calming hues of a municipal leisure complex – all peach and pink and pine. The prints on the walls were mass-produced pastel paintings of French doors opening onto beaches at sunrise. The building was called the Wellness Centre. I had caught the train here from London. I began to yawn uncontrollably around Kempton Park. This tends to happen to me in the face of stress. Apparently dogs do it too. They yawn when anxious.

Brian picked me up at the station and we drove the short distance to the hospital. We passed through two cordons – 'Do you have a mobile phone?' the guard asked me at the first. 'Recording equipment? A cake with a hacksaw hidden inside it? A ladder?' – and then on through gates cut out of high-security fence after fence after fence.

'I think Tony's the only person in the whole DSPD unit to have been given the privilege of meeting people in the Wellness Centre,' Brian said as we waited.

'What does DSPD stand for?' I asked.

'Dangerous and Severe Personality Disorder,' said Brian.

There was a silence.

'Is Tony in the part of Broadmoor that houses the *most dangerous* people?' I asked.

'Crazy, isn't it?' laughed Brian.

Patients began drifting in to sit with their loved ones at tables and chairs that had been fixed to the ground. They all looked quite similar to each other, quite docile and sad-eyed.

'They're medicated,' whispered Brian.

They were mostly overweight, wearing loose, comfortable T-shirts and elasticated sweatpants. There probably wasn't much to do in Broadmoor but eat.

I wondered if any of them were famous.

They drank tea and ate chocolate bars from the dispenser with their visitors. Most were young, in their twenties, and their visitors were their parents. Some were older, and their partners and children had come to see them.

'Ah! Here's Tony now!' said Brian.

I looked across the room. A man in his late twenties was walking towards us. He wasn't shuffling like the others had. He was sauntering. His arm was out-stretched. He wasn't wearing sweatpants. He was wearing a pinstripe jacket and trousers. He looked like a young businessman trying to make his way in the world, someone who wanted to show everyone that he was very, very sane.

And of course, as I watched him approach our table, I wondered if the pinstripe was a clue that he was sane or a clue that he wasn't.

We shook hands.

'I'm Tony,' he said. He sat down.

'So Brian says you faked your way in here,' I said.

'That's exactly right,' said Tony.

He had the voice of a normal, nice, eager-to-help young man.

'I'd committed GBH [grievous bodily harm],' he said. 'After they arrested me I sat in my cell and I thought, "I'm looking at five to seven years." So I asked the other prisoners what to do. They said, "Easy! Tell them you're mad! They'll put you in a county hospital. You'll have Sky TV and a PlayStation. Nurses will bring you pizzas." But they didn't send me to some cushy hospital. They sent me to bloody BROADMOOR.'

'How long ago was this?' I asked.

'Twelve years ago,' said Tony.

I involuntarily grinned.

Tony grinned back.

To remind yourself of how to apply AO1 skills on retrieving information and interpreting ideas, look back at the work you did in *Talking cats* (pages 118–121) and *Tough at the top* (pages 132–133).

Activity 1

a. Read the first two paragraphs again and select four things you learn about Broadmoor Psychiatric Hospital.

b. What impression does the writer give of the patients in Broadmoor?

c. How do you think the writer feels about visiting Broadmoor?

To remind yourself of how to apply AO2 skills on language, look back at the work you did in *Masters of the macabre* (pages 122–127) and *Crossing the line* (pages 138–141).

Activity 2

a. What is the effect of the writer describing the visitors' centre as 'all peach and pink and pine'?

b. Find two examples where the writer has adopted a comic tone and explain the effect on the reader of using humour in the text.

c. The writer uses a range of sentence forms. Select two examples from the text and explain the effects on the reader.

d. Using your answers to the above and any other examples of language that you find effective, answer the following question:

How does the writer use language to create a light-hearted tone?

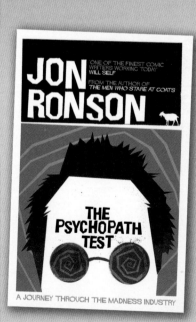

Now read the second extract. It is a newspaper article written by Fanny Fern, a 19th-century journalist. A 'lunatic asylum' was the term used in the 1800s for a psychiatric hospital.

My verdict after visiting a Lunatic Asylum is, […] what an immense improvement has modern humanity effected in the treatment of these unfortunates! What an advance upon the diabolical cruelty of blows and stripes, and iron cages, and nothing to do, and no room to do it in! Now, we have the elegant, spacious, well-ventilated and attractive building, surrounded with scenes of natural grandeur and beauty […]. One draws a long breath of relief to see them, under the eye of a watchful superintendent, raking hay in the sweet, fresh meadows, or walking about in the beautiful garden […]

How affecting, too, is the child-like confidence with which they approach a perfect stranger, to tell the sorrow that is eating their lives away. One sat at the window of a handsome room, watching with a smiling countenance the gravel-walk that led to the building. As I entered, she said, "I don't know when he will come; he said he would come and take me away, and I am going to sit here and wait for him;" and she turned again to the window and looked far off into the bright sunshine, and folded her hands in her lap in cheerful expectancy.

As the key was turned in one of the wards a woman rushed to the door, and said fiercely to the doctor, "Let me out, I say!" He calmly barred the entrance with his arm, and laying one hand soothingly on her shoulder, replied, "By and by – wait a little – won't you?" Her countenance grew placid; and she replied coaxingly, "Well, let me have one little peep out there then." – "Yes," said he, "you may go so far," pointing to a designated limit, but not accompanying her. She walked out delightedly, took a survey of the hall, and promptly returning, said, "I wanted my father, but I see he is not there." It seemed so humane to satisfy the poor creature, even though she might be a prey to some other fantasy the next minute.

It is a very curious sight, these lunatics – men and women, preparing food in the perfectly-arranged kitchen. One's first thought, to be sure, is some possibly noxious ingredient that might be cunningly mixed in the viands[1]; but further observation showed the impossibility of this, under the rigid surveillance exercised […] In fact I began to doubt whether our guide was not humbugging[2] us as to the real state of these people's intellects; particularly as some of them employed in the grounds, as we went out, took off their hats, and smiled and bowed to us in the most approved manner.

[1] viands – food
[2] humbugging – misleading

To remind yourself of how to apply AO2 skills on structure, look back at the work you did in *A bizarre start* (pages 130–131).

Activity 3

a. Write a summary sentence for each of the four paragraphs.

b. Identify how and where the writer's perspective shifts as the article progresses.

c. Choose either the first or the last sentence in the text and explain its effect on the reader.

d. Using your answers to the above and any other examples of structure that you find effective, answer the following question:

   How does the writer use structure to engage the reader's interest?

To remind yourself how to apply AO4 skills on evaluation, look back at the work you did in *A bizarre start* (pages 130–131) and *The milk's in the oven* (pages 142–143).

Activity (4)

a. Looking at the language and the use of contrast in the first paragraph, how has the writer revealed a particular view of the lunatic asylum?

b. Select three quotations which you think demonstrate the tone of the writer and analyse what effect this tone has on the reader.

c. What is the effect of including the conversation between one of the patients and the doctor in the third paragraph?

d. Using your answers to the above, and any other aspect of the text which you think is appropriate, answer the following question:

'Fanny Fern presents a view of the asylum which is almost too good to be true'. How far do you agree with this statement?

To remind yourself of how to apply AO1 skills on synthesizing evidence from different texts, look back at the work you did in *Talking cats* (pages 118–121) and *Crossing the line* (pages 138–141).

Activity (5)

Using details and quotations from both texts, summarize the differences between the attitudes of the two writers towards their experiences at the psychiatric hospitals.

To remind yourself of how to apply AO3 skills on comparison, look back at the work you did in *Masters of the macabre* (pages 122–127) and *Mind blowing* (pages 134–137).

Activity (6)

Compare how the patients are presented differently in the two texts. Remember to comment on the writers' use of language, structure and tone.

To remind yourself of how to apply writing skills (AO5 and AO6), look back at the work you did in *Tales of enchantment* (pages 128–129) and *Mind blowing* (pages 134–137).

Activity (7)

a. Write a description inspired by the picture on this page or describe an old person you know well.

b. 'Old people are useless. They should all be kept in care homes.'

Write a persuasive article for a local newspaper arguing either for or against this statement.

5 Town and country

In Britain we are a divided nation: divided between those of us who wake to the sound of a cockerel crowing at the crack of dawn and those of us who wake to the rumble of traffic in the streets outside. Some of us live in villages, on farms or isolated in the depths of the countryside, while the rest of us live in towns and cities – 64 million of us spread out across the landscape of Britain.

Cities are brilliantly exciting, bustling with activity and variety. They are vibrant, colourful, dynamic places. Between the towns and cities, however, lie vast areas of green fields, forests, coastal wetlands, moorlands and mountain ranges. The countryside is home to farming and those who have chosen a quieter life. The pace of life in the countryside is slower, more tranquil and more in tune with the seasons.

But wherever you live now, the time will come when you can choose for yourself where you would rather live. Do you long to escape the noise, pollution and endless activity of the town to enjoy the peace and tranquillity of the countryside? Or are you fed up of the boredom and inconvenience of being stuck in your village and crave the buzz and excitement of the city?

There are three units in this chapter:

- A novel setting
- People and places
- Assessment.

In the first two units, you will read both fiction and non-fiction texts, inviting you to taste something of the culture and experience of living in cities as well as the countryside. The first unit, *A novel setting*, takes you on a journey through different places found in fiction, seen through the eyes of the characters. The focus is on settings and characters, how they are presented and how readers respond to them.

The second unit, *People and places*, provides a range of non-fiction texts and the opportunity to engage with people's points of view about where they live and how they feel about it.

In the first two units you will have the opportunity to develop a number of reading and writing skills In the final unit, *Assessment*, you will put these skills into practice to make sure you can use them with confidence.

By the end of the chapter, you may have a clearer idea of whether you truly belong in the town or in the country!

Skills, Assessment Objectives and examination coverage

All the skills covered in this chapter focus on the Assessment Objectives and are directly relevant to the requirements of English Language.

Reading skills include how to:

- engage with ideas and meanings
- choose and use quotations to support ideas
- explore how language and structure are used
- compare ideas and perspectives from different texts
- evaluate the success of writers.

Writing skills include how to:

- write narrative, descriptive and discursive texts
- communicate clearly and imaginatively
- organize your ideas using different structural and grammatical features.

Activity

a. With a partner, discuss how you feel about where you live.

b. Make a list of the advantages and disadvantages.

c. Discuss where you would live if you had the choice and could live anywhere in Britain, and explain why.

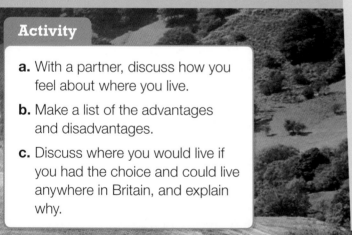

A novel setting

Take a tour of the cities and countryside featured in these novels and glimpse the very different worlds of the characters who live there.

Skills and objectives

- To identify explicit ideas in texts **(AO1)**
- To interpret implicit ideas and select evidence **(AO1)**

1 Brick Lane

The extracts below are from *Brick Lane*, a novel written in 2003 about Nazneen, a girl who travels from her home in Bangladesh to live in a city in Britain. The extracts describe what happens when she explores the city for the first time.

Extracts from *Brick Lane* by Monica Ali

Outside, small patches of mist bearded the lamp-posts and a gang of pigeons turned weary circles on the grass like prisoners in an exercise yard. A woman hurried past with a small child in her arms. The child screamed and kicked its legs against the kidnapper. The woman produced a plastic rattle with which to gag her victim. Nazneen pulled the end of her sari over her hair. At the main road she looked both ways, and then went left. Two men were dragging furniture out of a junk shop to display on the pavement. One of them went inside and came out again with a wheelchair. He tied a chain around it and padlocked it to an armchair as if arranging a three-legged furniture race. Nazneen changed her mind and turned around. She walked until she reached the big crossroads and waited at the kerb while the traffic roared from one direction and then the next. Twice she stepped into the road and drew back again. To get to the other side of the street without being hit by a car was like walking out in the monsoon and hoping to dodge the raindrops. A space opened up before her. God is great, said Nazneen under her breath. She ran.

A horn blared like an ancient muezzin*, ululating painfully, stretching his vocal cords to the limit. She stopped and the car swerved. Another car skidded to a halt in front of her and the driver got out and began to shout. She ran again and turned into a side street, then off again to the right onto Brick Lane.

***

Then she turned off at random, began to run, limped for a while to save her ankle, and thought she had come in a circle. The buildings seemed familiar. She sensed rather than saw, because she had taken care not to notice. But now she slowed down and looked around her. She looked up at a building as she passed. It was constructed almost entirely of glass, with a few thin rivets of steel holding it together. The entrance was like a glass fan, rotating slowly, sucking people in, wafting others out. Inside, on a raised dais, a woman behind a glass desk crossed and uncrossed her thin legs. She wedged a telephone receiver between her ear and shoulder and chewed on a finger-nail. Nazneen craned her head back and saw that the glass above became dark as a night pond. The building was without end. Above, somewhere, it crushed the clouds.

*muezzin – a Muslim crier who calls people to prayer from a mosque

When reading any text, we look for ideas and information. In this text there is **explicit** information, such as the fact that Nazneen waits before she crosses the road. There are also **implicit** ideas that we instinctively understand without being told, for example that Nazneen is nervous and uncertain about how to cross the road.

As readers, we can interpret ideas from the text, which means we can explain the meaning behind the ideas. An example of how the reader could interpret this text would be that Nazneen has perhaps never experienced traffic like this before because there were no major roads in her village in Bangladesh.

Reading tip

Using words and phrases such as 'perhaps', 'maybe' or 'it's possible that' suggest you are interpreting the text and coming up with original and interesting ideas of your own.

Activity 1

Show your understanding of the implicit meanings in the text by answering these questions in detail.

a. What are Nazneen's first impressions of the area outside her new home?

b. Why do you think Nazneen pulls her sari over her hair?

c. How do you think Nazneen feels as she watches the traffic?

d. Why do you think Nazneen runs away from the stopped cars?

e. Why had Nazneen 'taken care not to notice' the buildings she passed?

f. What do you think Nazneen thinks of the modern glass building?

Key terms

Explicit: stated clearly, exactly and openly

Implicit: implied or suggested but not stated openly; beneath the surface

Imagery: the use of figurative or other special language to convey an idea and create a particular effect on the reader

To show what you have understood in a text, you need to use quotations. This is evidence to show where in the text you have understood the implicit meanings.

For each idea you identify and interpret, you need to use a quotation from the text. For example:

> Nazneen sees a woman carrying a screaming child. She calls her 'the kidnapper' which suggests that Nazneen is unsure if the woman is really the child's mother. Perhaps Nazneen feels sorry for the woman because she describes how the child 'kicked its legs'.

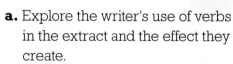

Activity 2

a. Explain what you understand about Nazneen's first experience of the city. Use quotations to support your answer.

b. How does the choice of narrative perspective influence the way the reader responds to the character of Nazneen?

 Stretch

a. Explore the writer's use of verbs in the extract and the effect they create.

b. How does the writer use **imagery** to suggest Nazneen's cultural identity and experience?

2 Mean streets

- To analyse how writers use language to create effects **(AO2)**
- To evaluate how effective writers are at creating character and settings through language **(AO4)**

The city streets are often chosen by writers as the backdrop or setting for certain genres (types) of fiction. The texts you are going to read on pages 153–156 are all from the same popular genre.

> I picked up my hat and my heaviest stick, but I observed that Holmes took his revolver from his drawer and slipped it into his pocket. It was clear that he thought our night's work might be a serious one.

From the very first line, there are clues to which genre of fiction this extract belongs. The 'revolver' is one clue, as is the name 'Holmes', or Sherlock Holmes as he is better known. The reference to 'our night's work' being 'serious' also suggests a mood or atmosphere of darkness and suspense. All these clues point to crime fiction as the genre.

Activity 1

a. There are many genres of fiction. Write a list of as many different genres as you can think of and share your list with a partner.

b. Complete the grid below to show the typical features you expect to find in each genre on your list. Hint: films have very similar genres to fiction, so thinking about films you have seen might give you some clues.

Genre	Plot	Characters	Settings	Themes	Language
Crime	murders, investigations, car chases, interviews	detectives, suspects, victims	streets, bars, wasteland, disused buildings	violence, betrayal, trust, suspicion	dialogue, imagery

Read the text opposite, which is a continuation of the above extract from *The Sign of Four*, written in 1890 by Sir Arthur Conan Doyle, the creator of the fictional detective Sherlock Holmes.

Key term

Connotation: an idea or feeling suggested by a word, in addition to the main meaning

Activity 2

What is the effect of using the following descriptive words and phrases? Explore the **connotations** of the words used.

a. 'Mud-coloured clouds'

b. 'the slimy pavement'

c. 'the endless procession of faces'

d. 'tortuous by-streets'

e. 'the coarse glare and tawdry brilliancy of public-houses'

**Extract from *The Sign of Four*
by Sir Arthur Conan Doyle**

It was a September evening and not yet seven o'clock, but the day had been a dreary one, and a dense drizzly fog lay low upon the great city. Mud-coloured clouds drooped sadly over the muddy streets. Down the Strand the lamps were but misty splotches of diffused light which threw a feeble circular glimmer upon the slimy pavement. The yellow glare from the shop-windows streamed out into the steamy, vaporous air and threw a murky shifting radiance across the crowded thorough-fare. There was, to my mind, something eerie and ghostlike in the endless procession of faces which flitted across these narrow bars of light. [...]

We had hardly reached the third pillar, which was our rendezvous, before a small, dark, brisk man in the dress of a coachman accosted us. [...] He gave a shrill whistle, on which a man led across a four-wheeler and opened the door. [He] mounted to the box, while we took our places inside. We had hardly done so before the driver whipped up his horse, and we plunged away at a furious pace through the foggy streets. [...]

At first I had some idea as to the direction in which we were driving; but soon, what with our pace, the fog, and my own limited knowledge of London, I lost my bearings and knew nothing save that we seemed to be going a very long way. Sherlock Holmes was never at fault, however, and he muttered the names as the cab rattled through squares and in and out by tortuous by-streets.

'Rochester Row,' said he. 'Now Vincent Square. Now we come out on the Vauxhall Bridge Road. [...] You can catch glimpses of the river.'

We did indeed get a fleeting view of a stretch of the Thames, with the lamps shining upon the broad, silent water; but our cab dashed on and was soon involved in a labyrinth of streets upon the other side.

'Wordsworth Road,' said my companion. '[...] Cold Harbour Lane. Our quest does not appear to take us to very fashionable regions.'

We had indeed reached a questionable and forbidding neighbourhood. Long lines of dull brick houses were only relieved by the coarse glare and tawdry brilliancy of public-houses at the corner. Then came rows of two-storeyed villas, and then again interminable lines of new, staring brick buildings – the monster tentacles which the giant city was throwing out into the country. At last the cab drew up at the third house in a new terrace. None of the other houses were inhabited, and that at which we had stopped was as dark as its neighbours, save for a single glimmer in the kitchen-window.

Activity ③

Read the student example below about language in the extract and write a similar paragraph for each of the following quotations:

- 'a dense drizzly fog lay low'
- 'a labyrinth of streets'
- 'the monster tentacles which the giant city was throwing out'
- 'new, staring brick buildings'

By using the phrase 'a murky shifting radiance', the writer is creating an oxymoron, an image which is made up of opposite ideas: 'murky' suggests the sinister darkness of the evening and 'radiance' refers to the glaring, almost pure, brightness of the street lamps. He creates an image which is a contrast between light and dark to convey a sense of being caught between the two — not quite day or night. By using the word 'shifting' he also adds a feeling of the light changing so that you are not sure what you are seeing. It creates a mood of uncertainty and mystery which matches the genre. Light and dark are also used as symbols of good and evil which creates another level of meaning in a crime story...

Fifty years later, another writer in a different city, was writing crime fiction and developing a new genre: hard-boiled crime fiction.

Raymond Chandler wrote *Farewell, My Lovely* in 1940. It was one of several stories about the detective Philip Marlowe, who lived and worked on the streets of Los Angeles, USA. In the extracts below, Marlowe observes a man behaving strangely, 'a big man but not more than six feet five inches tall and not wider than a beer truck'.

Extracts from *Farewell, My Lovely* by Raymond Chandler

He wore a shaggy borsalino hat, a rough grey sports coat with white golf balls on it for buttons, a brown shirt, a yellow tie, pleated grey flannel slacks and alligator shoes with white explosions on the toes. From the outer breast pocket cascaded a handkerchief of the same brilliant yellow as his tie. There were a couple of colored feathers tucked into the band of his hat, but he didn't really need them. Even on Central Avenue, not the quietest dressed street in the world, he looked about as inconspicuous as a tarantula on a slice of angel food.

***

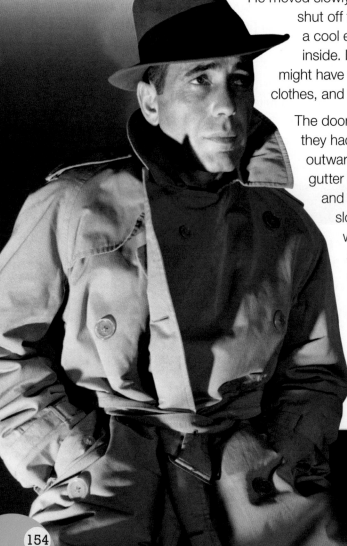

He moved slowly across the sidewalk to the double swinging doors which shut off the stairs to the second floor. He pushed them open, cast a cool expressionless glance up and down the street, and moved inside. If he had been a smaller man and more quietly dressed, I might have thought he was going to pull a stick-up. But not in those clothes, and not with that hat, and that frame.

The doors swung back outwards and almost settled to a stop. Before they had entirely stopped moving they opened again, violently, outwards. Something sailed across the sidewalk and landed in the gutter between two parked cars. It landed on its hands and knees and made a high keening noise like a cornered rat. It got up slowly, retrieved a hat and stepped back onto the sidewalk. It was a thin, narrow-shouldered brown youth in a lilac-coloured suit and a carnation. It had slick black hair. It kept its mouth open and whined for a moment. People stared at it vaguely. Then it settled its hat jauntily, sidled over to the wall and walked silently splay-footed off along the block.

Silence. Traffic resumed. I walked along to the double doors and stood in front of them. They were motionless now. It wasn't any of my business. So I pushed them open and looked in.

Activity 4

Discuss with a partner how you can tell that this story is set in America. Write down all the clues you can find.

Chandler uses a range of language features, as well as American dialect words, to create a vivid sense of the setting and characters.

Activity 5

a. Identify which language feature is used in each of these quotations and analyse the effect created by the writer.

   i. 'as inconspicuous as a tarantula on a slice of angel food'

   ii. 'But not in those clothes, and not with that hat, and that frame.'

   iii. 'It got up slowly'

   iv. 'Silence. Traffic resumed.'

b. How does the writer use language to engage the reader's interest in this opening extract?

These extracts introduce the character of Moose Malloy, a gangster who has left prison to search for his old girlfriend, Velma, who used to work in the 'dine and dice emporium'. The larger-than-life characters and exaggerated language give Chandler's stories a comic book atmosphere.

The following extract picks up the story inside the bar.

Extract from *Farewell, My Lovely* by Raymond Chandler

There was a dull flat sound at the back of the place, behind the closed door. It might have been a slammed door. I didn't think it was. The barman didn't think so either.

The barman froze. His mouth drooled. I listened. No other sound. I started quickly for the end of the counter. I had listened too long.

The door at the back opened with a bang and Moose Malloy came through it with a smooth heavy lunge and stopped dead, his feet planted and a wide pale grin on his face.

A Colt Army .45 looked like a toy pistol in his hand.

'Don't nobody try to fancy pants,' he said cosily. 'Freeze the mitts on the bar.'

The barman and I put our hands on the bar.

Moose Malloy looked the room over with a raking glance. He shifted his feet and moved silently across the room. His grin was taut, nailed on. He looked like a man who could take a bank single-handed – even in those clothes.

The writer continues in the same style. The plot is harsh (shooting and killing Mister Montgomery); the setting is hard (a drinking, gambling den); the characters are violent (Moose Malloy throws a man through a door); the themes are serious (violence and revenge) and the language is also tough. However, Chandler's purpose is clearly to entertain rather than terrify the reader.

Activity 6

How does Chandler use language and tone to create a comic book feel of cartoon violence in these extracts?

The crime genre continues to develop. Modern crime writers use similar features in a contemporary way. The following is an extract from *Loss*, written by Tony Black in 2010, about a Scottish detective called Gus Dury.

Extract from *Loss* by Tony Black

Debs had got up early and locked herself in the bathroom. I heard her snivelling inside but left her be. I wanted her to understand I couldn't just let my brother's murder go, but now wasn't the time to tell her.

I tweaked the dog's ear, then put on my Crombie*. The car keys hung by the door. The rank smell in the stair had got worse – I held my breath again on the way down. Outside the street looked whitewashed by the snow. It was too early for footprints, or to see the roads turned to slush. Everywhere lay silent and still beneath the pure-white blanket. I felt the cold seize me, go for my chest. I fastened my coat and raised the collar.

As I trudged down towards the car the grey sky suddenly turned to a black mass. A vast group of starlings swirled into view, cutting treacherous angles as they darted in first one, then another direction. I watched the darkness form and dissemble then re-form again. Nature amazed me; I felt sure I was of its lowest order.

The windscreen of Deb's Punto was frozen over. I cleared it with the scraper, but then the engine refused to turn over. Automatic choke chugged a bit; when it bit, the tyres span on the road. I dropped into second to give more traction to the hill start. Got a break at the lights and took a steady pace on the quiet roads all the way to the Grange.

My brother and his family stayed in Edinburgh's millionaires' row. A house round here was said to have set you back the best part of three mill until recently. After the banks crashed and demand plummeted, it wiped a third off the valuation. As I reached their home, I checked for any signs of movement. I rolled down the car window and sparked up a Marlboro. Got about two drags in when I saw a bloke appear from round the side of the house, dragging a wheelie bin behind him. He looked about six-two, early twenties, with a shaved head and broad shoulders. He clocked me sitting in the motor and frowned. I got out.

'I can help you?' he had an Eastern European accent. We had so many in the city now it was hardly worth noting.

*Crombie – a luxury coat

Key term

Tone: a way of writing which conveys the writer's or narrator's attitude, for example an apologetic or angry tone

Activity 7

a. What similarities can you find between these three texts?

b. Write down one word to describe the **tone** of each text.

c. Write a summary of the similarities between two of the texts.

d. How do you think the crime fiction genre has developed in 100 years?

Support — Think about how Tony Black uses slang, details about people, the weather, driving terms, the narrator's attitudes to people and the dialogue. Are these the same as in the other texts or different? Are they more extreme?

Stretch — Why do you think the crime genre is dominated by male writers and male detectives? Why is the writer's choice of narrative perspective so important in crime friction? Why do you think crime writers often choose to write a whole series of novels about the same detective?

When evaluating a text, you are giving an **opinion** about how effective you think the writer is. You should explain your opinion and refer to the range of skills the writer demonstrates. You should refer to how well you think they present characters, settings and themes. You should also refer to the way they use language, **structure** and tone to present them.

Activity 8

In a review of Tony Black's crime novel *Loss*, one critic wrote: 'Black's novel is a perfect example of the crime genre; it transports the reader to a dark, dismal city in the hands of a dark and dangerous detective.'

How far do you agree with this review?

Support

Plan your answer in paragraphs. **SPAG**

1 Introduce your answer by explaining what you know about crime fiction.

2 Write at least one paragraph each about the following:
   • characters   • setting   • themes.
   When you write about these features, remember to use quotations to support your ideas. Make sure you comment on the language, structure and tone that the writer uses.

3 Conclude your answer by giving your own opinion about the critic's statement and explaining how far you agree.

Stretch

What is it about the city that makes it such a compelling setting for novelists, particularly crime writers?

3 Rambling into danger

The countryside is often chosen by writers as the setting for their stories. The following extract, from the opening chapter of Ross Raisin's contemporary novel *God's Own Country*, takes place on the Yorkshire Moors.

Extract from *God's Own Country* by Ross Raisin

Ramblers. Daft sods in pink hats and green hats. It wasn't even cold. They moved down the field swing-swaying like a line of drunks, addled with the air and the land, and the smell of manure. I watched them from up top, their bright heads peeping through the fog.

Sat on my rock there I let the world busy itself below, all manner of creatures going about their backwards-forwards same as always, never mind the fog had them half-sighted. But I could see above the fog. It bided under my feet, settled in the valley like a sump-pool spreading three miles over to the hills at Felton.

The ramblers hadn't marked me. They'd walked past the farm without taking any notice, of me or of Father rounding up the flock from the moor. Oi there ramblers, I'd a mind for shouting, what the bugger are you doing, talking to that sheep? Do you think she fancies a natter, eh? And they'd have bowed down royal for me then,

no doubt. So sorry, Mr Farmer, we won't do it again, I hope we haven't upset her. For that was the way with these – so respect-minded they wouldn't dare even look on myself for fear of crapping up Nature's balance. The laws of the countryside. And me, I was real, living, farting Nature to their brain of things, part of the scenery same as a tree or a tractor. I watched as the last one over the stile fiddled with a rock on top the wall, for he thought he'd knocked it out of place weighting himself over. Daft sods these ramblers. I went towards them.

Halfway down the field the fog got hold of me, feeling around my face so as I had to stop a minute and tune my eyes, though I still had sight of the hats, no bother. They were only a short way into the next field, moving on like a line of chickens, their heads twitching side to side. What a lovely molehill. Look, Bob, a cuckoo behind the drystone wall. Only it wasn't a cuckoo, I knew, it was a bloody pigeon.

The main character in this story is the narrator, Sam Marsdyke. The reader learns a lot about Sam from what he says, does and thinks.

Activity 1

Answer the following questions, using quotations to support your ideas.

a. How old do you think Sam is? Give reasons for your answer.

b. How does Sam react to the ramblers?

c. What do you understand about how Sam feels about the countryside?

d. What tone does the writer use in this extract? Explain the effect on the reader.

e. Summarize how Sam thinks the ramblers feel about the countryside.

Stretch

a. Do you think Sam is going to be a hero or anti-hero on the basis of this introduction? Explain your reasons.

b. What advantages are there in using a **first-person narrative** to present the character of Sam?

Key terms

Summarize: to give the main points of something briefly

First-person narrative: story or account told from the point of view of a character or person involved, typically using the pronoun 'I'

Contrast: the use of opposing ideas and words in order to emphasize differences

Activity 2

The writer uses humour in the extract. Explain what makes it funny and what effect the humour has on the reader.

Structure is the way a writer organizes the text. Writers use a range of structural features to influence readers. The words and phrases in italics below are useful terms to use when writing about structure.

The extract begins with a clear *focus* on the ramblers. The first three words *identify* the ramblers as the focus of the narrator's contempt and ridicule. The *effect* is to establish a **contrast** between the *narrator* and the ramblers.

The *focus* moves from the *narrow detail* of the ramblers' hats to a *wider perspective* of the fields and fog. The effect is to *establish the setting* for the reader so they can *visualize the scene*.

The *focus shifts* to the narrator himself, sitting on a rock. The writer wants the reader to *engage* with the *main character*, so this description of him sitting alone watching the ramblers *creates sympathy* for him.

The writer uses a *flashback*, where the action moves back in time to show what happened earlier when the ramblers passed the farm. This gives additional *background information* for the reader about the characters.

The *dialogue* Sam imagines between himself and the ramblers about the sheep begins a section of the text which shows the reader Sam's thoughts and imagination. It is a move from the real *exterior world* to the psychological *interior world*. This is very important for the reader to understand and *empathize* with Sam.

Activity 3

How effective is the writer in using structure and language to introduce the main character in the novel?

159

4 Tales from the dairy

Skills and objectives

- To explore how writers use language and structure to create effects **(AO2)**
- To write a narrative piece, using a range of structural and linguistic features **(AO5, AO6)**

Thomas Hardy was a 19th-century novelist who set many of his novels in the countryside. The extract below is from *Tess of the d'Urbervilles*. Tess is a dairymaid on a farm in Dorset. She has fallen in love with Angel Clare, a gentleman, who is learning to be a farmer.

Extract from *Tess of the d'Urbervilles* by Thomas Hardy

Amid the oozing fatness and warm ferments of the Froom Vale, at a season when the rush of juices could almost be heard below the hiss of fertilization, it was impossible that the most fanciful love should not grow passionate. [...]

July passed over their heads, and the [...] weather which came in its wake seemed an effort on the part of Nature to match the state of hearts at Talbothays Dairy. [...] Its heavy scents weighed upon them, and at mid-day the landscape seemed lying in a swoon. [...]

They milked entirely in the meads for coolness and convenience, without driving in the cows. [...] On one of these afternoons four or five unmilked cows chanced to stand apart from the general herd, behind the corner of a hedge, among them being Dumpling and Old Pretty, who loved Tess's hands above those of any other maid. When she rose from her stool under a finished cow, Angel Clare, who had been observing her for some time, asked her if she would take the aforesaid creatures next. She silently assented, and with her stool at arm's length, and the pail against her knee, went round to where they stood. Soon the sound of Old Pretty's milk fizzing into the pail came through the hedge, and then Angel felt inclined to go round the corner also [...]

She did not know that Clare had followed her round, and that he sat under his cow watching her. The stillness of her head and features was remarkable: she might have been in a trance, her eyes open, yet unseeing. Nothing in the picture moved but Old Pretty's tail and Tess's pink hands, the latter so gently as to be a rhythmic pulsation only, as if they were obeying a reflex stimulus, like a beating heart.

How very lovable her face was to him. Yet there was nothing ethereal[1] about it; all was real vitality, real warmth, real incarnation[2]. [...]

Clare had studied the curves of those lips so many times that he could reproduce them mentally with ease: and now, as they again confronted him, clothed with colour and life, they sent an *aura* over his flesh, a breeze through his nerves [...]

Resolutions, reticences[3], prudences, fears, fell back like a defeated battalion. He jumped up from his seat, and, leaving his pail to be kicked over if the milcher had such a mind, went quickly towards the desire of his eyes, and, kneeling down beside her, clasped her in his arms.

[1] ethereal – light and delicate, often associated with something heavenly
[2] incarnation – the taking of human form
[3] reticences – thoughts and feelings that are kept hidden

Hardy's language is evocative and sensuous, meaning that he uses words which create feelings and give pleasure to the senses.

Activity 1

Explore the connotations and effects of the following words and phrases.

a. 'Amid the oozing fatness and warm ferments'

b. 'the rush of juices'

c. 'heavy scents'

d. 'the desire of his eyes'

Hardy also uses a range of language features, including onomatopoeia. Two students wrote about this feature in the text.

Key terms

Symbolism: the use of symbols to represent something else; often a simpler portrayal of something more complicated or abstract

Personification: the representation of a quality or idea as a person

Student A

Hardy uses the word 'hiss' in the text. This is an example of onomatopoeia, which is when the word sounds like the noise it is describing. He uses the word 'hiss' to make us think about the noise it makes.

Student B

Hardy uses onomatopoeia to bring alive the sounds of summer. He refers to the 'hiss of fertilisation' which is the sound Hardy imagines is made by plants and animals as they reproduce. It suggests a soft, continuous sound, like the buzzing of insects and contributes to the overall effect of natural sensuality which is the setting for Tess and Angel Clare to fall in love. The word 'hiss', however, reminds the reader of snakes and therefore might be symbolic of sin.

Activity 2

a. With a partner, discuss how Student B adds so much more to their answer than Student A. Identify where Student B makes reference to the characters, the setting, the **symbolism** and the effect on the reader.

b. Using Student B's answer as a model, write about the effects of each of the following features in the extract, using quotations from the text to support your ideas.

- **Personification**
- Lists
- **Alliteration**
- **Simile**
- **Metaphor**

Stretch

Thomas Hardy's main theme in the novel is the purity of nature; he calls Tess 'A Pure Woman'. Writers often use symbols to represent those themes. Analyse how each of the following has symbolic value in the extract and how each might contribute to the main theme: summer, the heat, the cows, Tess's lips.

Key terms

Simile: a comparison showing the similarity between two quite different things, stating that one is *like* the other

Metaphor: a comparison showing the similarity between two quite different things, stating that one actually *is* the other

Alliteration: repetition of the same letter or sound at the beginning of several words

On page 158 you saw how the writer structured an extract by starting from a detailed view of the characters, then broadening that view to take in a wider perspective of the landscape. Here, Hardy does the reverse. He begins with a wide perspective of the setting: the landscape and the weather, and then gradually shifts the focus to zoom in on Tess and Angel in particular.

The fourth paragraph brings another structural change as the writer freezes the action to create a still image of the lovers milking. He even writes 'Nothing in the picture moved' to emphasize this special moment, just before the lovers embrace. The delay in the action creates a feeling of increased anticipation and pleasure for the reader. Hardy continues with this structural delay by narrowing the focus to Angel's thoughts as he watches her, almost as if the writer wants the reader to fall in love with Tess too.

Activity ③

How does Thomas Hardy use language and structure to engage the reader in the romance between Tess and Angel?

You have seen how Thomas Hardy used the countryside as the setting for a romantic story. Now you are going to write a short narrative of your own where the setting has an effect on the action.

Stage 1: Planning

Consider and make notes on the following:
- Plot – think about what will happen in your story. It is better to write in detail about a short sequence of events than a whole lifetime.
- Setting – think about where the action will happen. The setting is everything from the locations where the action takes place, to the time of year, the time of day, the weather, the period in history and the social, cultural or political events taking place.

- Characters – for a short narrative, the fewer characters the better. Try to picture them and imagine their voices.
- Language – the type of language you use will depend on the genre of your story. Think about how much emphasis you will give to description, dialogue and action.
- Tone – it is useful to consider before you start what tone you will adopt, whether you want to write a fast-paced, thrilling narrative or a more reflective, dreamlike story, for example.
- Structure – think about how you will direct the focus of the reader and organize your ideas. Choose what sort of narrative perspective you will use.

Activity ④

Plan what you will include in each paragraph of your narrative. Make sure you refer to the development of plot, characters and setting in each paragraph.

Support

Remember the main reasons why you would start a new paragraph:
- Shift in time
- Shift in place
- Shift in perspective
- Shift in purpose

Stage 2: Writing

The opening sentence of your story has to intrigue the reader and draw them into the world you are creating. It offers a glimpse of the setting, the characters or the plot. The closing sentence is also important as it gives the reader a sense of closure once the story has ended, or a sense of anticipation in reaching a climax.

Activity 5

a. With a partner, discuss the following sentences and decide how they could work as the opening or closing sentences to a story and what impact they would have on the reader.

 With a cheerful wave from Sophie, they turned into the busy street and disappeared.

 Through the dense forest, like silent monks, the hooded soldiers marched.

b. Using the notes and plans you have made, write the first draft of your story.

Stage 3: Proofreading

All writers make changes to their first drafts. It is an opportunity to add to the richness of your writing.

Activity 6

 SPAG

a. Find examples of nouns in your story that sound uninteresting. Consider how you could use adjectives and adverbs to build noun phrases and bring the words alive. For example:

> There were *dark, sinister* clouds lurking *ominously* in the sky.

b. Check the variety of sentence structures and lengths you have used. Try using two or three very short sentences for impact. You could also use **connectives** to extend and link sentences. For example:

> There were dark, sinister clouds lurking ominously in the sky *while* beneath the trees crouched the tiny figure of a child. He was alive!

c. Make sure all your paragraphs start differently. Use a variety of phrases to let the reader know where the story is taking them. For example:

> *By evening*, there were dark, sinister clouds...

d. Check that you have included a range of vocabulary and that your spelling, punctuation and grammar are accurate. Then write a second draft of your narrative.

Key term

Connective: a word that joins phrases or sentences, such as: 'whereas', 'although', 'while', 'despite', 'therefore', 'alternatively', 'because'

People and places

Everyone has a view about where they live. This unit offers a variety of perspectives on the city and the country. Some are very positive while others are much less so.

Skills and objectives

- To summarize and compare writers' ideas, with reference to the language they use **(AO3)**
- To write clearly and organize ideas **(AO5)**

5 Sounds of the city

Cities are busy places, full of people, activity, traffic and noise. This is nothing new, according to a journalist's account of spring in the city written in 1871.

Extract from 'Budding Spring – In the City' written by Fanny Fern

We of the city do not appreciate the blessing of closed windows and silence, until budding Spring comes. The terrific war-whoop of the milkman inaugurates the new-born day long before we should otherwise recognize it. Following him is the rag-man, with his handcart, to which six huge jangling, terrific cow-bells are fastened, as an accompaniment to the yet louder yell of 'r-a-g-s'. Then comes the 'S-t-r-a-w-b-e-r-r-y' man, with lungs of leather, splitting your head, as you try to sip your coffee in peace. Close upon his heels, before he has hardly turned the corner, comes the pine-apple man, who tries to outscreech *him*. Then the fish-man, who blows a hideous tin trumpet, loud enough and discordant enough to set all your nerves jangling, if they had not already been taxed to the utmost.

You jump up in a frenzy to close the window, only to see that the fish-man has stopped his abominable cart at the door of a neighbor, where he is deliberately cleaning and splitting them, and throwing the refuse matter in the street, as a bouquet for your nostrils during the warm day. [...] By this time comes a great mob of boys, with vigorous lungs, tossing each other's caps in the air, and screeching with a power perfectly inexplicable at only six, ten, or twelve years of practice. Indeed, the smaller the boy the bigger is his war-whoop, as a general rule. [...]

By this time your hair stands on end, and beads of perspiration form upon your nose. You fly for refuge to the back of the house. Alas! In the next house is a little dog barking as if his last hour was coming; while upon the shed are two cats, in the most inflamed state of bristle, glaring like fiends, and '*maow*'-ing in the most hellish manner at each other's whiskers. You go down into the parlor, and seat yourself there. Your neighbor, Tom Snooks, is smoking at his window, and puffing it right through yours over your lovely roses, the perfume of which he quite extinguishes with his nasty odor.

Heavens! And this is 'Spring'!

The journalist presents a clear perspective in this article: the city is noisy. However, there are more details about this point of view that you need to be able to identify and support with quotations.

Activity 1

Find a quotation from the extract to support the following statements.

a. The milkman arrives early in the morning.

b. The rag-man's bells are noisy.

c. The journalist wants peace and quiet.

d. It is not only the noise that is annoying.

To identify the writer's perspective, you need to read the article carefully, starting at the beginning, asking yourself after every sentence: 'What point is the writer making here? Is this the same point or a new one?' There is no need to repeat what the writer says; you need to identify what the writer *thinks* or *feels* about it. For example:

Student A

> The writer goes to the back of the house because of all the noise at the front of the house. There is a dog barking, cats screeching and a man is 'smoking at his window'.

Student B

> The writer tries to escape from the noise by saying 'fly for refuge', which shows how desperate the writer is, but there is a dog barking and cats screeching in the garden at the back of the house too. The word 'Alas!' shows the writer's surprise and distress at not finding any peace there either.

What Student A writes is true, but does not explain how the writer feels about it. Student B makes it clear that the writer feels desperate to escape, and is both surprised and distressed at the continuing noise.

Activity 2

Using quotations, summarize the writer's perspective on noise in the city.

The writer has chosen her language carefully to present this point of view.

Activity 3

Analyse how the writer uses language in the following phrases.

a. 'with lungs of leather'   **c.** 'two cats, in the most inflamed state of bristle'

b. 'a bouquet for your nostrils'

Stretch

a. What effect does the writer's use of pronouns and tenses have on the reader?

b. Is there any hint of **irony** in this article? If so, what effect does it have?

Key term

Irony: the use of words that mean the opposite of what is said, for humour or emphasis

A second article, written in 2010, offers a very different perspective on sound in the city.

Why we love sounds of the city jungle

For some, living in a city is a loud, unpleasant babble of intrusive noise. For others it is a soundscape of calming tones that lift the spirits and brighten the day. Now a £1m research project is building a database of noises that people say improve their environment. It will translate those findings into design principles to help architects create sweeter-sounding cities.

Among the urban sounds researchers have found to be surprisingly agreeable are car tyres on wet, bumpy asphalt, the distant roar of a motorway flyover, the rumble of an overground train and the thud of heavy bass heard on the street outside a nightclub.

Other sounds that are apparently kind to the ear include a baby laughing, skateboarders practising in underground car parks and orchestras tuning up.

'Sound in the environment, especially that made by other people, has overwhelmingly been considered purely as a matter of volume and generally in negative terms, as both intrusive and undesirable,' said Dr Bill Davies of Salford University, who is leading the Engineering and Physical Sciences Research Council-funded project Positive Soundscapes. [...]

According to the latest National Noise Incidence Study, moves to bring in quieter transport and urban noise barriers are falling short. Traffic noise is audible in 87 per cent of homes in England and Wales, and 54 per cent of the population is exposed to levels beyond the World Health Organisation guidelines for avoiding serious irritation.

Davies would like to see more water features and sound-generating sculptures next to busy roads. Buildings and trees can also be used to scatter, deaden or reflect sound, to create peaceful, quieter spaces or vibrant, exciting-sounding areas. [...]

Sounds are not, the study found, judged solely on volume. 'The frequency [pitch] of a noise is a huge issue,' said Davies. 'A high-pitched sound is unpleasant even if it is very quiet, like the whine of a wasp trapped in a room, while a sound like bass coming through the wall of a nightclub, which is loud but low, can be very soothing.'

Both articles explore the issue of urban noise. Writing a summary of the articles means you need to identify and interpret ideas from both texts and make connections between them. You also need to synthesize (or bring together) quotations from the texts.

Activity 4

Write a summary of the differences between the sounds of the city in 1871 and in 2010.

Support Make a list of all the sounds described in the first article. Do the same for the second article. Do any of these sounds appear in both articles? Use your lists to answer the question.

Activity 5

What does each of these quotations tell you about the writer's perspective in the second text?

a. 'For some… For others…'

b. 'surprisingly agreeable'

c. 'both intrusive and undesirable'

d. 'to create peaceful, quieter spaces or vibrant, exciting-sounding areas'

e. 'can be very soothing'

When comparing writers' perspectives, you need to identify *what* those perspectives are, as well as comparing *how* they present them to the reader. The methods they use could be language, structure and/or tone.

It is very important to plan your response when comparing texts. Although it is possible to write about each text separately, it is better to write about both texts together, so you can compare them more closely. Your plan might look like this:

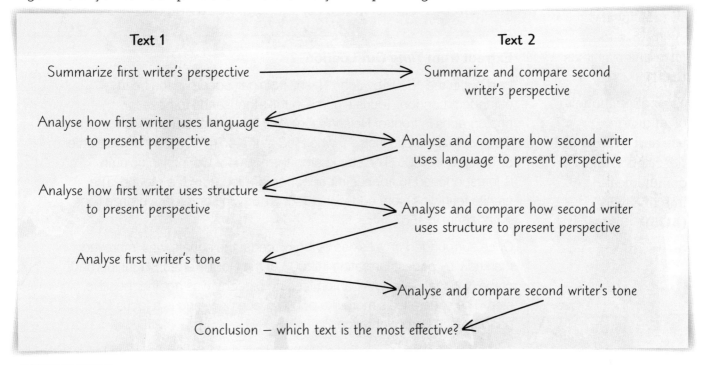

Text 1

Summarize first writer's perspective

Analyse how first writer uses language to present perspective

Analyse how first writer uses structure to present perspective

Analyse first writer's tone

Text 2

Summarize and compare second writer's perspective

Analyse and compare how second writer uses language to present perspective

Analyse and compare how second writer uses structure to present perspective

Analyse and compare second writer's tone

Conclusion – which text is the most effective?

Activity 6

Compare how attitudes to city sounds are presented differently in the two texts.

Plan your answer first, using the model above, giving one or two examples of language, structure and tone from each text.

Now you are going to write an article to present your own perspective on noise.

● Use what you have learned about language, structure and tone from the two texts you have read.

● Aim to write an introduction, four or five paragraphs and a conclusion.

● Plan what you will write in each paragraph before you start writing.

Writing tip

When the purpose of your writing is to argue, you need to present your ideas directly and forcefully, using a range of powerful language features.

Activity 7

'We left the city to find peace and quiet in the countryside – now we have to listen to sheep bleating, tractors roaring and pub music blaring. There is no escape from the horror of noise in the modern world.'

Write an article arguing your point of view about noise in the modern world.

6 Trafalgar Square

London is the biggest city in Britain, home to more than 8 million people. It is also popular with tourists. On average, 30 million people visit London every year. Below is an extract from a contemporary travel guide.

- To identify and synthesize ideas from different texts **(AO1)**
- To explore models of language use and write a description to communicate imaginatively **(AO5)**

Extract from *Time Out* London

Laid out in the 1820s by John Nash, Trafalgar Square is the heart of modern London. Tourists come in their thousands to pose for photographs in front of Nelson's Column. It was erected in 1840 to honour Vice Admiral Horatio Nelson, who died at the point of victory at the Battle of Trafalgar in 1805. The statue atop the 150-foot Corinthian column is foreshortened to appear in perfect proportion from the ground. The granite fountains were added in 1845; Sir Edwin Landseer's bronze lions joined them in 1867.

Once surrounded on all sides by busy roads, the square was improved markedly by pedestrianisation in 2003 of the North Terrace, right in front of the National Gallery. A ban on feeding pigeons was another positive step. The square feels more like public space now, and is a focus for performance and celebration.

Around the perimeter are three plinths bearing statues of George VI and two Victorian military heroes, Henry Havelock and Sir Charles James Napier. The long-empty fourth plinth, which never received its planned martial statue, has been used since 1998 to display temporary, contemporary art. At the square's north-east corner is the refurbished St Martin-in-the-Fields.

Key term

Fact: something that can be proved to be true

Activity 1

a. Find as many examples of these language features as you can in the text:

  i. Facts

  ii. Figures

  iii. Present tense

  iv. Specialist vocabulary

b. What is the effect of using each of these language features and what do they suggest about the purpose of this text?

Activity 2

Which of the following statements are true and which are false, according to the text?

a. Nelson died at the Battle of Trafalgar in 1840.

b. Art and drama are major attractions for tourists visiting the square.

c. One of the statues is of King George V.

d. Pigeons have been banned from the square.

e. The lions are made of metal.

f. Nelson's Column is 150 ft high.

g. Restricting the flow of traffic has made the Square pleasanter.

h. The fourth plinth permanently displays a piece of contemporary art.

One visitor to London in 1960 was an American poet, Sylvia Plath. She wrote down her impressions of the city in a journal in note form.

Extract from *The Journals of Sylvia Plath* 1950–1962

Trafalgar Square: "wooden benches, back to Nat. Gallery – hot June sun – sparkling & sheen: lavender-pink metalled neck of brown pigeons – bums asleep under newspapers – round yellow-orange eye of pigeons, pink feet – red & white checked flag flapping in blue sky over Canadian-pacific clock – white & grey domes – back of black Lord Nelson on pillar – 9:30am – fountains begin – spurt – drift of water vapor slicking the green back of the dolphins & mermaids

roar of traffics – red tops of great double decker busses moving to right, black cabs – white highlights – sun high at left – front – green leaves in granite oblong basins – gleam of brown metal desk lamps

traffic roar, squeal of brakes like high struck glass – guardian lions – white metal on metal flanks – dark squadrons of pigeons

derricks & cranes: skeletal buildings in background – cool clear lucid air – drifted over by smoke, exhaust fumes, fountain spray – two wide fountain basins, light from pool reflecting on underside – flap & flight of hundreds of pigeons wheeling – woman in black passing – pigeons in basket, about sandalled feet – statue of mermaids – limpid & flowing green

huge flapping wheel of pigeons round & round base of Nelson's pillar – rainbow in spray – green water – white shit on paving – church spire – blue clock face – gilt hands – pediment"

Activity 3

Discuss with a partner which features of Trafalgar Square are included in each text and which text you prefer as an introduction to this London attraction.

Stretch

If you were the editor of a London travel guide, would you include this extract from Sylvia Plath's journal? Consider both sides of the argument and justify your conclusion.

Activity 4

Find quotations to support references to Trafalgar Square and complete a grid like the one started below.

Feature	Travel guide	Journal
Lions	'Landseer's bronze lions'	'guardian lions'
Traffic	'pedestrianised'	'red tops of great double decker busses'

Summarizing the similarities and differences between two texts means you are expected to do three things.

1 Identify and interpret the similarities between the ideas.

2 Identify and interpret the differences between the ideas.

3 Use quotations from both texts to support your answer.

Look at the response below to see how one student has done this.

Both of the texts include references to the lions. The travel guide refers to them as 'Sir Edwin Landseer's bronze lions', which gives us factual details about who designed and created the lions and what they were made of. The journal also refers to the lions, but this time as 'guardian lions'. The writer uses her imagination to make the lions seem almost human, as if they are guarding Nelson on his column. The difference between these two accounts is because the purpose of the travel guide is to inform the reader and give precise details about the square, whereas the purpose of the journal is to create a vivid snapshot of a scene, like taking a photograph.

Activity 5

Using the quotations from your grid, summarize the similarities and differences between the two writers' views of Trafalgar Square.

Plath uses vivid language to describe what she could *see*. She uses a combination of nouns, adjectives and verbs to describe what is going on around her. The words she uses have been chosen to create particular effects. For example:

Onomatopoeia echoes the repetitive, whipping sound of the flag in the wind. The alliteration here echoes the sound of the flag moving, adding a soundtrack to the visual description of the scene.

'flag flapping...'

The verb describes how the spray has made the statues wet, slippery and shiny – bringing them alive. Connotations of 'slick' suggest shiny dark hair or a black oily sheen, indicating something extravagant or maybe dangerous.

'drift of water vapor slicking the green back of the dolphins & mermaids...'

A simple adjective highlights how water has affected the colour of the metal, giving a sense of the age of the statue.

'dark squadron of pigeons'

An adjective emphasizes the sinister, military nature of the birds, in contrast to the brightness of the rest of the description.

A metaphor, comparing birds to an army, creates the idea of pigeons as soldiers – organized and united, maybe even aggressive and preparing to attack.

Activity 6

How does Sylvia Plath use language to create a vivid description of Trafalgar Square?

You should refer to a range of language features, as well as any other words you find particularly effective.

Remember to use quotations to support your answer.

> **Stretch**
>
> Sylvia Plath's writing style has been described by critics as both 'cinematic' and 'fragmentary'. Analyse Plath's style in this extract and how she uses structural features to create specific effects.

Now you are going to write a description of a place. Unlike Sylvia Plath's description, you will need to write in full sentences, but you should still include a collection of vivid images and impressions.

As you plan your work, think about the following:

- Subject: choosing a place to write about. It could be somewhere near where you live or somewhere you have visited.
- Structure: writing in full sentences and paragraphs. You can achieve a similar impact to Plath by grouping words and using lists of nouns, verbs, adjectives and adverbs. You can also use sentences of different lengths.
- Language: using a variety of language features to create a description that appeals to many senses, for example, sight, sound and smell.
- Mood: choosing a mood that you want to convey to the reader.

> **Writing tip**
>
> **SPAG**
>
> Using very short sentences can have a big impact on the reader. As long as a sentence has a subject and a verb it works. For example: 'He vanished' or 'Rain fell'.

Activity 7

a. Jot down some ideas of descriptive words or phrases you could include. **SPAG** Think about the sights, sounds, activities and atmosphere of the place.

b. Try grouping some of your descriptive phrases into clusters to see how they work together.

c. Look back at how Plath uses a combination of simile, metaphor, alliteration, onomatopoeia and personification, as well as a wide range of words with rich connotations. Write some examples of each and share your ideas with a partner.

d. Decide what mood or atmosphere you want to create in your description. It could be dark and serious, busy and bustling or calm and serene.

e. Write your description. When you have finished, share your work with a partner. Invite suggestions for improving your description.

f. Finally, proofread your work, checking that you have included a range of vocabulary and that your punctuation and spelling are accurate.

Skills and objectives

7 Selling the air

- To analyse how writers use language to persuade readers of their perspective **(AO2)**
- To write imaginatively **(AO5, AO6)**

Some writers have very strong views on the city and the countryside. The poet Laurie Lee wrote this article entitled 'An Obstinate Exile', published in 1975.

Extract from 'An Obstinate Exile' by Laurie Lee

Everything I see in this city, even those things that give me greatest pleasure, I view always in terms of comparison with their country equivalents. When I look at the great Thames, I do not see the river god that rules the Port of London; I see a body of water, thick, brown, reechy, coated with tar and feathers, and I think only of the springs near my home where the young Thames rises, clear as bubbled glass from a bank of moss.

And this translation seems to me to be a symbol of the change which everything undergoes on its way from country to city. All things that grow, for instance, by the time they have reached the city seem to suffer such a loss of virtue that only by legal courtesy can they any longer be called by their original country names.

Why doesn't someone find a new name for city flowers and city vegetables? In my village, in the full tide of summer, we had to cut down the roses with a sickle to get to our front door. If you left them for a week they swept over the house like flames, cracking the windows and breaking through the roof. As they grew, in great blowsy perfumed masses all over the garden, you could jump on them, or hack them with knives, or even drive the cows through them, and they still flourished as persistent and lusty as weeds.

But look at those London roses – scentless, puny, plastic-coloured shades, mass-produced in market gardens, sold for a shilling and dead in a night. Fancy having to buy flowers anyway. I can never get used to it. We used to chuck them like rubbish at the neighbour. Primroses, tenpence a withered bunch; dry little violets sprayed with hair-oil. Step out of our back door and you'd tread on a pound's worth before you'd gone a yard. And cowslips – very rare in the London streets and costing a packet in season – we used to pick them by the bucketful and make wine out of them. I've even seen people selling cow-parsley and beech leaves up here. It's like selling the air.

Activity 1

Summarize Lee's perspective on the city, using quotations to support your answer.

Laurie Lee uses language, structure and tone to convey his point of view.

Language: Lee uses a variety of language features to engage the reader in his argument. If they can visualize what he sees and imagine the same tastes and smells as he describes, then they are more likely to agree with him.

Structure: Contrast is used throughout the article, forcing the reader to see how much better the country is than the city.

Tone: The tone he uses creates an emotional response in the reader and helps Lee to persuade the reader to agree with him.

Activity 2

How does Laurie Lee use language, structure and tone to convey his attitude to flowers?

Using a picture as the starting point for a piece of writing can give you a lot of ideas. You can take inspiration from the details, the background, the colours and the mood. If there are people in the picture, you could create a story about how they came to be there.

Activity 3

Write a piece of descriptive or narrative writing suggested by one of these pictures.

SPAG

a. Plan your work, thinking carefully about the language, structure and tone.

b. Write with care, varying your sentence structures for effect, using a range of vocabulary, and using paragraphs to focus on different aspects of your narrative or description.

c. Proofread your work, checking punctuation and spelling.

Support Note down words and phrases suggested by the images. Use adjectives and adverbs to build up phrases and clauses around the key nouns.

shiny, wet cobbled **streets**, iridescent in the moonlight

raindrops drip delicately, like streaks of light

dark, sinister figures of **people**, retreating silently into the distance

Skills and objectives

8 The pig issue

- To analyse how writers use language, particularly humour, to create effects **(AO2)**

- To compare how writers present ideas and perspectives **(AO3)**

We laugh every day for one reason or another, but rarely stop to think why something is funny. On pages 174–177, you will read humorous texts and explore what makes them funny.

The extracts below comes from an autobiographical book called *The Farm*, written by Richard Benson in 2009. Here he describes what happens when a pig escapes from the farmyard into his neighbour's garden.

Extracts from *The Farm* by Richard Benson

The Twist's lawn is stately-home pristine, their weedless, geometrically perfect flower beds full of unusual and brilliant plants, their antique stone sundial juxtaposed perfectly with the bank of ornamental grasses. Just setting foot on the lawn is enough to make you feel elevated above the untidy chores of day-to-day life; it is the sort of garden I used to imagine Mrs Hirst [Richard's English teacher] in, discussing politics with poets and her admirers.

The drawback, of course, was its location next to our yard. One of the flowery borders was overlooked by my dad's muck-cart, and this presented a particular problem. When we were herding young pigs from one shed to another, we moved along holding boards against the ground to stop them running past us. If you watched the pigs closely, you could usually anticipate any about to make a break for freedom, and head them off by either moving the board, or in extreme cases, throwing it so that it landed in front of their snout and scared them into doubling back. However, if they went underneath the muck-cart they were away. We couldn't follow them there, and so we had to try to get around the back of it, hoping we made it before they realized that if they carried on through the bushes and shrubs, and then across the flowery border, they had an escape route into the most inviting and tasty little landscape a pig could dream of.

As a child I had wondered why neither my dad or Major Twist had put up a fence, and I wondered again now as I ran with my brother and sister from the old barn to join my parents, Mal and Major Twist on the Major's lawn. They were surrounding a panting foot-high porker whose little hooves had left indents the size of chestnuts across the grass. The human faces concentrated hard on the pig. The pig, looking slightly stunned, concentrated back.

'Reinforcements on the flank!' cried the Major, who loved a military metaphor.

***

Suddenly Guy lunged for the pig's back leg, missed, and sent it scuttling off towards the gap between me and Major Twist. The Major snatched at empty air and I dived to my left, missed the animal and knocked the edge off a flower bed with my knee. Seeing the pig break through the circle and head for the gate, my dad tossed his board ahead of it. The pig skidded to a halt, then jackknifed back past Mal. Mal grabbed, but his hands came up empty. Deep in his belly, he growled.

The pig picked its way through the grasses and then paused, panting again, in front of the conservatory, where it deposited a sloppy, steaming stream of turds.

'Calm down!' my mum said to it.

I noticed Guy nip back into the farmyard.

The pig calmed down, its panting growing slower. We closed in around it. I sprang forward and grabbed its back leg, which is usually the best place to grab a pig because the crook of the knee is easy to get hold of. This is not true, however, if the leg has been lubricated by sweat and liquid excrement; the pig slipped away and then went past my dad, who in lurching to reach it almost collided with the sundial.

There was a fleeting look of terror on my dad's face as he realised he had just missed what he assumed to be an expensive antique, but Major Twist was enjoying the chase. 'Six men including a trained soldier to hunt him down!' he boomed, fringe flopping into his glittering eyes. 'We could do with a few pigs like this in Her Majesty's Forces!'

Activity 1

Discuss with a partner what you find funny in this extract. Look for examples where you think the writer intended to create humour. Explain why you think it might be funny.

Humour does not always mean laughing out loud and rolling on the floor, particularly when it is written down. It is more likely to make the reader smile and feel amused or to see things in a light-hearted way.

Activity 2

There are several different types of humour used in the extract. Copy and complete the grid below, finding an example of each type of humour.

Type of humour	Example in the extract
Incongruity: when something completely unexpected is introduced – for example, placing something where it isn't normally seen or people behaving unexpectedly	A pig belongs in a farmyard, not the Twists' beautiful garden, full of 'weedless, geometrically perfect flower beds'.
Hyperbole: when the writer uses language to exaggerate a description to make it laughable	
Farce: where events take place which are highly unlikely or absurd, often in quick succession	
Slapstick: action humour which usually involves people tripping and falling, hitting and slapping, without anyone getting hurt	
Stereotyping: an oversimplified, often exaggerated, presentation, usually of a type of person or character	

Activity 3

Using the extracts on pages 174–175, Identify what form of humour the writer uses in the quotations below and explain how the humour works. Remember, there is often more than one reason why something is funny.

a. '"Calm down!" my mum said to it.'

b. 'There was a fleeting look of terror on my dad's face as he realised he had just missed what he assumed to be an expensive antique.'

c. '... an escape route into the most inviting and tasty little landscape a pig could dream of.'

d. 'We could do with a few pigs like this in Her Majesty's Forces!'

In the 19th century, there was a fashion for training pigs to perform in public. Toby was trained by his owner Nicholas Hoare to pick out letters and answer questions from the audience. In order to promote the show, Hoare wrote an autobiography, pretending it had been written by the pig himself. It was published in 1817 and cost a penny to buy. Read the extract below and then complete Activity 4.

Extract from *The Life and Adventures of Toby, the Sapient Pig, with his Views on Men and Manners* by Nicholas Hoare

I was born in a place, [...] called Avershall, on the Duke of Bedford's demesnes. My father was an independent gentleman, who roamed at large over his Grace's lands; and my Mother a spinster, in the service of a person whose name I have forgot (he kept an inn, or road-side house, called the Green Man) [...]. She was of a prolific nature and I was one, among many more, who were the offsprings of an illicit amour between her and my father. On my natal day, the first of April, 1816, [...] the gentleman, who has since been my friend and preceptor, and to whom I owe every comfort I now enjoy, from the great care he has all along taken in the cultivation of my mind and manners, was travelling that road. The above sign attracted his notice, under which was written the following words:

"You may go further and fare worse."

Being somewhat fatigued, he took the advice and entered accordingly. At that moment an elderly man came in at the back door of the house, which, by the bye, was no other than my mother's master. [...] Highly pleased at the event, he exclaimed "Dame! Bess," (for that was my mother's name), "is farrowing." [...] The whole house was in a bustle at the news; and all [...] hastened [...] to the place of her accouchement*, which was in an outhouse hard by, just as I came forth – they all instantly expressed their admiration of me; and on their return to the house it was agreed between the gentleman and my mother's master, that [...] I should be placed under his care; my mother having so large a family [...] Alas! to gratify his ruling passion, the dearest of all "Nature's ties" (the separation of an affectionate mother from her tender babe at so early a period) "were torn asunder." [...]

From the moment I left the place of my nativity, my preceptor became my constant companion by day and by night; asleep or awake he was but few removes from me. I wish all Tutors would discharge their duties in the like manner; if they did, we should not have so many blockheads in the world as we see every day: and truly they are a very numerous race.

*accouchement – where a mother gives birth

Activity 4

a. What do we learn from the extract about Toby's parents?

b. When and where was Toby born?

c. What happened to Toby after his birth?

d. What are Toby's views on education?

Some of the forms of humour from the first extract can be found in this text, but there are also some different forms too. For example:

- Parody: a way of mocking a specific genre. Here, the writer mocks the genre of autobiography, using a pompous, superior tone, inappropriate for a pig writing about being born in an 'outhouse'. He describes his father as 'an independent gentleman, who roamed at large over his Grace's lands', when in reality the pig's father was just a pig in a field.

- Irony: a form of humour where the writer says one thing but the reader understands that the opposite is true. An example from the extract would be where Toby writes about how if only everyone had a tutor like his 'we should not have so many blockheads in the world'. This is ironic because it is usually pigs that are considered to lack intelligence rather than humans.

Activity 5

Compare how the writers of these extracts use humour in a similar way to present their views on pigs.

 Stretch

a. Explore why these two writers have chosen to use humour and what effect the comedy creates for the reader.

b. Try writing your own autobiographical account, making humour a feature of the writing.

Progress check

Use the chart below to review the skills you have developed in this chapter. For each Assessment Objective, start at the bottom box and work your way up towards the highest achievement in the top box. Use the box above your current achievement as your target for the next chapter. If you're at the top, can you stay there?

AO1	AO2	AO3	AO4	AO5	AO6
I can analyse ideas and synthesize evidence from different texts.	I can analyse a writer's choice of language and structure.	I can make detailed comparisons and analyse how writers' methods convey ideas.	I can evaluate the effect of a variety of writers' choices, using a range of quotations.	I can write convincingly, employing a range of complex linguistic and structural features.	I can use a range of effective sentences and spelling and punctuation are precise.
I can interpret ideas, select evidence and make clear connections between texts.	I can explain clearly the effects of language and structure.	I can compare ideas from different texts and explain how they are conveyed.	I can explain the effect of writers' methods, using relevant quotations.	I can write clearly and effectively, using linguistic and structural features appropriately.	I can use sentences for effect and spelling and punctuation are mostly accurate.
I can understand some ideas, linking evidence from different texts.	I can identify and comment on features of language and structure.	I can make comparisons between texts, commenting on how ideas are conveyed.	I can comment on writers' methods and use some quotations.	I can write with some success, using some linguistic features and paragraphs.	I can use a variety of sentence forms, with some accurate spelling and punctuation.
I can find information and ideas and make references to texts.	I can find examples of language and structure.	I can identify similarities and differences between texts.	I can give my views on texts and support them with evidence from the text.	I can write in a simple way to communicate my ideas.	I can write in sentences, using basic punctuation and some accurate spelling.

Assessment

This unit tests all the reading and writing skills that you have learned in this chapter to see if you are able to apply them to different texts.

Read the extracts below and complete the activities that follow. The extracts are taken from an account of a country childhood written in 1959 called *Cider with Rosie*.

Extracts from *Cider with Rosie* by Laurie Lee

Walking downstairs there was a smell of floorboards, of rags, sour lemons, old spices. The smoky kitchen was in its morning muddle, from which breakfast would presently emerge. Mother stirred the porridge in a soot-black pot. Tony was carving bread with a ruler, the girls in their mackintoshes were laying the table, and the cats were eating the butter. I cleaned some boots and pumped up some fresh water; Jack went for a jug of skimmed milk.

'I'm all behind,' Mother said to the fire. 'This wretched coal's all slack.'

She snatched up an oil-can and threw it all on the fire. A belch of flame roared up the chimney. Mother gave a loud scream, as she always did, and went on stirring the porridge.

'If I had a proper stove,' she said. 'It's a trial getting you off each day.'

I sprinkled some sugar on a slice of bread and bolted it down while I could. How different again looked the kitchen this morning, swirling with smoke and sunlight. Some cut-glass vases threw jagged rainbows across the piano's field of dust, while Father in his pince-nez up on the wall looked down like a scandalized god.

At last the porridge was dabbed on our plates from a thick and steaming spoon. I covered the smoky lumps with treacle and began to eat from the sides to the middle. The girls round the table chewed moonishly, wrapped in their morning stupor. Still sick with sleep, their mouths moved slow, hung slack while their spoon came up; then they paused for a moment, spoon to lip, collected their wits, and ate. Their vacant eyes stared straight before them, glazed at the sight of the day. Pink and glowing from their dreamy beds, from who knows what arms of heroes, they seemed like mute spirits hauled back to the earth after paradise feasts of love.

'Golly!' cried Doth. 'Have you seen the time?'

They began to jump to their feet.

'Goodness, it's late.'

'I got to be off.'

'Me too.'

'Lord, where's my things?'

'Well, ta-ta Ma; ta boys – be good.'

***

But what should we boys do, now they had all gone? If it was school-time, we pushed off next. If not, we dodged up the bank to play, ran snail races along the walls, or dug in the garden and found potatoes and cooked them in tins on the rubbish heap. We were always hungry, always calling for food, always seeking it in cupboards and hedges. But holiday mornings were a time of risk, there might be housework or errands to do. Mother would be ironing, or tidying-up, or reading books on the floor. So if we hung around the yard we kept our ears cocked; if she caught us, the game was up.

'Ah, there you are, son. I'm needing some salt. Pop to Vick's for a lump, there's a dear.'

Or: 'See if Granny Trill's got a screw of tea – only ask her nicely, mind.'

Or: 'Run up to Miss Turk and try to borrow half-crown; I didn't know I'd got so low.'

'Ask our Jack, our Mother! I borrowed the bacon. It's blummin'-well his turn now.'

To remind yourself of how to apply AO1 skills on identifying and interpreting ideas, look back at the work you did in *Brick Lane* (pages 150–151) and *Trafalgar Square* (pages 168–171).

Activity 1

a. List four things the writer does in the morning.

b. What do you learn from the extracts about the writer's family?

c. What do you learn about the kitchen?

d. How do you think the writer feels about his childhood home?

To remind yourself of how to apply AO2 skills on analysing language, look back at the work you did in *Mean streets* (pages 152–157), *Tales from the dairy* (pages 160–163), *Selling the air* (pages 172–173) and *The pig issue* (pages 174–177).

Activity 2

a. Explore how the writer uses lists in the extracts to create effects.

b. What is the effect of the description of his father's picture on the wall?

c. Why do you think the writer describes his sisters as 'chewing moonishly'?

d. Using your answers to the above and any other examples of language that you find effective, answer the following question:

How does the writer use language to create a vivid impression of family life?

To remind yourself of how to apply AO2 skills on structure, look back at the work you did in *Rambling into danger* (pages 158–159) and *Tales from the dairy* (pages 160–163).

Activity 3

a. How does the writer organize his memories from childhood?

b. What is the effect of the writer pausing to reflect on his surroundings in the fifth paragraph?

c. Why do you think the writer chooses to include dialogue in this description?

d. What is the effect of using a first-person narrative in this extract?

e. How does the writer use structure to focus the reader's interest in this extract?

To remind yourself of how to apply AO4 skills on evaluating texts, look back at the work you did in *Mean streets* (pages 152–157) and *Rambling into danger* (pages 158–159). To remind yourself how to identify types of humour, look back at *The pig issue* (pages 174–177).

Activity (4)

a. Some of the writer's descriptions are amusing. Find examples of incongruity in the extract and explain the effect on the reader.

b. How successful has the writer been in presenting the character of his mother?

c. Using what you have learned about language, structure and tone, evaluate how effective you think the writer is in capturing the reader's interest in his memories of childhood.

The following extract is taken from *Mrs Beeton's Book of Household Management*, which was first published in 1861. This extract gives guidance to women on how they should run their households.

Extract from *Mrs Beeton's Book of Household Management* by Isabella Beeton

HAVING THUS INDICATED some of the more general duties of the mistress, [...] we will now give a few specific instructions on matters having a more practical relation to the position which she is supposed to occupy in the eye of the world. To do this the more clearly, we will begin with her earliest duties, and take her completely through the occupations of a day.

HAVING RISEN EARLY, [...] and having given due attention to the bath, and made a careful toilet, it will be well at once to see that the children have received their proper ablutions[1], and are in every way clean and comfortable. The first meal of the day, breakfast, will then be served, at which all the family should be punctually present, unless illness, or other circumstances, prevent.

AFTER BREAKFAST IS OVER, it will be well for the mistress to make a round of the kitchen and other offices, to see that all are in order, and that the morning's work has been properly performed by the various domestics[2]. The orders for the day should then be given, and any questions which the domestics desire to ask, respecting their several departments, should be answered, and any special articles they may require, handed to them from the store-closet.

In those establishments where there is a housekeeper, it will not be so necessary for the mistress, personally, to perform the above-named duties.

AFTER THIS GENERAL SUPERINTENDENCE of her servants, the mistress, if a mother of a young family, may devote herself to the instruction of some of its younger members, or to the examination of the state of their wardrobe[3], leaving the later portion of the morning for reading, or for some amusing recreation.

[1] ablutions – washing
[2] domestics – servants
[3] wardrobe – clothing

Both of these texts give the reader a perspective on family life.

To remind yourself of how to apply AO1 skills on summarizing, look back at the work you did in *Sounds of the city* (pages 164–167) and *Trafalgar Square* (pages 168–171).

Activity 5

Using quotations from both texts, summarize the similarities and differences between the role of the mother, as described in the extracts.

To remind yourself of how to apply AO3 skills on comparison, look back at the work you did in *Sounds of the city* (pages 164–167) and *The pig issue* (pages 174–177).

Activity 6

Compare how the two texts present a different perspective on family life.

To remind yourself of how to apply AO5 and AO6 writing skills, look back at the work you did in *Tales from the dairy* (pages 160–163), *Sounds of the city* (pages 164–167) and *Selling the air* (pages 172–173).

Activity 7

a. Write the text for a booklet for modern parents, providing guidance on how to manage a household and raise a family.

b. Write a piece of descriptive or narrative writing about your own childhood.

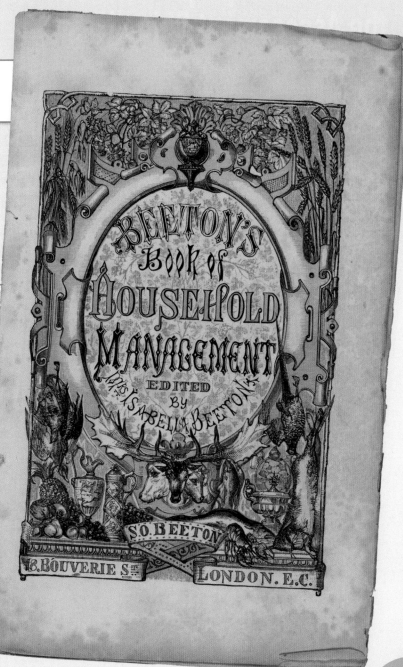

6 Now is the time to understand more

Assessment preparation: revisiting the Assessment Objectives

So far in this book you have encountered a range of writing from different genres and different centuries, and you have learned and practised a number of reading and writing skills.

This chapter is different. It looks ahead to next year's work when you will be using the skills you have learned to prepare for your GCSE English Language examination. For this exam, you will sit two different papers, and your work will be marked according to Assessment Objectives.

This chapter revisits each of the Assessment Objectives in turn, showing you exactly *where*, *when* and *how* to apply the relevant skills.

The title of this chapter is part of a quotation from Marie Curie, a famous scientist, who said: 'Nothing in life is to be feared, it is only to be understood. Now is the time to understand more, so that we may fear less.' The more you understand what you have to do in examinations, the less scary they become. By being fully prepared, you will hopefully 'understand more' and 'fear less'.

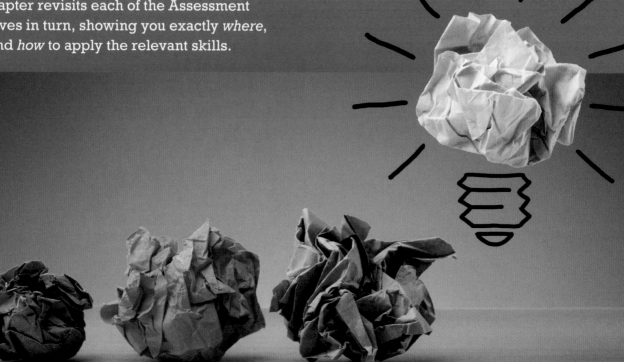

Assessment Objective 1 (AO1)

Read and understand a range of texts to:
- Identify and interpret explicit and implicit information and ideas
- Select and synthesize evidence from different texts

The first place AO1 is tested is in Paper 1, Question 1 and Paper 2, Question 1. This is where you have to demonstrate your understanding of a text by retrieving explicit and implicit information and ideas contained in it and, more importantly, to interpret the information and ideas. This is one of the most important skills you can possess: it forms a stepping stone to everything else you do in the examination because you have to be able to understand a text before you can analyse its language or structure, evaluate it, or compare it with another text.

You have already practised this skill in several units in the book. It does not matter which genre or which century your text is from; the skill you apply is exactly the same.

In the following newspaper article, Tony Parsons offers his views on the subject of tattoos.

Making my skin crawl: Tattoos scream for attention

As soon as the sun starts shining, I realise with a sinking heart that Britain is now a tattooed nation.

Tattoos are everywhere. You see them on firm young flesh and on wobbly, middle-aged flab,
5 as common now on the school run and in the supermarket queue as they are on some footballer or his wife.

I feel like the last man left alive whose skin crawls at the sight of these crass daubings*. I feel like the
10 only person in the world who sees David Beckham modelling his swimming pants on the cover of *Elle* magazine and thinks – oh, how much better a handsome guy like you would look, David, without all those dumb ink stains stitched into your skin. I feel
15 like nobody else looks at little Cheryl Cole – so pretty, so smiley – and recoils at the sight of the florist shop she has permanently engraved on her lovely body.

[...] Tattoos scream for attention. Tattoos say – look at me! I guess the person with the tattoo imagines that
20 – somehow – having a martial arts symbol or a badly drawn flower or a sentimental heart expresses their individuality. The end result is a million simple souls all with exactly the same primitive daubings, all telling you what an individual they are.
25 On Tuesday, a tattooed lady called Joanna Southgate – pretty, blonde, young – swerved past the dress code at Royal Ascot by waiting until she was inside before revealing that her arms are covered in what looks like a three-year-old's finger paintings. Joanna looked so proud. But why? She has ravaged her natural good 30 looks with what, at best, looks like cartoons done by someone who flunked their art GCSE.

Tattoos were her choice. But tattoos are self-mutilation. Tattoos are a tragedy. Having tenth-rate art on your body for life is now part of the national fabric. 35

Did I say that Britain is a tattooed nation? Strike that – Britain is *the* tattooed nation. [...]

Tattoos are so widespread, so ugly and so very, very permanent. You can, in theory, have them removed – but a large chunk of your living flesh will go with it. 40

The tattooed nation will live to regret this voluntary disfigurement. Already I sense that some of our celebs are covering up – you don't see Cheryl Cole's florist shop nearly as often as you used to. It used to be that you made a mark on your body because you couldn't 45 make a mark on the world. With adored multi-millionaires like Beckham stoking the tattoo craze, that is clearly no longer the case. But some things never change.

A tattoo doesn't make you look like an individual. 50 A tattoo makes you look a thicko. You'll all look silly when you're 60.

*daubing – rough, amateurish picture

For AO1, one of the skills you have to demonstrate is to identify explicit information. Remember, if something is explicit it is clearly stated and all you have to do is retrieve it from the text.

Activity 1

Read again lines 1 to 7. List four things from this part of the text about the type of people who have tattoos.

Another of the skills you have to demonstrate for AO1 is to look beneath the surface to identify implicit information. Remember, if something is implicit it is just suggested and you have to interpret the text to work it out for yourself.

Activity 2

Read again lines 8 to 17. Choose four statements below which are true.

| The writer dislikes tattoos. | The writer thinks that everyone has the same attitude as him about tattoos. | The writer says that David Beckham has appeared on the cover of *The Sunday Times* magazine. | The writer feels that David Beckham would look better without tattoos. |

| The writer thinks David Beckham is attractive. | Cheryl Cole has tattoos of hearts on her body. | Cheryl Cole's tattoos are only temporary. | The writer believes Cheryl Cole is pretty. |

One of the most important skills you have to demonstrate for AO1 is to interpret information and ideas. Remember, to show your understanding you have to interpret using your own words but also select supporting quotations from the text to show how you have come to this understanding. The more perceptive and detailed your interpretation, the better your response will be.

Activity 3

a. Read again lines 18 to 24. How is Tony Parsons being ironic when he says: 'The end result is a million simple souls all with exactly the same primitive daubings, all telling you what an individual they are'?

b. Read again lines 25 to 32.

    i. What do the phrases 'pretty, blond, young', 'looked so proud' and 'ravaged her natural good looks' tell us about Tony Parson's attitude towards Joanna Southgate and her tattoos?

    ii. What other words and phrases in this paragraph support this view?

c. Read again from line 33 to the end of the article. What further points does Tony Parsons make to develop his views about tattoos?

d. Using all the work you have done so far on AO1, write your response to the following:

    What do you understand about Tony Parson's views on the subject of tattoos? Use your own words but also quote from the text to support what you say.

AO1 is also tested in Paper 2, Question 2. This is where you have to demonstrate your ability to synthesize information and ideas from two texts and produce new material in the form of a summary. Remember, you need to interpret and make connections between the information and ideas in both texts. This is an important skill as it forms a stepping stone to Paper 2, Question 4, where you have to include a comparison of information and ideas in two texts.

You have already practised this skill in several units in the book. It does not matter which genre or which century your texts are from; the skill you apply is exactly the same.

Read the account 'Tattooed Royalty' which was written in 1898. It is also about tattoos, but this time the attitude towards them is very different.

Tattooed Royalty. Queer Stories of a Queer Craze

When royalty hangs onto a craze, you may be assured that the rest of the exclusive world of wealth and power soon follow in the same path, and annex the peculiarities of the pleasures of which have given
5 amusement to their heroes born in the purple.

What wonder, then, that tattooing is just now the popular pastime of the leisured world? For one of the best-known men in high European circles, the Grand Duke Alexis of Russia, is most elaborately tattooed.
10 And Prince and Princess Waldemar of Denmark, [...] with many others of royal and distinguished rank, have submitted themselves to the tickling, but painless and albeit pleasant, sensation afforded by the improved tattooing needle. [...]

15 The present fancy for being tattooed [...] mainly exists among men who have travelled much; while ladies have also taken a strong liking to this form of personal decoration, which, from a woman's point of view, is about as expensive as a dress, but not so costly as good jewellery. [...] For the purpose of passing her (20) time in the 'off' season, the lady about town now consents to be pricked by the tattoo artist's operating needle, and to have her forearm or shoulder adorned with perhaps such a mark as this – a serpent holding its tail in its mouth – a symbol representing eternity. (25)

In order to form an idea of the kind of work that is wanted by those who give their patronage to this specific class of fine art, a close examination of these illustrations will assist you. The skill of the tattoo artist, to be realized properly and fairly, must be seen (30) in beautiful colours on a white skin – work which is amazing. The sketches he employs are made in various coloured inks. His great skill is in the faithful reproduction of any symbol or picture desired by the sitter. These designs vary in size from a small fly, or (35) bee, to that of an immense Chinese dragon, occupying the whole space offered by the back or chest, or a huge snake many inches in thickness coiling round the body from the knees to the shoulders.

Activity 4

Summarize the different views of tattoos in the two texts. Use your own words but also quote from both texts to support what you say.

In particular you could include:

- the type of people who have tattoos
- the types of tattoos that are worn
- the popularity of tattoos
- the quality of the artwork
- the different attitudes towards the idea of tattoos.

Assessment Objective 2 (AO2)

Explain, comment on and analyse how writers use language and structure to achieve effects and influence readers, using linguistic terminology to support your views

The first place AO2 is tested is in Paper 1, Question 2 and Paper 2, Question 3. This is where you have to demonstrate your ability to analyse language. Remember, language is deliberately chosen by the writer to add to your understanding of a text and create an effect on the reader. It includes words, phrases and language features, plus sentence forms. This is an important skill as it forms a stepping stone to Paper 1, Question 4, where you have to include an evaluation of the writer's use of language, and Paper 2, Question 4, where you have to include a comparison of the writers' methods in two texts.

You have already practised this skill in several units in the book. It does not matter which genre or which century your text is from; the skill you apply is exactly the same.

Read the following extract which is the opening of a short story called 'The Pedestrian', written in 1951 by Ray Bradbury, an American writer known in particular for his science-fiction works. The main character, Leonard Mead, enjoys an evening stroll around his neighbourhood, a pastime that is forbidden in the year AD 2053 because such simple pleasures have been prohibited by a totalitarian government.

Extract from 'The Pedestrian' by Ray Bradbury

To enter out into that silence that was the city at eight o'clock of a misty evening in November, to put your feet upon that buckling concrete walk, to step over grassy seams and make your way, hands in pockets, through the silences, that was what Mr. Leonard Mead most dearly loved to do. He would stand upon the corner of an intersection and peer down long moonlit 5 avenues of sidewalk in four directions, deciding which way to go, but it really made no difference; he was alone in this world of A.D. 2053, or as good as alone, and with a final decision made, a path selected, he would stride off, sending patterns of frosty air before him like the smoke of a cigar.

Sometimes he would walk for hours and miles and return only at midnight 10 to his house. And on his way he would see the cottages and homes with their dark windows, and it was not unequal to walking through a graveyard where only the faintest glimmers of firefly light appeared in flickers behind the windows. Sudden grey phantoms seemed to manifest upon inner room walls where a curtain was still undrawn against the night, or there 15 were whisperings and murmurs where a window in a tomb-like building was still open.

On this particular evening he began his journey in a westerly direction, toward the hidden sea. There was a good crystal frost in the air; it cut the nose and made the lungs blaze like a Christmas tree inside; you could feel the cold light going on and off, all the branches filled with invisible snow. He listened to the faint push of his soft shoes through autumn leaves with satisfaction, and whistled a cold quiet whistle between his teeth, occasionally picking up a leaf as he passed, examining its skeletal pattern in the infrequent lamplights as he went on, smelling its rusty smell. `20` `25`

For AO2, one of the skills you have to demonstrate is the ability to select appropriate examples from the text on which to comment. Remember, selection is an important skill because if you do not choose wisely you will have very little to say.

In the opening paragraph, the writer sets the scene by using vivid descriptive language. An appropriate example of language to select would be the phrase 'a misty evening in November'. November has many connotations, some positive and some negative: it is a clear, crisp time of the year but also notoriously cold and damp. The adjective 'misty' is equally ambiguous: it may suggest a scene that is pretty and ethereal, but could also evoke an atmosphere of potential danger.

Activity 1

Read again lines 1 to 9. Find a simile in this opening paragraph that creates a similar effect to 'a misty evening', and explain how this choice of language adds to your understanding of the setting.

The opening of the story continues in the following extract.

Extract from 'The Pedestrian' by Ray Bradbury

In ten years of walking by night or day, for thousands of miles, he had never met another person walking, not once in all that time.

He came to a cloverleaf intersection which stood silent where two main highways crossed the town. During the day it was a thunderous surge of cars, the gas stations open, a great insect rustling and a ceaseless jockeying for position as the scarab beetles, a faint incense puttering from their exhausts, skimmed homeward to the far directions. But now these highways, too, were like streams in a dry season, all stone and bed and moon radiance. `30`

He turned back on a side street, circling around toward his home. He was within a block of his destination when the lone car turned a corner quite suddenly and flashed a fierce white cone of light upon him. He stood entranced, not unlike a night moth, stunned by the illumination, and then drawn toward it. `35`

A metallic voice called to him: 'Stand still. Stay where you are! Don't move!'

One of the most important skills you have to demonstrate for AO2 is to analyse the writer's choice of language and explain its effect on the reader. Remember, you should always consider the context of the language and be precise when commenting on the effect. The more perceptive and detailed your analysis, the better your response will be.

Activity 2

a. Read again lines 10 to 17. In this paragraph, Bradbury confirms our suspicions that the atmosphere is negative by employing an extended metaphor of death. Write about the connotations and effects of the following words and phrases within the context of the story. The first one has been done for you:

   i. 'it was not unequal to walking through a graveyard':

> This gives the reader a haunting sense of dread. It is as if the neighbourhood is a final resting place for dead people, and a cold, dark stillness surrounds Leonard Mead as he walks the streets. Everything is silent and every minute sound amplified. The buildings appear architecturally lifeless and the people inside them lacking in humanity. Society seems to be literally and metaphorically decaying around him.

   ii. 'grey phantoms seemed to manifest upon inner room walls'

   iii. 'tomblike building'

b. Read again from line 18 to the end (line 39), and comment on the effects of the writer's use of contrast. Focus in particular on the following:

- hot and cold imagery, such as 'There was a good crystal frost in the air; it cut the nose and made the lungs blaze like a Christmas tree inside.' What could this suggest about Leonard Mead's place in this society?

- the area by night and by day, such as 'During the day it was a thunderous surge of cars…'. What do the language choices suggest about Leonard Mead's attitude to this society?

- natural versus unnatural imagery, such as 'He stood entranced, not unlike a night moth, stunned by the illumination' and 'A metallic voice called to him'.

c. Using all the work you have done so far on AO2 and any other examples of language in the text that you find effective, write your response to the following question:

How does Bradbury's use of language influence our impressions of this futuristic society?

The other place AO2 is tested is in Paper 1, Question 3. This is where you have to demonstrate your ability to analyse structure. Remember, writers shape and structure their ideas to help the reader understand their meaning. They do this at a whole text level, at a paragraph level and at a sentence level. This is an important skill as it forms a stepping stone to Paper 1, Question 4, where you have to include an evaluation of the writer's structure, and Paper 2, Question 4, where you have to include a comparison of the writers' methods in two texts.

You have already practised this skill in several units in the book. It does not matter which genre or which century your text is from; the skill you apply is exactly the same.

The structure of the extract from 'The Pedestrian' follows Leonard Mead's journey through his neighbourhood, but each paragraph shifts the reader's focus.

Activity ③

a. How does the whole text structure follow Leonard Mead's journey through his neighbourhood? Which directions does he take and where does he go?

b. Where does the text shift between what is happening in the present and what has happened in the past? What effect does this have on the reader?

c. The text is a combination of both external actions and internal thoughts. How does this affect our view of Leonard Mead?

d. Why does Bradbury choose to begin his story with a long complex sentence that ends in '…that was what Mr. Leonard Mead most dearly loved to do'? How does this contrast with the sentence forms in the final line of the text, and why?

e. What is the significance of the single sentence paragraph in lines 26 to 27? What other key sentences or phrases contribute structurally to the reader's growing apprehension?

f. Using your answers to the above and anything else in the story that is structurally relevant, write your response to the following:

How has Ray Bradbury structured his story to build up to the climax in the final line?

Assessment Objective 3 (AO3)

Compare writers' ideas and perspectives, as well as how these are conveyed, across two or more texts

AO3 is tested in Paper 2, Question 4. This is where you have to demonstrate your ability to compare two texts, focusing on either the similarities or the differences. Remember, you are comparing both the ideas and perspectives in the texts and also the methods used by the writers to convey them.

You have already practised this skill in several units in the book. It does not matter which genre or which century your text is from; the skill you apply is exactly the same.

In the following newspaper article, Max Davidson offers his views on the subject of neighbours.

How to get on with the neighbours

by Max Davidson

If ever a statistic leapt out and hit me between the eyes, it was that a million Britons have moved house because of disputes with their neighbours.

This finding, from new research by the insurance company CPP,
5 reveals a worrying trend. If you're living next door to someone, surely it's common sense that you should bend over backwards to get on with them? Why make a mortal enemy out of someone with so much power to irritate you?

But common sense, it seems, has gone out of the window. From
10 fences to barbecues to parking spaces to crying babies, minor nuisances have been allowed to escalate to the point where people have moved out of a neighbourhood, rather than deal with disputes in a grown-up way.

Personally, I have had a very mixed bag of neighbours. Some have
15 become good friends, while others held all-night Abba parties, built dodgy extensions, chucked cigarette-ends over the garden fence and had miniature poodles who bayed like the Hound of the Baskervilles. But I wouldn't have let the most annoying of them drive me from my home. It would have felt like a defeat.

20 Others seem to be less positive, judging by the CPP research. The live-and-let-live attitudes embedded in English culture are unravelling.

If anti-social behaviour is on the rise, so is irritability at the anti-social behaviour of others. People who would once have
25 shrugged at smoke from a bonfire, now get on their high horse and hawk their complaints to the council. Often with disastrous consequences.

There is a lot of pent-up anger behind those twitching net curtains. But in many cases improved communication skills would help defuse tensions with neighbours and prevent feuds spiralling out 30 of control.

'Bad relationships between neighbours reflect the hectic pace of modern life,' says psychologist Dr Rob Yeung. 'People don't have time to build healthy relationships with those living next door. They need to develop the art of empathy, and see things from 35 their neighbour's point of view rather than rushing to judgment.'

Fail to empathise, assume your neighbours are beyond the pale because their lifestyles are different from yours, and you get trapped in repetitive loops of behaviour. Every day brings fresh flashpoints and accusations fly like tracer bullets across the 40 garden fence.

Good neighbours breed good neighbours, just as bad neighbours breed bad neighbours. But if you want good neighbours, the best way to get them is to be a good neighbour yourself. A few more smiles on the street wouldn't hurt, would they? 45

The following account, written in the 1800s, focuses on one specific neighbour, the 'old lady upstairs', and what it is like to live near her.

She is a mysterious being; you never see her, and you hear of her perpetually; she must be a complication of nerves and headaches, an invalid of the most delicate order, and an Argus* whom nothing escapes. She is the bar to comfort, the extinguisher of fun [...]. Everybody is afraid of her, and she is afraid of nobody.

5

Jenkins, newly married, gives a housewarming, in his first floor; Dobkins is asked because he can sing a comic song, Miss Smith because she knows all the operas by heart; Twangle comes with his guitar, Traddles with his flute, and you are expected to bring a repertoire of jokes and good things. The bride is smilingly happy, the bridegroom jovial, and all promises to go swimmingly. Dobkins begins his comic song, and roars of laughter follow.

10

Alas! Scarcely have the echoes died away, when rat-tat-tat at the door comes Biddy, with the request that 'If ye please, ye'll make no more noise, for the old lady upstairs is very bad with nervousness, and can't abear it.'

15

Cold water is dashed upon the assemblage. The hostess grows pale. Twangle's guitar and Traddles' flute are useless. The soprano of Miss Smith is unheard. Your jokes are whispered, and no one smiles. Cake and wine are handed round stealthily, and you take leave at nine o'clock. [...]

You make your way to the bachelor establishment of your cousin Twiggs. You find him in despair, and after much pressing, he groans forth the reason.

20

'I can never stay out after ten o'clock; the old lady upstairs has ordered the door to be locked at that hour, and takes the key to bed with her.' It is the old lady upstairs who sows seeds of discontent and anger in the neighbourhood: she discovers that you use Dobkins' coal; that brother John stays out till three in the morning, and that sister Ann flirts shamefully. She is aware of the household expenses, and reveals them to the neighbours. She will have the door open in winter, that her pet cat may freely exit, and will not allow it to be unclosed in summer on account of flies. She objects to company, and to mirth; she has no sympathy for childhood or youth, for people who laugh, or sing, or dance [...], and appears to live that others may not enjoy themselves. It is possible that she may have once been young, but the natural conclusion would be that she was born and will remain for ever the old lady upstairs, and nothing else.

25

30

*Argus – a mythological giant with one hundred eyes

When you are comparing two texts, you need to demonstrate many of the same skills that have already been tested elsewhere in the examination, including interpretation of ideas and perspectives, and analysis of language and structure. It is also appropriate to compare other areas, such as viewpoint and tone.

Viewpoint could be discussed in an introductory paragraph before comparing the two texts in more detail. For example:

> Both of these texts are about neighbours but they are written in different centuries and from different perspectives. 'How to get on with the neighbours' at first appears to be an objective article. With the exception of one personal paragraph, it takes an overview of the subject matter and includes statistical evidence. However, it is written in the first person and includes many opinions as well as facts. On the other hand, the 19th-century text is a subjective narrative account of one particular evening. It is written in the second person from the point of view of someone who personally knows the neighbours of 'the old lady upstairs' and witnesses her anti-social behaviour.

Activity 1

Find evidence to support each of the highlighted points in the above statements. What is the effect of the writers adopting these different methods?

For AO3, one of the skills you have to demonstrate is the ability to compare ideas and perspectives. Remember, you have to interpret as well as identify the ideas and perspectives in order to show your understanding.

Activity 2

a. Find some examples of the anti-social behaviour of neighbours in both texts.

b. One way that people react to bad neighbours in the first text is to move house.

   i. In what other way do they react?

   ii. What is the writer's attitude towards these reactions?

c. One way that people react to their bad neighbour in the second text is that 'cake and wine are handed round stealthily' (lines 18 to 19).

   i. In what other ways do they react, and what does this suggest about them?

   ii. How are these reactions different from the first text?

d. How does each writer try to explain the reasoning behind the neighbours' anti-social behaviour? Which explanation do you find more convincing?

Another of the skills you have to demonstrate for AO3 is to compare the writers' use of language. Remember to select appropriately, analyse the words, phrases, language features or sentence forms in context and be precise when commenting on the effect on the reader.

Activity 3

a. The first text uses several examples of colloquial (commonly spoken) language – for example, in the opening sentence 'If ever a statistic leapt out and hit me between the eyes…'.

   i. Find some other examples of colloquial language.

   ii. What tone does this create in the article, and why do you think the writer adopts this method to convey his ideas?

b. Read again lines 1 to 5 in the second text. The old lady is described as 'a complication of nerves and headaches' and 'an Argus whom nothing escapes'.

   i. What effect do these metaphors create in the reader?

   ii. Can you find any other examples of effective metaphors in this opening paragraph?

   iii. How do the sentence forms add to the effect created?

Another of the skills you have to demonstrate for AO3 is to compare the writers' use of structure. Remember, you can comment on the structure of the whole text, the paragraphs or the sentences.

Activity 4

a. The first text presents a logical argument to the reader.

   i. How does the whole text structure influence the reader to support the writer's point of view?

   ii. How does this compare with the whole text structure of the second text?

b. Find some examples of sentence forms in each text that you find structurally significant and explain their effect.

Activity 5

Using all the work you have done so far on AO3, write your response to the following:

Compare how the writers convey the subject of neighbours. Use your own words but also quote from both texts to support what you say.

Assessment Objective 4 (AO4)

Evaluate texts critically and support this with appropriate textual references

AO4 is tested in Paper 1, Question 4. This is where you have to demonstrate your ability to evaluate a text or part of a text. To 'evaluate' means to judge something in a carefully considered way, and in order to evaluate a text 'critically', you need to go beyond your own opinion and recognize the strengths of the text, regardless of your own personal views. Remember, you are evaluating both the content of the text and also the methods used by the writer.

You have already practised this skill in several units in the book. It does not matter which genre or which century your texts are from: the skill you apply is exactly the same.

The following extract is the opening of a short story called 'Next Term, We'll Mash You', written in 1978 by Penelope Lively. The parents of seven year old Charles are taking him to visit a private Sussex boarding school recommended to them by their rich friends, the Wilcoxes. They have arranged to meet with the Headmaster and his wife.

Extract from 'Next Term, We'll Mash You' by Penelope Lively

Inside the car it was quiet, the noise of the engine even and subdued, the air just the right temperature, the windows tight-fitting. The boy sat on the back seat, a box of chocolates, unopened, beside 5 him, and a comic, folded. The trim Sussex landscape flowed past the windows: cows, white-fenced fields, highly-priced period houses. The sunlight was glassy, remote as a coloured photograph. The backs of the 10 two heads in front of him swayed with the motion of the car.

His mother half-turned to speak to him. 'Nearly there now, darling.'

The father glanced downwards at his wife's 15 wrist. 'Are we all right for time?'

'Just right, nearly twelve.'

'I could do with a drink. Hope they lay something on.'

'I'm sure they will. The Wilcoxes say 20 they're awfully nice people. Not really the schoolmaster-type at all, Sally says.'

The man said, 'He's an Oxford chap.'

'Is he? You didn't say.'

'Mmn.' 25

'Of course, the fees are that much higher than the Seaford place.'

'Fifty quid or so. We'll have to see.'

The car turned right, between white gates and high, dark tight-clipped hedges. 30 The whisper of the road under the tyres changed to the crunch of gravel. The child, staring sideways, read black lettering on a white board: *St. Edward's Preparatory School. Please Drive Slowly.* He shifted 35 on the seat, and the leather sucked at the bare skin under his knees, stinging.

The mother said, 'It's a lovely place. Those must be the playing-fields. Look darling, there are some of the boys.' She clicked open her handbag, and the sun caught her mirror and flashed in the child's eyes; the comb went through her hair and he saw the grooves it left, neat as distant ploughing. 40

'Come on then, Charles, out you get.' The building was red brick, early nineteenth century, spreading out long arms in which windows glittered blackly. Flowers, trapped in neat beds, were alternate red and white. They went up the steps, the man, the woman, and the child, two paces behind. 45 50

The woman, the mother, smoothing down a skirt that would be ridged from sitting, thought: I like the way they've got the maid all done up properly. The little white apron and all that. She's foreign, I suppose. Au pair. Very nice. If he comes here there'll be Speech Days and that kind of thing. Sally Wilcox says it's quite dressy – she got that cream linen coat for coming down here. You can see why it costs a bomb. Great big grounds and only an hour and a half from London. 55 60

They went into a room looking out onto a terrace. Beyond, dappled lawns, gently shifting trees, black and white cows grazing behind 65

iron railings. Books, leather chairs, a table with magazines – *Country Life*, *The Field*, *The Economist*. 'Please, if you would wait here. The Headmaster won't be long.'

Alone, they sat, inspected. 'I like the atmosphere, don't you, John?' 70

'Very pleasant, yes.' Four hundred a term, near enough. You can tell it's a cut above the Seaford place, though, or the one at St Albans. Bob Wilcox says quite a few City people send their boys here. One or two of the merchant bankers, those kind of people. It's the sort of contact that would do no harm at all. You meet someone, get talking at a cricket match or what have you... Not at all a bad thing. 75 80

'All right, Charles? You didn't get sick in the car, did you?'

The child had black hair, slicked down smooth to his head. His ears, too large, jutted out, transparent in the light from the window, laced with tiny, delicate veins. His clothes had the shine and crease of newness. He looked at the books, the dark brown pictures, his parents. Said nothing. 85 90

When you are evaluating a text or part of a text, you need to demonstrate many of the same skills that have already been tested elsewhere in the examination, including interpretation of ideas and analysis of language and structure. However, you may find it more helpful to take a slightly different approach than in previous questions and structure your response around the characters and events.

We learn a lot about the characters in this extract: the things they say and do, and the way they interact with one another are gradually revealed to the reader and these, together with the writer's choice of language to describe them and their surroundings, determine our understanding of them.

The central character in the story is Charles, and immediately the reader forms a clear impression of him.

Activity 1

a. Read the first paragraph again.

   i. Why is it important that the box of chocolates is 'unopened' and the comic 'folded'?

   ii. What are your initial impressions of Charles from these details and the rest of this opening paragraph?

b. As the car drives into the grounds of the school we are told: 'He shifted on the seat, and the leather sucked at the bare skin under his knees, stinging' (lines 35 to 38). What does the writer's choice of language suggest about Charles at this point?

c. When Charles and his parents enter the school building we learn: 'They went up the steps, the man, the woman, and the child, two paces behind' (lines 49 to 51). What does this suggest about the relationships between the family members?

d. Charles has no dialogue in this extract, although it is easy to miss this fact when reading the story. Why are the final two words 'Said nothing' structurally significant? How does the physical description of Charles in the final paragraph add to our understanding of him?

On the surface, the character of the mother appears to be caring and attentive, but there are hints throughout the text that she may be more concerned with herself than her son.

Activity 2

a. Look at the dialogue spoken by the mother.

   i. How does it influence your impression of her?

   ii. What does it convey about her relationship with her husband and her son?

b. Read again lines 40 to 44.

   i. How do the mother's actions suggest a superficiality about her character?

   ii. Where else in the extract is the same impression created?

c. When the mother tends to her hair, the grooves from the comb are described as 'neat as distant ploughing'. How does Lively's choice of imagery reinforce our impressions of her?

d. Read again lines 51 to 62.

   i. Why is it structurally significant to learn of her thoughts at this point in the text?

   ii. How concerned do you think she is about Charles's best interests?

On the surface, the character of the father is similar to the mother, but again, Lively hints that he may have things on his mind other than the welfare of his son.

Activity 3

a. Look at the dialogue spoken by the father.

   i. How does it influence your impression of him?

   ii. What does it convey about his relationship with his wife and his son?

b. Read again lines 72 to 81.

   i. Why is it structurally significant to learn of his thoughts at this point in the text?

   ii. How concerned do you think he is about Charles's best interests?

There may well be aspects of a text that are important to evaluate as well as the characters and the events. In this case, the description of the setting is particularly significant – for example, 'white-fenced fields' and 'highly-priced period houses' create an idyllic scene. However, there is also an extended metaphor of imprisonment throughout the story, beginning with car windows that are 'tight-fitting', implying there is no escape for Charles.

At times, the writer even combines both positive and negative ideas within the same image. For example, 'The building was red brick, early nineteenth century, spreading out long arms…' sounds welcoming, a place that metaphorically will wrap its 'long arms' round a child to nurture him and keep him safe, but this is then followed by 'in which windows glittered blackly', suggesting maybe the initial welcome is deceptive and behind the pleasant exterior, there is a shadow of darkness or even danger.

Activity 4

a. Find some other examples in the text that make the setting appear to be perfect. How does this affect our initial impression of the place?

b. Find some other examples of words, phrases or language features that suggest a feeling of being trapped. How might this change our initial impression of the place?

c. Find some other examples of images where the initial positive connotation is then twisted into something negative.

Activity 5

Using all the work you have done on AO4, write your response to the following question:

The title of this story is 'Next Term, We'll Mash You', which is a comment made to Charles by one of the pupils on the day of the visit, threatening to bully him if he joins the school.

To what extent does the opening extract prepare you, the reader, for this undercurrent of unpleasantness?

Assessment Objectives 5 and 6 (AO5, AO6)

AO5 Communicate clearly, effectively and imaginatively, selecting and adapting tone, style and register for different forms, purposes and audiences

Organize information and ideas, using structural and grammatical features to support coherence and cohesion of texts

AO6 Use a range of vocabulary and sentence structure for clarity, purpose and effect, with accurate spelling and punctuation

AO5 and AO6 are tested in both Paper 1, Question 5 and Paper 2, Question 5. This is where you have to demonstrate your writing skills rather than your reading skills. The subject matter of your writing is thematically linked to the reading sources in Section A. The purpose of your writing in each Paper is different: in Paper 1 you have to narrate or describe and in Paper 2 you have to explain your point of view on a given statement, but the skills you have to demonstrate are the same.

Remember, the key to success is how effectively you communicate. For AO5, this means addressing the correct purpose and audience and adapting your tone, style and register accordingly, plus organizing your writing for impact. For AO6, this means varying your sentence structure for effect, employing correct spelling and punctuation and writing in Standard English.

Remember, there are three stages to any response: planning, writing and proofreading. While most of your time will be spent on writing, you should always spend the first few minutes planning your work and leave a few minutes at the end to read it through.

Paper 1: Explorations in creative reading and writing

In Paper 1 you have to demonstrate your ability to narrate or describe. You are given a choice of task, although not always a choice of purpose: there may be the option to narrate or describe, but equally you may have to select from two tasks that focus on description or two tasks that require you to narrate a story.

Whatever the combination, both tasks will have a written prompt and one will include a picture to suggest ideas for the task. Remember, you do not need to take the picture literally: 'suggest' means you can use it as a starting point to stimulate your imagination.

Narrative writing

For AO5, one of the skills you have to demonstrate is the ability to use your imagination. When writing a narrative story, the first place to start is with some ideas: your plot (the sequence of events that will take place in your story); your setting (the place and time your story will be set); and your characters (who the story is about).

Activity 1

Look at the image on this page and start to use your imagination. Make notes on the plot, setting and characters for your story.

Another of the skills you have to demonstrate for AO5 is being able to organize your narrative. This involves deciding on your viewpoint (who is narrating the story) and your structure (how the story will begin, what conflict will be encountered by your characters and how it will be resolved). It is also useful to address tone at this point and decide what sort of mood or atmosphere you want to create.

Activity 2

Make notes on the viewpoint, structure and tone for your story.

Another of the skills you have to demonstrate in AO5 is the ability to craft your narrative. This includes engaging your reader through your choice of language, for example, effective vocabulary choices, or imagery such as similes and metaphors.

Activity 3

a. Make a note of any words, phrases or language features that you could include in your story to engage your reader.

b. Using all the work you have done so far on AO5, write a narrative suggested by the picture above.

The skills you have to demonstrate for AO6 include using a range of appropriate sentence forms, using correct spelling, punctuating your narrative correctly and writing in Standard English.

Activity 4

Read through your story to check that what you have written is clear and accurate. Make any changes that would improve your demonstration of AO6 skills.

Descriptive writing

Remember, a description is a picture made up of words. It needs to contain vivid details so that the reader can experience every aspect of the person, place, thing or event being described.

When writing a description, the first place to start is with some ideas: think of some sensory details that appeal to the reader's senses (what they can see, hear, touch, smell or taste). As with narrative writing, it is also important to decide how you are going to organize these ideas (for example, order of importance, chronological order or spatial order). Again, the ability to craft your description is vital. This includes:

- engaging your reader through your choice of language, for example, effective vocabulary choices (specific adjectives and adverbs and powerful verbs that bring the description to life)

- imagery, such as similes and metaphors

- tone: it is useful to address tone at this point and decide what sort of mood or atmosphere you want to create.

Activity 5

a. Look at the image below and start to use your imagination. Make notes on how you could apply the above characteristics to a description of your own.

b. Using the notes you have made, write a description suggested by this picture.

c. Read through your description to check that what you have written is clear and accurate. Make any changes that would improve your AO6 skills.

Paper 2: Writers' viewpoints and perspectives

In Paper 2 you have to demonstrate your ability to explain your point of view on a given statement.

For AO5, one of the skills you have to demonstrate is the ability to present a considered explanation. When writing your response, the first thing to decide is what your opinion is on the given statement. Then you need to think about the reasons why you hold this point of view. Remember, it is also useful to consider any alternative viewpoints at this stage so that you can effectively dismiss them in your response and thereby strengthen your argument.

Activity 6

a. Read the following statement and decide if you agree with it, disagree with it or agree with it in some ways but not others.

> **A research scientist recently said: 'We have no idea of the long-term impact of mobile phones, and therefore they should not be used by anyone under the age of 18.'**

b. List reasons for and against this statement. Think of as many aspects as you can, for example, enjoyment, health, communication and privacy. Then select two or three main reasons that support your point of view that you can discuss and develop in detail.

Another of the skills you have to demonstrate for AO5 is the ability to organize your essay. Remember, one effective way is to discuss each of your reasons in a separate paragraph, making sure your point of view is developed and sustained, and that the paragraphs are linked together in a logical order. It is also useful at this point to consider the tone you wish to adopt.

Activity 7

Plan your response to the following task:

Write a letter of reply to the research scientist in which you explain your point of view on this statement.

Remember, it is important to engage your reader immediately with a strong introduction and leave them satisfied with a conclusion that sums up your point of view.

Another of the skills you have to demonstrate for AO5 is the ability to craft your response. When offering a point of view, the aim is to convince your reader to think the same way as you. Some strategies to achieve this include:

- offering evidence in the form of other people's opinions, facts or anecdotes
- including effective vocabulary choices and language features, such as language for emotive effect, rhetorical questions, similes and metaphors, or repetition.

Activity 8

a. Make a note of any evidence you could offer in support of your point of view.

b. Make a note of any effective vocabulary choices you could include in your letter that would help to convince your reader.

c. Make a note of any language features you could include in your letter that would help to convince your reader.

d. Using all the work you have done so far on AO5, write a letter in response to the given statement.

e. Read through your letter to check that what you have written is clear and accurate. Make any changes that would improve your demonstration of AO6 skills.

Full sample papers

Paper 1: Explorations in creative reading and writing

Source A

This extract is the opening of a short story by John Wyndham. Although written in 1952, it is set in the future. In this section, a shuttle bus is taking the next group of volunteers to a space ship, ready to depart for Mars.

Survival

As the spaceport bus trundled unhurriedly over the mile or more of open field that separated the terminal building from the embarkation hoist*, Mrs Feltham stared intently forward across the receding
5 row of shoulders in front of her.

The ship stood up on the plain like an isolated silver spire. Near its bow she could see the intense blue light which proclaimed it all but ready to take off. Among and around the great tailfins, dwarf vehicles
10 and little dots of men moved in a fuss of final preparations. Mrs Feltham glared at the scene, at this moment loathing it and all the inventions of men with a hard, hopeless hatred.

Presently she withdrew her gaze from the distance
15 and focused it on the back of her son-in-law's head, a yard in front of her. She hated him, too.

She turned, darting a swift glance at the face of her daughter in the seat beside her. Alice looked pale; her lips were firmly set, her eyes fixed straight
20 ahead.

Mrs Feltham hesitated. Her glance returned to the spaceship. She decided on one last effort. Under cover of the bus noise, she said: 'Alice, darling, it's not too late, even now, you know.'

25 The girl did not look at her. There was no sign that she had heard, save that her lips compressed a little more firmly. Then they parted.

'Mother, please!' she said.

But Mrs Feltham, once started, had to go on.

'It's for your own sake, darling. All you have to do 30 is say you've changed your mind.'

The girl held a protesting silence.

'Nobody would blame you,' Mrs Feltham persisted. 'They'd not think a bit worse of you. After all, everybody knows that Mars is no place for –' 35

'Mother, please stop it,' interrupted the girl.

The sharpness of her tone took Mrs Feltham aback for a moment. She hesitated. But time was growing too short to allow herself the luxury of offended dignity. She went on: 'You're not used 40 to the sort of life you'll have to live there, darling. Absolutely primitive. No kind of life for any woman. After all, dear, it is only a five-year appointment for David. I'm sure if he really loves you he'd rather know that you *are* safe here and waiting –' 45

The girl said, harshly: 'We've been over all this before, Mother. I tell you it's no good. I'm not a child. I've thought it out, and I've made up my mind.'

Mrs Feltham sat silent for some moments. 50 The bus swayed on across the field, and the rocketship seemed to tower further into the sky.

'If you had a child of your own –' she said, half to herself. 'Well, I expect some day you will. Then you will begin to understand...' 55

*embarkation hoist – take off platform for the space ship

Section A: Reading

1 Read again the first part of the source, lines 1 to 5.

List **four** things from this part of the text about Mrs Feltham's journey.   **[4 marks]**

2 Look in detail at this extract from lines 6 to 16 of the source:

> The ship stood up on the plain like an isolated silver spire. Near its bow she could see the intense blue light which proclaimed it all but ready to take off. Among and around the great tail fins, dwarf vehicles and little dots of men moved in a fuss of final preparations. Mrs Feltham glared at the scene, at this moment loathing it and all the inventions of men with a hard, hopeless hatred.
>
> Presently she withdrew her gaze from the distance and focused it on the back of her son-in-law's head, a yard in front of her. She hated him, too.

How does the writer use language here to describe the space ship and Mrs Feltham's response to it?

You could include the writer's choice of:
* words and phrases
* language features and techniques
* sentence forms.   **[8 marks]**

3 You now need to think about the **whole** of the source.

This text is from the opening of a short story.

How has the writer structured the text to interest you as a reader?

You could write about:
* what the writer focuses your attention on at the beginning
* how and why the writer changes this focus as the extract develops
* any other structural features that interest you.   **[8 marks]**

4 Focus this part of your answer on the rest of the source, from line 17 to the end.

A novelist once said: 'Mothers and daughters with strong personalities might see the world from very different points of view.'

To what extent do you agree?

In your response, you should:
* write about what impressions Mrs Feltham and Alice make on the reader
* evaluate how the writer has created these impressions
* support your opinions with quotations from the text.   **[20 marks]**

Section B: Writing

5 You are going to enter a creative writing competition.

Either:

Write a description suggested by this picture:

Or

Write a story about tension between a mother and daughter.

(24 marks for content and organization,

16 marks for technical accuracy)

[40 marks]

Paper 2: Writers' viewpoints and perspectives
Source A

The following newspaper article was written by Tanith Carey, a parenting expert, in response to the Channel 4 programme, *Child Genius*.

Cruellest reality TV show ever

At the tender age of eight, Tudor Mendel-Idowu has been picked to play soccer for no fewer than three Premier League junior teams: QPR, Tottenham and Chelsea. This achievement alone would be enough to make most fathers' hearts burst with pride. But, unfortunately for Tudor, he appears to have a very long way to go before he meets the sky-high expectations of his demanding dad, Tolu.

So far, the most heart-rending scenes on Channel 4's reality series *Child Genius* – in which 20 gifted children are subjected to a terrifying barrage of tests – have been the sight of this small boy hiding his face in his hands as he weeps. The reason? He has not scored as well as his father tells him he should have done. [...] Yet rather than commiserate with his son after a disappointing performance, it is Tolu, who declares that he finds the contest 'emotionally draining'. He then tells Tudor: 'Maybe you're not as good as we thought.' [...]

Even for a nation well used to the mercenary exploitation of spy-on-the-wall television, this has raised concern. As one worried viewer pointed out, the series would more aptly be named 'Lunatic Parents'. For it is really all about the Eagle Dads and Tiger Mums, who want to show off how much work they have invested in their youngsters.

The show first aired in its current format last year, and – as the author of a book looking at the damage caused by competitive parenting – I had thought we would not see a return of this toxic mix of reality TV and hot-housing*. I had expected the sight of children as young as eight crying to prick the conscience of the commissioning editors.

A vain hope, of course. [...]

Child Genius has tapped into an increasingly dangerous trend in parenting; the misguided belief that your offspring is a blank slate and if you hot-house them enough, you can be solely responsible for their success. Parenting is turning into a form of product development. Increasingly, we are falling for the notion that if we cram enough facts into their little brains we can make sure they come out on top. The end result is a rise in depression and anxiety among a generation who believe they are losers if they fail, or could always do better if they win.

Like all offspring of pushy parents, who feel their family's affection is conditional on their success, children like Tudor are not just weeping because they didn't score well. When he tries to cover his tears with his hands, saying 'What I achieved was absolutely terrible', he is facing a much darker fear: That he will lose his father's love if he does not come up to scratch. [...]

Of course, the goal of reality TV is to entertain — but should dramatic story-lines really come ahead of a child's emotional well-being?

[...] Perhaps it's a measure of their state of mind that some parents, such as psychologists Shoshana and Sacha, who featured in the first two episodes,
60 saw nothing harmful in describing their approach to bringing up their daughter Aliyah, nine, as though she is 'a well-bred race-horse'. Shoshana openly pities parents left to bring up children without her skill set. She was blissfully oblivious to the fact
65 that the rest of us were watching, slack-jawed in disbelief at how hard she pushes her child. Far from rushing to adopt such techniques, parents have reacted in horror. The internet has been buzzing with viewers saying they found the series 'upsetting
70 to watch', 'heartbreaking' and expressing concern that it 'verges on abuse'. [...]

No doubt the reality is that Tolu is also a loving father, who sincerely believes he is doing the best for his son, and the producers have edited the programme to make him look like the ultimate 75 caricature of an overbearing father.

But for me, one question remains: How much longer are we going to allow Channel 4 to encourage extreme parents to push their helpless children to breaking point in the name of entertainment? 80

*hot-housing – intensely educating a gifted child

Source B

The following newspaper article was written in the 19th century. It also offers views on how to raise children.

Children

It is a mistake to think that children love the parents less who maintain a proper authority over them. On the contrary, they respect them more. It is a cruel and unnatural selfishness that indulges
5 children in a foolish and hurtful way. Parents are guides and counsellors to their children. As a guide in a foreign land, they undertake to pilot them safely through the shoals and quicksands of inexperience. If the guide allows his followers all
10 the freedom they please; if, because they dislike the constraint of the narrow path of safety, he allows them to stray into holes and precipices that destroy them, to quench their thirst in brooks that poison them, to loiter in woods full of wild beasts
15 of deadly herbs, can he be called a sure guide?

And is it not the same with our children? They are as yet only in the preface, or as it were, in the first chapter of the book of life. We have nearly finished it, or are far advanced. We must open the pages
20 for these younger minds.

If children see that their parents act from principle – that they do not find fault without reason – that they do not punish because personal offence is taken, but because the thing in itself is wrong – if they see that while they are resolutely but 25 affectionately refused what is not good for them, there is a willingness to oblige them in all innocent matters – they will soon appreciate such conduct. If no attention is paid to the rational wishes – if no allowance is made for youthful spirits – if they are 30 dealt with in a hard and unsympathising manner – the proud spirit will rebel, and the meek spirit be broken. [...]

A pert* or improper way of speaking ought never to be allowed. Clever children are very apt to be 35 pert, and if too much admired for it, and laughed at, become eccentric and disagreeable. It is often very difficult to check our own amusement, but their future welfare should be regarded more than our present entertainment. It should never be 40 forgotten that they are tender plants committed to our fostering care, that every thoughtless word or careless neglect may destroy a germ of immortality.

*pert – cheeky

Section A: Reading

1 Read again **source A**, *Cruellest reality TV show ever*, from lines 1 to 19.

Choose **four** statements below which are TRUE.   **[4 marks]**

    A.   Tudor has been picked to play soccer for three Premier League junior teams.

    B.   Tolu's heart is bursting with pride at his son's achievements.

    C.   *Child Genius* is a TV programme on Channel 3.

    D.   Tudor hides his face in his hands as he weeps.

    E.   Tudor does not score as well as his father thinks he should.

    F.   Tolu sympathizes with Tudor over his disappointing performance.

    G.   Tudor finds the contest emotionally draining.

    H.   Tudor may not be as good as his father thought.

2 You need to refer to the whole of **source A**, and **source B**, lines 34 to 44 for this question.

Use details from **both** sources. Write a summary of the different ways to raise a child who is clever.   **[8 marks]**

3 You now need to refer only to **source B**, *Children*, lines 1 to 20.

How does the writer use language to describe the role of parents?   **[12 marks]**

4 For this question, you need to refer to the whole of **source A** and the whole of **source B**.

Compare the two writers' views on raising children.

In your answer, you should:
* compare the different viewpoints of the writers
* compare the methods the writers use to convey these viewpoints
* support your ideas with quotations from both texts.   **[16 marks]**

Section B: Writing

5 'Children need strict discipline from their parents when they are young or they will grow into teenagers who are out of control.'

Write a magazine article in which you explain your point of view on this statement.

(24 marks for content and organization,
16 marks for technical accuracy)
[40 marks]

OXFORD
UNIVERSITY PRESS

Great Clarendon Street, Oxford, OX2 6DP,
United Kingdom

Oxford University Press is a department of the University of Oxford.

It furthers the University's objective of excellence in research, scholarship, and education by publishing worldwide. Oxford is a registered trade mark of Oxford University Press in the UK and in certain other countries

© Oxford University Press 2015

First published in 2015

British Library Cataloguing in Publication Data

Data available

ISBN 978-019-834074-4

10 9 8 7 6 5

Printed in Great Britain by Ashford Print and Publishing Services, Gosport

Acknowledgements

The authors and publisher are grateful for permission to reprint extracts from the following copyright material:

Monica Ali: *Brick Lane* (Doubleday, 2003), copyright © Monica Ali 2003, reprinted by permission of The Random House Group Ltd and Scribner, a Division of Simon & Schuster, Inc.

Samantha and Laurence Barlow with Sue Williams: *Left for Dead* (Michael Joseph, Penguin Australia, 2013), reprinted by permission of Penguin Australia Pty Ltd.

Floella Benjamin: *Coming to England: An Autobiography* (Walker Books, 2009), copyright © Floella Benjamin 1995, 2009, reprinted by permission of Walker Books Ltd, London SE11 5HJ, www.walker.co.uk.

Richard Benson: *The Farm: the story of one family and the English Countryside* (Hamish Hamilton, 2005), copyright © Richard Benson 2005, reprinted by permission of Penguin Books Ltd.

Tony Black: *Loss* (Arrow Books, 2010), copyright © Tony Black 2010, reprinted by permission of The Random House Group Ltd and the author.

Ray Bradbury: 'The Pedestrian', copyright © 1951 by the Fortnightly Publishing Company, © renewed 1979 by Ray Bradbury, first published in *The Reporter*, Aug 1951, from *The Golden Apples of the Sun* (Bantam Books, 1954), reprinted by permission of Don Congdon Associates, Inc.

Tanith Carey: 'Cruellest Reality TV: Brilliant children reduced to tears', *Daily Mail*, 3 Aug 2013, copyright © Daily Mail 2013, reprinted by permission of Solo Syndication.

Rachel Carlyle: 'A Bug's life: Bed bugs are back and living under a mattress near you!', *The Express*, 5 Feb 2013, reprinted by permission of Express Newspapers.

Raymond Chandler: *Farewell, My Lovely* (Penguin, 2010), copyright © Raymond Chandler 1940, reprinted by permission of Penguin Books Ltd.

Liz Cleere: 'Turtle Trap' – Travel Writing Competition, theguardian.com, 22 Nov 2013, copyright © Guardian News & Media Ltd 2013, reprinted by permission of Guardian News & Media Ltd.

Max Davidson: 'How to get on with your neighbours', *Daily Telegraph*, 5 Aug 2011, copyright © Telegraph Media Group Ltd 2011, reprinted by permission of TMG.

Neil Gaiman: *Coraline* (Bloomsbury, 2012), copyright © Neil Gaiman 2002, reprinted by permission of Bloomsbury Publishing plc.

Robert Graves: *Goodbye to All That: and other Great War writings* (Carcanet, 2007), reprinted by permission of Carcanet Press.

Gordon Grice: *Deadly Animals: Savage Encounters Between Man and Beast* (Penguin, 2012), first published in the UK as *The Book of Deadly Animals*, 2011, copyright © Gordon Grice 2012, reprinted by permission of Penguin Books Ltd.

Katy Guest: 'Gender-specific books demean all our children' *The Independent on Sunday*, 16 March 2014, copyright © The Independent 2014, reprinted by permission of Independent Print Ltd.

Rachel Halliwell: 'Dad forced me into marriage, but then saved me', theguardian.com, 12 Oct 2013, copyright © Guardian News & Media Ltd 2013, reprinted by permission of Guardian News & Media Ltd.

Alex Hannaford: '127 Hours: Aron Ralston's story of survival', *The Telegraph*, 6 Jan 2011, copyright © Telegraph Media Group Ltd 2011, reprinted by permission of TMG.

Eugene Henderson: 'I've got it nice says killer as he brags of easy life in jail', *The Express*, 24 June 2012, reprinted by permission of Express Newspapers.

Patricia Highsmith: 'The snail watcher' from *Eleven* (Bloomsbury, 2007), copyright © Patricia Highsmith 1970, reprinted by permission of the Little Brown Book Group Ltd by arrangement with Diogenes Verlag AG

Amelia Hill: 'Why we love sounds of the city jungle', *The Observer*, 23 September 2007, copyright © Guardian News & Media Ltd 2007, reprinted by permission of Guardian News & Media Ltd.

Dr Martin Luther King Jr: 'I Have a Dream', spoken at a Civil Rights rally in Washington DC, 1963, copyright © 1963 Dr Martin Luther King Jr, © renewed 1991 by Coretta Scott King, reprinted by arrangement with the Heirs to the Estate of Martin Luther King Jr., c/o Writers House as agent for the proprietor, New York, NY, USA.

Hanif Kureishi: *The Buddha of Suburbia* (Faber, 2009), copyright © Hanif Kureishi 2009, reprinted by permission of the publisher, Faber & Faber Ltd.

David Leafe: 'Ready, Steady, Slow!' *Daily Mail*, 20 July 2009, copyright © Daily Mail 2009, reprinted by permission of Solo Syndication.

Laurie Lee: 'An Obstinate Exile' from *I Can't Stay Long* (Penguin, 1977), copyright © Laurie Lee 1975, and *Cider with Rosie* (Vintage, 2011), copyright © Laurie Lee 1959, reprinted by permission of the Curtis Brown Group Ltd, London on behalf of the Beneficiaries of The Estate of Laurie Lee.

Andrea Levy: *Small Island* (Headline Review, 2009), copyright © Andrea Levy 2004, reprinted by permission of Headline Publishing Group and David Grossman Literary Agency for the author.

Penelope Lively: 'Next Term, We'll Mash You' from *Pack of Cards: Stories 1978–1986* (Penguin, 1987), copyright © Penelope Lively 1987, reprinted by permission of David Higham Associates.

Nelson Mandela: *Long Walk to Freedom* (Little Brown/Abacus 2013), reprinted by permission of Little Brown Book Group Ltd.

Erin Morgenstern: *The Night Circus* (Harvill Secker, 2011), reprinted by permission of The Random House Group Ltd.

George Orwell: *Nineteen Eighty-Four* (Viking, 2008), copyright © George Orwell 1949, reprinted by permission A M Heath & Co Ltd, Authors' Agents on behalf of Bill Hamilton as the Literary Executor of the Estate of the Late Sonia Brownell Orwell.

Tony Parsons: 'Making my skin crawl: Tattoos scream for attention', *The Mirror*, 23 June 2012, copyright © Tony Parson 2012, reprinted by permission of Curtis Brown Group Ltd, London, on behalf of Tony Parsons,

Sylvia Plath: *The Journals of Sylvia Plath 1950–1972* (Faber, 2000), reprinted by permission of the publishers, Faber & Faber Ltd.

Terry Pratchett: 'Those of us with Dementia need a little help from our friends', *The Guardian*, 13 May 2014, reprinted by permission of Colin Smythe on behalf of the author.

Horacio Quiroga: 'The Feather Pillow' from *The Decapitated Chicken and Other Stories*, translated by Margaret Sayers Peden, copyright © 1976, reprinted by permission of the University of Texas Press.

Ross Raisin: *God's Own Country* (Viking, 2008), copyright © Ross Raisin 2008, reprinted by permission of Penguin Books Ltd.

Jon Ronson: *The Pyschopath Test: a journey through the madness industry* (Picador, 2011), copyright © Jon Ronson 2011, reprinted by permission of the publishers, Pan Macmillan UK.

Salman Rushdie: *The Enchantress of Florence* (Cape, 2008), copyright © Salman Rushdie 2008, reprinted by permission of The Random House Group Ltd.

Siegfried Sassoon: 'Finished with War – A Soldier's Declaration', first published in *Hansard*, July 1917, copyright © Siegfried Sassoon, reprinted by permission of the Barbara Levy Literary Agency on behalf of the Estate of George Sassoon.

Paullina Simons: *Eleven Hours* (Flamingo, 1998), copyright © Paullina Simons 1998, reprinted by permission of HarperCollins Publishers Ltd.

Jonny Wilkinson: *Jonny: My Autobiography* (Headline, 2011), copyright © 2011 Jonny W Ltd reprinted by permission of Headline Publishing Group

John Wyndham: 'Survival' from *The Seeds of Time* (Penguin, 1959), reprinted by permission of David Higham Associates.

Malala Yousafzai with Christina Lamb: *I Am Malala: the girl who stood up for education and was shot by the Taliban* (Weidenfeld & Nicholson/ Little Brown, 2013), copyright © Salarzai Ltd, reprinted by permission of Little Brown & Company, Hachette Book Group, Inc.

Benjamin Zephaniah: 'Me? I thought, OBE me? Up Yours, I thought', *The Guardian*, 27 Nov 2003, copyright © Benjamin Zephaniah 2003, reprinted by permission of United Agents (www.unitedagents.co.uk), on behalf of Benjamin Zephaniah.

and to the following for their permission to reprint extracts from copyright material:

The Queen's Printer for Scotland for extract from 'Just because they're sold as legal, doesn't mean they're safe' from Know the Score, the national drugs helpline for Scotland, a Scottish Government website, © Crown Copyright, reprinted under the Open Government Licence.

Guardian News & Media Ltd for 'Maria: Child Poverty: A 43-year-old mother writes of struggling to make ends meet', theguardian.com, 5 September 2012, copyright © Guardian News & Media Ltd 2012.

ITN (Independent Televison News) for Lawrence McGinty interview 'Stephen Hawking: I'm a scientist not a celebrity', ITV News, 16 Sept 2013.

Time Out London for 'Trafalgar Square' in Time Out London (Time Out Guides Ltd, 2013).

Solo Syndication for 'Autumnwatch presenter Chris Packam slams *I'm a Celebrity* for killing animals and cruelty to bugs and insects', *Daily Mail* online, 10 Sept 2012, copyright © Daily Mail 2012.

Stonewall for 'FA and Premier League slammed by fans for failure to tackle anti-gays abuse', from www.stonewall.org.uk/media.

Telegraph Media Group Ltd for 'Rare Amnesia leaves mother with 17 year memory gap', *The Telegraph*, 29 July 2011, copyright © Telegraph Media Group Ltd 2011.

Approval message from AQA

This textbook has been approved by AQA for use with our qualification. This means that we have checked that it broadly covers the specification and we are satisfied with the overall quality. Full details of our approval process can be found on our website.

We approve textbooks because we know how important it is for teachers and students to have the right resources to support their teaching and learning. However, the publisher is ultimately responsible for the editorial control and quality of this book.

Please note that when teaching the AQA GCSE English Language course, you must refer to AQA's specification as your definitive source of information. While this book has been written to match the specification, it does not provide complete coverage of every aspect of the course.

A wide range of other useful resources can be found on the relevant subject pages of our website: www.aqa.org.uk.